Fodor's
New
THIRTEENTH EDITION

Madrid &
Barcelona

Reprinted from *Fodor's Spain*

Fodor's Travel Publications, Inc.
New York • Toronto • London • Sydney • Auckland

Thirteenth Edition

ISBN 0–679–02734–3

Fodor's Madrid & Barcelona

Editor: Christopher Billy
Contributors: Steven Amsterdam, Hilary Bunce, Philip Eade, Echo Garrett, Anita Guerrini, Sean Hignett, Michael Jacobs, Dawn Lawson, Deborah Luhrman, Bevin McLaughlin, Mark Potok, Mary Ellen Schultz, George Semler, Nancy van Itallie
Creative Director: Fabrizio La Rocca
Cartographer: David Lindroth
Illustrator: Karl Tanner
Cover Photograph: Peter Guttman

Design: Vignelli Associates

Special Sales

Fodor's Travel Publications are available at special discounts for bulk purchases for sales promotions or premiums. Special editions, including personalized covers, excerpts of existing guides, and corporate imprints, can be created in large quantities for special needs. For more information, contact your local bookseller or write to Special Markets, Fodor's Travel Publications, 201 East 50th Street, New York, NY 10022. Inquiries from Canada should be directed to your local Canadian bookseller or sent to Random House of Canada, Ltd., Marketing Department, 1265 Aerowood Drive, Mississauga, Ontario L4W 1B9. Inquiries from the United Kingdom should be sent to Fodor's Travel Publications, 20 Vauxhall Bridge Road, London, England SW1V 2SA.

Contents

Maps

Foreword

We would like to express our gratitude to Pilar Vico, Director of Public Relations, and Roberta Cores of the Spanish National Tourist Office in New York City for their valuable assistance during the preparation of this edition of *Fodor's Madrid & Barcelona*.

While every care has been taken to ensure the accuracy of the information in this guide, the passage of time will always bring change, and consequently, the publisher cannot accept responsibility for errors that may occur.

All prices and opening times quoted here are based on information supplied to us at press time. Hours and admission fees may change, however, and the prudent traveler will avoid inconvenience by calling ahead.

Fodor's wants to hear about your travel experiences, both pleasant and unpleasant. When a hotel or restaurant fails to live up to its billing, let us know and we will investigate the complaint and revise our entries where the facts warrant it.

Send your letters to the editors of Fodor's Travel Publications, 201 E. 50th Street, New York, NY 10022.

Highlights'95 and Fodor's Choice

Highlights '95

Visitors to Spain in 1995 will likely face **climbing hotel and restaurant** prices brought on by the tourism boom of last summer. The biggest price hikes, however, will be at coastal resorts and in the Balearic and Canary islands. Prices in Madrid and Barcelona should remain relatively stable, with especially good deals for tourists who schedule their city visits on weekends.

Securing accommodations in rural areas is an increasingly popular budget option for travelers in Spain. Catering to a trend toward rural tourism, numerous small privately owned inns have opened, many in historic buildings, and these make a charming alternative to the civil service attitudes of the paradors and the impersonality of the high-rise chains. Farmhouses are also being converted into charming bed-and-breakfast inns throughout the country. Besides providing a low-cost way to travel, these lodgings usually also make it easier for visitors to mix with the locals. Ask in small-town tourism offices for accommodations in *turismo rural* or *agroturismo*. Majorca has an especially well developed system of rural inns in comfortable farmhouses, where you are treated like one of the family and have a unique opportunity to learn about traditional ways of life on the island.

In 1995 the citizens of **Granada** will grab the spotlight in Spain, first by hosting the **World Ski Championships** in February and then continuing throughout the year with celebrations promoting the Moorish heritage of Andalucía. The Spanish National Tourist Office has launched a program called **"The Andalus Legacy,"** which includes the creation of 10 different tourism routes through the region's most picturesque and historic pueblos. All itineraries terminate in Granada, home of the magical Alhambra palace and the last capital of the Moors in Spain.

In addition, organizers are mounting 10 exhibitions showcasing aspects of Spanish life that derive from the country's 800-year legacy of Moorish rule. One of these shows will focus on the ingenious irrigation methods employed by the Moors to provide relief from the scorching Andalusian sun. Others will focus on the architectural, agricultural, and scientific contributions made by the Moors, as well as the influence of Arabic on the Spanish language. These expositions will be held April–August in all the provincial capitals of Andalucía and in Ronda, Almuñécar, and Algeciras. Further information and brochures describing the tourism routes are available from the Oficina de Comunicacíon, El Legado Andalusi, Callejon Atarazana Vieja 1, 18010 Granada, tel. 958/20–64–62, fax 958/20–63–58.

Also new to Spain in 1995 is the **Port Aventura theme park** in Salou on the Costa Dorada, which is scheduled to open in April. Owned in part by the U.S. brewery Anheuser Busch, the park will have five main theme areas: Polynesia, China, Mexico, the Wild West, and Catalonia.

Fodor's Choice

No two people will agree on what makes a perfect vacation, but it can be fun and helpful to know what others think. We hope you'll have a chance to experience some of Fodor's Choices yourself while visiting Madrid and Barcelona. For detailed information on individual entries, see the relevant sections of this guidebook.

Castles and Palaces

Palacio Real, Aranjuez

Palacio Real, La Granja

Palacio Real, Madrid

Palau Güell, Barcelona

Churches and Monasteries

Convent of Las Dueñas, Salamanca

Convent of the Descalzas Reales, Madrid

El Escorial, Madrid

La Moreneta shrine, Montserrat

New Cathedral, Salamanca

Santa Maria del Mar, Barcelona

Temple Expiatori de la Sagrada Família, Barcelona

Museums

Centro de Arte Reina Sofía, Madrid

Fundació Miró, Barcelona

Museu Picasso, Barcelona

Prado, Madrid

Thyssen-Bornemísza, Madrid

Squares and Parks

Parc Güell, Barcelona

Parque del Retiro, Madrid

Plaza de España, Madrid

Plaza Mayor, Madrid

Plaza Mayor, Salamanca

Hotels

Palace, Madrid, *$$$$*

Ritz, Barcelona, *$$$$*

Colón, Barcelona, *$$$*

Parador Nacional Castillo de Sigüenza, Sigüenza, *$$$*

Reina Victoria, Madrid, *$$$*

Restaurants

Eldorado Petit, Barcelona, *$$$$*

Zalacaín, Madrid, *$$$$*

El Asador de Aranda, Barcelona, *$$*

La Pampa, Madrid, *$$*

Other Sights

Palau de la Música, Barcelona

University, Salamanca

Spain

Bay of Biscay

El Ferrol
La Coruña
Villalba
Ribadeo
Luarca
Gijón
Ribadesella
Santander
Oviedo
Cangas
de Onis
Bilbao
Santiago de
Compostela
Lugo
Mieres
PICOS DE
EUROPA
Muros
CANTABRIAN MTS.
Ponferrada
León
Pontevedra
Orense
Astorga
Burgos
Vigo
Benavente
Palencia
Log
Tui/Túy
Zamora
Tordesillas
Valladolid
Duero
Salamanca
Adanero
Segovia
SIERRA DE GUADARR
Ciudad
Rodrigo
Avila
Guadala
El Escorial
MADRID
PORTUGAL
SIERRA DE GREDOS
Toledo
Plasencia
Talavera
de la Reina
Aranjuez
Tajo
Guadalupe
Alcázar de
San Juan
Cáceres
Trujillo
Guadiana
Ciudad
Real
Mérida
Abenójar
Valdepeñas
Badajaz
Zafra
Almadén
Jerez de los
Caballeros
SIERRA MORENA
Fregenal
de la Sierra
Bailén
Linares
Ube
Córdoba
Aroche
Jaén
Baeza
Seville
Guadalquivir
Ecija
Baena
Carmona
Guadix
Huelva
Lucena
Granada
SIERRA
Antequera
Loja
*Gulf of
Cadiz*
Sanlúcar de
Barrameda
Ronda
Nerja
COSTA DE LA LUZ
Cádiz
Jerez de
la Frontera
Torremolinos
Málaga
Motril
Estepona
Fuengirola
ATLANTIC
OCEAN
Marbella
COSTA DEL SOL
Algeciras
Gibraltar
TO CANARY
ISLANDS
Strait of Gibraltar

Introduction

By George Semler

How to get a Catalan to speak Spanish? Misunderstand the price by a peseta. Madrid bureacrats don't work after lunch? No, that's in the morning; after lunch they don't even show up.

Catalan avarice, Madrid sloth: old standbys in the arsenal of barbs the citizens of Spain's two largest cities routinely toss at each other.

Beneath the humor lies a well-aged and historically rooted bitterness combining elements of the world's great internecine feuds—Québec and the rest of Canada, Milan and Rome, even the United States' North–South resentment more than a century after the American Civil War.

Though largely undetectable to a visitor, traces of this rivalry crop up everywhere. Cars with Madrid license plates may encounter extra discourtesies in Catalonia; Madrileños have little patience with the Catalan language and typically insist upon being addressed exclusively in Spanish; Catalans, in turn, seem to "forget" their Spanish, and so on. A foolproof way to ruin a social gathering in Madrid is to prosyletize the Catalan point of view vis à vis its own history and culture. Meanwhile, in Barcelona, the "language of Cervantes" can be a surefire soporific for dinner parties that would crackle with humor and innuendo in Catalan.

This mutual antipathy has been centuries in the making and will not go away any time soon, even though feelings have cooled considerably since the 1714 siege and conquest of Barcelona by Spain's first Bourbon monarch, Felipe V. Armed conflict between the two is no longer even a remote possibility. Catalans are basically a peaceful people who have always managed to prosper no matter whose army was manning the cannon overlooking Barcelona, and besides, the two cities are now so intertwined and interdependent that the Spanish minister of defense, for one, was, until recently, Narcis Serra, a Catalan, formerly mayor of Barcelona and presently vice president of Spain.

The squaring-off between Barcelona, medieval capital of an opulent Mediterranean empire, and Madrid, once the nerve center for one of the greatest global empires ever assembled, may be the nearest Spain comes to a two-party system. The cities debate every national issue from politics to sports to the economy, even as Iberia Airlines daily shuttles 5,000–6,000 commuting executives and bureaucrats back and forth between the two.

Fundamental to the Barcelona versus Madrid (Catalonia versus Castile, really) antagonism is the time-honored northern Europe–southern Europe animus. Catalonian national pride is, quite simply, an affront to Madrid's. When Catalonia insists upon recognition of its language and cultural identity, Madrid hears echoes and overtones of "We're Europeans, and better than you." Castilians reply, "You're an Iberian people just as we are, and not as different as you would like to think. And besides, what's the matter with being like us?"

The dramatic changes of the last 20 years—the end of Franco, the establishment of the constitutional monarchy—have actually reversed some of the more stereotypical qualities that have traditionally characterized the two cities. Thus, whereas Barcelona was always considered Spain's most European city up to 1975, Catalonia's zealous restoration of its long-suppressed language and culture has made it somewhat self-absorbed and cost it a few points in cosmopolitanism. Madrid, on the other hand, has burst back onto the world stage with a vigor and energy unimaginable when it was the seat of Franco's reactionary and repressive regime. The capital's legendary bureaucratic indolence has been replaced by a frenzy of activity in the arts and business and a powerful new international orientation and appeal.

But some things don't change. Madrid remains open; Barcelona—despite its seaport—is less so. Even the topography reinforces this notion: Madrid stands on a promontory at the center of Spain's central steppe, Barcelona nestles in a crease between the hills and the sea. Barcelona is moist, pungent, even fetid, slippery. Madrid is high, arid, brittle. Madrid's streets are broader and seem to embrace the sky, while Barcelona's are predominantly darker and narrower, leafier and more intimate, older, tunnels back into the city's medieval past. Barcelona is, after all, 2,000 years old, to Madrid's mere millennium.

Even, maybe especially, the air is different. Barcelona's steamy and passionate Mediterranean breath is a far thing from Madrid's legendary highland air with its sharp and icy lightness.

Catalans are more private and self-contained, feline, Gallic. Madrileños are a little of everything, coming as they do from all corners of the peninsula and the world, but they are known for a more gregarious, accessible, open, generous spirit. In Madrid they *give* you things—tapas, hot broth, the time of day. In Barcelona, trade is absolutely fundamental to every nuance of social contact.

Catalonia's *fets diferencials* or "differentiating facts" are based on linguistic and historical realities often dismissed as fantasy by non-Catalans educated during the unity-oriented Franco regime. Barcelona is geographically closer to Marseilles than to Madrid, and medieval Catalonia included much of what is today southern France. The Rousillon, or French Catalonia, stretched as far north as Avignon and Nîmes, where the Catalan language is still spoken. Grammatically closer to Provençal French than to Castilian Spanish, Catalan lacks the fricative phonemes and nearly all of the Arabic-rooted vocabulary modern Spanish inherited from 700 years of Moorish occupation. Catalonia, sacked but never colonized by the Moors, was the border zone for Charlemagne's Frankish empire, finally gaining independence from the Carolingians in 988, only a few years after Madrid was made a military outpost by the Moorish command defending regional headquarters at Toledo. When Catalonia became, through royal marriage, part of the House of Aragon in 1137, Barcelona's commercial and maritime power made it the kingdom's nerve center and royal court. But in 1469, when Isabella of Castile married Ferdinand of Aragon, Barcelona found itself left dangling on the eastern edge of an Iberian power about to turn its attention west across the Atlantic.

The "discovery" of the New World and the great enterprise undertaken to exploit its riches definitively sealed Catalonia's fate as a declining power within the new unified Spain. Legally excluded from participation in Castile's colonization and plunder of the Americas, Catalonia did manage to retain a measure of home rule and cultural identity until 1714, when, as a reprisal for having supported Archduke Carlos of Austria in the War of the Spanish Succession, Felipe V stripped Catalonia of all of its institutions and privileges.

Barcelona, deprived of the easy loot pouring in from the New World, developed an industrial power base which led into a resurgence of Catalonian nationalism—*la Renaixença*—during the latter half of the 19th century. Limited home rule returned from 1914 to 1924 and later during the Second Republic from 1931 to 1936, but after the 1936–1939 Spanish Civil War, the Franco regime's "National Movement" endeavored to eradicate all traces of the Catalan language and culture, along with any political parties that might threaten the national fabric of church, state, oligarchy, and the army. Officially suppressed but never abandoned, Catalan language and culture have returned more powerfully than ever since Franco's death in 1975.

Madrid's history, shorter but less checkered, took the city from military observation post to provincial town to world capital in just over 500 years. When the until-then itinerant royal court was permanently established there in 1561, riches were already pouring in from the Spanish empire's far-flung colonies. Soon Madrid was a teeming boom town with a burgeoning population and government subsidies promoting architecture, theater, and especially, painting. Rubens and Velázquez shared a studio; Cervantes and Lope de Vega (the "Spanish Shakespeare") exchanged acerbic sonnets; the city's literary quarter was a crush of poets, actors, composers, and playwrights. The lavish cultural spending of Spain's Golden Century left a legacy of artistic masterpieces that today fill the Prado and other museums, as well as convents, churches, foundations, and over a hundred art galleries.

Madrid, from the twisting streets of its early Moorish and Jewish quarter, through the stately and austere Hapsburg architecture of the 16th and 17th centuries and the broad avenues of the 18th- and 19th-century Bourbon monarchy, has grown into a sprawling industrial and cultural giant of (like Barcelona) more than four million inhabitants.

Comparing the pros and cons and respective assets of these two cities—an endless exchange of proposals and rebuttals—may only be valuable as a means of better defining and characterizing each of the two. Certainly, they seem perfectly organized for debate. Madrid's landlocked, highland monochrome, for example, contrasts with Barcelona's vivid and varied palette, a rich mixture of Pyrenees, Mediterranean, and metropolitan hues. Madrid offers convenient access to all of the Iberian Peninsula, whereas Barcelona is nearly equidistant from Rome and London, as close to Geneva as it is to Madrid. Madrid is most appealing in winter, when the hearty Castilian cuisine of roasts and thick stews makes the most sense, whereas Barcelona's sweetest season is springtime, between the lovers' fiesta of Sant Jordi in late April and the all-night bonfires of Sant Joan on Midsummer's Eve. Madrid's treasury of paintings is countered by Barcelona's relentless innovation in art, architecture, and design and by the legacies of Picasso, Miró, Dalí, and Gaudí. Barcelona has delicious markets such as the central Boqueria; Madrid has its Sunday flea market, the Rastro, and bookstall browsing along the Cuesta de Moyanes. Madrid's superb side visits—Toledo, Segovia, El Escorial—are balanced by Barcelona's excellent beaches on the Costa Brava to the north and the Delta del Ebro to the south. Madrid is centered around its peerless and peaceful Plaza Mayor, whereas Barcelona has its meandering Rambla. Madrid has a midtown forest in the stately Retiro, while Gaudí's Güell Park hovers on a hill above Barcelona. Madrid's oldest quarters are a jumble of red clay-tiled rooftops, while Barcelona's are Roman, Romanesque, and Gothic stone.

Ultimately, Barcelona's Mediterranean vitality draws heavily on its rich triangle of mountains, sea, and city life, whereas modern Madrid, brisk and lively, is broader and more universal, the melting pot of the many Spains.

Today, both cities are riding a wave of excitement that even severe economic woes can't seem to discourage. Barcelona still basks in the afterglow of the Olympic Games, its greatest domestic and international triumph since the glory days of its 12th-century Mediterranean prominence. Madrid, meanwhile, has reassumed an energy and outlook comparable only to that of its own Golden Century.

1 Essential Information

Before You Go

Government Information Offices

Contact the Spanish government tourist offices for information on all aspects of travel to and in Spain.

In the U.S. 665 5th Ave., New York, NY 10022, tel. 212/759–8822, fax 212/980–1053; Water Tower Pl., Suite 915, 845 N. Michigan Ave., Chicago, IL 60611, tel. 312/642–1992, fax 312/642–9817; 1221 Brickell Ave., Miami, FL 33131, tel. 305/358–1992, fax 305/358–8223; 8383 Wilshire Blvd., Suite 960, Beverly Hills, CA 90211, tel. 213/658–7188, fax 213/658–1061.

U.S. Government Travel Briefings The Department of State's **Overseas Citizens Emergency Center** (Room 4811, Washington, DC 20520; enclose S.A.S.E.) issues Consular Information Sheets, which cover crime, security, political climate, and health risks as well as embassy locations, entry requirements, currency regulations, and other routine matters. For the latest information, stop in at any passport office, consulate, or embassy; call the interactive hotline (tel. 202/647–5225, fax 202/647–3000); or, with your PC's modem, tap into the Bureau of Consular Affairs' computer bulletin board (tel. 202/647–9225).

In Canada 102 Bloor St. W, Suite 1450, Toronto, Ontario M5S 1M8, tel. 416/961–3131, fax 416/961–1992.

In the U.K. 57–58 St. James's St., London SW1A 1LD, tel. 0171/499–0901, fax 0171/629–4257.

Tours and Packages

Should you buy your travel arrangements to Spain packaged or do it yourself? There are advantages either way. Buying packaged arrangements saves you money, particularly if you can find a program that includes exactly the features you want. You also get a pretty good idea of what your trip will cost from the outset. You have two options: fully escorted tours and independent packages. Escorted tours mean having limited free time and traveling with strangers. Escorted tours are most often via motorcoach, with a tour director in charge. Your baggage is handled, your time rigorously scheduled, and most meals planned. Escorted tours are therefore the most hassle-free way to see Spain, as well as generally the least expensive. Independent packages allow plenty of flexibility. They generally include airline travel and hotels, with certain options available, such as sightseeing, car rental, and excursions. Independent packages are usually more expensive than escorted tours, but your time is your own.

While you can book directly through tour operators, you will pay no more to go through a travel agent, who will be able to tell you about tours and packages from a number of operators. Whatever program you ultimately choose, be sure to find out exactly what is included: taxes, tips, transfers, meals, baggage handling, ground transportation, entertainment, excursions, sports or recreation (and rental equipment if necessary). Ask about the level of hotel used, its location, the size of its rooms, the kind of beds, and its facilities and amenities, such as pool, room service, or programs for children, if they're important to you. Find out the operator's cancellation penalties. Nearly everyone charges them, and the only way to avoid them is to buy trip-cancellation insurance (*see* Insurance, *below*). Also ask about the single supplement, a surcharge assessed to solo travelers. Some operators do not make you pay it if you agree to be matched up with a roommate of the same sex, even if one is not found by departure time. Remember that a program that has features you won't use may not be the most cost-wise choice.

Fully Escorted Tours
Escorted tours are usually sold in three categories: deluxe, first-class, and tourist or budget class. The most important differences are the price and the level of accommodations. Some operators specialize in one category, while others offer a range. In the deluxe category, try **Maupintour** (Box 807, Lawrence, KS 66044, tel. 913/843–1211 or 800/255–4266) or the "Club Petrabax" tours sponsored by **Petrabax** (97-45 Queens Blvd., Rego Park, NY 11374, tel. 718/897–7272 or 800/367–6611). First-class programs are offered by **Abreu Tours** (317 E. 34th St., New York, NY 10016, tel. 212/532–6550 or 800/223–1580), **Caravan** (401 N. Michigan Ave., Chicago, IL 60611, tel. 800/227–2862), **Certified Vacations** (Box 1525, Fort Lauderdale, FL 33302, tel. 305/522–1414 or 800/233–7260), **Collette Tours** (162 Middle St., Pawtucket, RI 02680, tel. 401/725–3805 or 800/832–4658), **El Corte Inglés** (500 5th Ave., Suite 1044, New York, NY 10110, tel. 212/944–9400 or 800/333–2469), **Gadabout Tours** (700 E. Tahquitz Way, Palm Springs, CA 92262, tel. 619/325–5556 or 800/952–5068), **Globus** (5301 S. Federal Circle, Littleton, CO 80123, tel. 303/797–2800 or 800/221–0090), **Petrabax**, **Perillo Tours** (Perillo Plaza, 577 Chestnut Ridge, Woodcliff Lake, NJ 07675, tel. 201/307–1234 or 800/431–1515), **Tauck Tours** (11 Wilton Rd., Box 5027, Wilton, CT 06881, tel. 800/468–2825, fax 203/454–3081), and **Trafalgar Tours** (21 E. 26th St., New York, NY 10010, tel. 212/689–8977 or 800/854–0103). In the budget category, look into **Cosmos Tourama,** a sister company of Globus (*see above*), and the "Cost Saver" programs offered by **Trafalgar Tours.**

Also look into programs from **Abreu Tours** (*see above*), **Bravo Tours** (182 Main St., Ridgefield, NJ 07660, tel. 201/641–0655 or 800/272–2674), **Hispanidad Holidays** (99 Tulip Ave., Floral Park, NY 11001, tel. 516/488–4700 or 800/274–4400), **Spanish Heritage Tours** (116–47 Queens Blvd., Forest Hills, NY 11375, tel. 718/544–2752 or 800/221–2580), and **V E Tours** (1150 N.W. 72nd Ave., Suite 450, Miami, FL 33126, tel. 800/222–8383).

Most itineraries are jam-packed with sightseeing, so you see a lot in a short amount of time (usually one place per day). To judge just how fast-paced the tour is, review the itinerary carefully. If you are in a different hotel each night, you will be getting up early each day to head out, travel to your next destination, do some sightseeing, have dinner, and go to bed; then you'll start all over again. If you want some free time, make sure it's mentioned in the tour brochure; if you want to be escorted to every meal, confirm that any tour you consider does that. Also, when comparing programs, be sure to find out if the motorcoach is air-conditioned and has a restroom on board. Make your selection based on price and stops on the itinerary.

Independent Packages
Independent packages, which travel agents call FITs (for foreign independent travel), are offered by airlines, tour operators who may also do escorted programs (such as American Express Vacations, Gadabout, Petrabax, and most of the others), and any number of other companies from large, established firms to small, new entrepreneurs.

U.S. **American Airlines Fly AAway Vacations** (tel. 800/321–2121), **Continental Airlines' Grand Destinations** (tel. 800/634–5555), and **Delta Dream Vacations** (tel. 800/872–7786) have Barcelona and Madrid city packages; airline operators also include **TWA Getaway Vacations** (tel. 800/438–2929) and **United Airlines' Vacation Planning Center** (tel. 800/678–0949). Other programs are available from **El Corte Inglés** (*see above*), **Spain Tours and Beyond** (261 W. 70th St., New York, NY 10023, tel. 212/595–2400), **Travel Bound** (599 Broadway, New York, NY 10012, tel. 212/334–1350 or 800/456–8656), **V E Tours** (*see above*), **Wright Travel** (57 E. 77th St., New York, NY 10021, tel. 212/570–0969 or 800/877–3240) for Marbella, and **Odysseys Adventures** (537 Chestnut St., Cedarhurst, NY 11516, tel. 516/569–2812 or 800/344–0013).

U.K. **Mundi Color** (276 Vauxhall Bridge Rd., London SW1V 1BE, tel. 0171/828–6021) is an established, Spanish-owned specialist in Spanish holidays.

When to Go

May and October, when the weather is generally warm and dry, are considered the best months for touring Spain. May gives you more hours of daylight for sightseeing. April is good for catching a glimpse of some of the spectacular Semana Santa (Holy Week) fiestas.

Because Spain is the number-one destination for European tourists, the months of June, July, August, and September tend to be crowded and more expensive, especially along the coasts. Most people find the waters of the Mediterranean too cold for swimming the rest of the year. August is the month when Spaniards take vacations; the annual migration to the beach causes huge traffic jams on August 1 and 31. During August big cities are delightfully relaxed and empty. Small shops and some restaurants shut down for the entire month, but museums remain open.

Summers in Spain are hot; temperatures frequently hit 100°F (38°C), and air-conditioning is not widely used. Try to limit your touring to the morning hours and take a siesta in the afternoon. Warm summer nights are one of the most enjoyable things about Spain.

Winters in Spain are mild and rainy along the coasts. Elsewhere winter blows bitterly cold. Snow is infrequent except in the mountains, where skiing is possible from December to March in the Pyrenees and other resorts near Granada, Madrid, and Burgos.

Climate The following are average daily maximum and minimum temperatures for Madrid and Barcelona.

Madrid

Jan.	48F	9C	**May**	70F	21C	**Sept.**	77F	25C
	36	2		50	10		57	14
Feb.	52F	11C	**June**	81F	27C	**Oct.**	66F	19C
	36	2		59	15		50	10
Mar.	59F	15C	**July**	88F	31C	**Nov.**	55F	13C
	41	5		63	17		41	5
Apr.	64F	18C	**Aug.**	86F	30C	**Dec.**	48F	9C
	45	7		63	17		36	2

Barcelona	Jan.	55F	13C	May	70F	21C	Sept.	77F	25C
		43	6		57	14		66	19
	Feb.	57F	14C	June	77F	25C	Oct.	70F	21C
		45	7		64	18		59	15
	Mar.	61F	16C	July	82F	28C	Nov.	61F	16C
		48	9		70	21		52	11
	Apr.	64F	18C	Aug.	82F	28C	Dec.	55F	13C
		52	11		70	21		46	8

Information Sources For current weather conditions and forecasts for cities in the United States and abroad, plus the local time and helpful travel tips, call the **Weather Channel Connection** (tel. 900/932–8437; 95¢ per minute) from a touch-tone phone.

Festivals and Seasonal Events

From solemn pre-Easter processions to hilarious wine and tomato battles, Spain has a fiesta for every occasion.

January: Epiphany, on the 6th, is a Spanish child's Christmas. Youngsters leave their shoes on the doorstep to be filled with gifts by the three wise men, or Three Kings. In towns throughout Spain the Kings arrive by camel or car in a parade the night of January 5.

February: Carnival dances through Spain as a final fiesta before Lent. One of the most flamboyant parades takes place in Sitges (Barcelona).

April: April 9 to 15 is **Semana Santa,** Spain's most spectacular fiesta.

May: San Isidro (May 15) begins two weeks of the best bullfighting in Spain in honor of the patron saint of Madrid.

June: Corpus Christi (June 25) is celebrated with processions throughout Spain, but one of the most magnificent is in Sitges (Barcelona).

July and August: Veranos de la Villa cools off Madrid's summer nights with a series of outdoor films, and concerts of everything from flamenco to rock and roll all summer long.

September: La Merced is celebrated in Barcelona on September 24 with concerts, fireworks, and parades featuring people wearing giant papier-mâché heads.

December: New Year's Eve ticks away at Madrid's Puerta del Sol, where crowds gather to eat 12 grapes, one on each stroke of midnight.

What to Pack

Pack light. Although baggage carts are free and plentiful in most Spanish airports, they are rare in train and bus stations.

Clothing On the whole, Spaniards dress up more than Americans or the British. What you bring will depend a great deal on what time of year you visit. Summer will be hot nearly everywhere, but don't forget a raincoat or an umbrella. Visits in winter, fall, and spring call for warm clothing and boots.

It is sensible to wear casual, comfortable clothing and shoes when sightseeing, but dressier outfits are required for the cities, especially at fine restaurants and nightclubs. American tourists can be spotted easily in Spain because they are the ones wearing sneakers. If you want to blend in, wear leather shoes.

On the beach, anything goes; it is common to see females of all ages wearing only bikini bottoms, and many of the more remote beaches allow nude bathing. Bring a cover-up to wear over your bathing suit when you leave the beach.

Electricity The electrical current in Spain is 220 volts, 50 cycles alternating current (AC); the United States runs on 110-volt, 60-cycle AC current. Unlike wall outlets in the United States, which accept plugs with two flat prongs, outlets in Spain take continental-type plugs, with two round prongs.

Adapters, To use U.S.-made electric appliances abroad, you'll need an adapter
Converters, plug. Unless the appliance is dual voltage and made for travel, you'll
Transformers also need a converter. Hotels sometimes have 110-volt outlets for low-wattage appliances marked "For Shavers Only" near the sink; don't use them for a high-wattage appliance like a blow-dryer. If you're traveling with an older laptop computer, carry a transformer. Newer laptop computers are auto-sensing, operating equally well on 110 and 220 volts (so you need only the appropriate adapter plug). When in doubt, consult your appliance's owner's manual or the manufacturer. Or get a copy of the free brochure "Foreign Electricity is No Deep Dark Secret," published by adapter-converter manufacturer Franzus Company (Customer Service, Dept. B50, Murtha Industrial Park, Box 142, Beacon Falls, CT 06403, tel. 203/723–6664; send a stamped, self-addressed envelope when ordering).

Miscellaneous Bring an extra pair of eyeglasses or contact lenses in your carry-on luggage. If you have a health problem that requires a prescription drug, pack enough to last the duration of the trip or have your doctor write a prescription using the drug's generic name, because brand names vary from country to country. Always carry prescription drugs in their original packaging to avoid problems with customs officials. Don't pack them in luggage that you plan to check in case your bags go astray. Pack a list of the offices that supply refunds for lost or stolen traveler's checks.

Luggage Free airline baggage allowances depend on the airline, the route,
Regulations and the class of your ticket; ask in advance. In general, on domestic flights and on international flights between the United States and foreign destinations, you are entitled to check two bags—neither exceeding 62 inches, or 158 centimeters (length + width + height), or weighing more than 70 pounds (32 kilograms). A third piece may be brought aboard; its total dimensions are generally limited to less than 45 inches (114 centimeters), so it will fit easily under the seat in front of you or in the overhead compartment. In the United States, the Federal Aviation Administration gives airlines broad latitude to limit carry-on allowances and tailor them to different aircraft and operational conditions. Charges for excess, oversize, or overweight pieces vary.

If you are flying between two foreign destinations, note that baggage allowances may be determined not by the piece method but by the weight method, which generally allows 88 pounds (40 kilograms) of luggage in first class, 66 pounds (30 kilograms) in business class, and 44 pounds (20 kilograms) in economy. If your flight between two cities abroad *connects* with your transatlantic or transpacific flight, the piece method still applies.

Safeguarding Before leaving home, itemize your bags' contents and their worth in
Your Luggage case they go astray. To minimize that risk, tag them inside and out with your name, address, and phone number. (If you use your home address, cover it so that potential thieves can't see it.) Put a copy of your itinerary inside each bag, so that you can easily be tracked. At check-in, make sure that the tag attached by baggage handlers bears the correct three-letter code for your destination. If your bags

do not arrive with you, or if you detect damage, immediately file a written report with the airline before you leave the airport.

Taking Money Abroad

Traveler's Checks Traveler's checks are preferable in metropolitan centers, although you'll need cash in rural areas and small towns. The most widely recognized are **American Express, Citicorp, Diners Club, Thomas Cook,** and **Visa,** which are sold by major commercial banks. Both American Express and Thomas Cook issue checks that can be countersigned and used by you or your traveling companion. Typically the issuing company or the bank at which you make your purchase charges 1% to 3% of the checks' face value as a fee. Some foreign banks charge as much as 20% of the face value as the fee for cashing traveler's checks in a foreign currency. Buy a few checks in small denominations to cash toward the end of your trip, so you won't be left with excess foreign currency. Record the numbers of checks as you spend them, and keep this list separate from the checks.

Currency Exchange Banks offer the most favorable exchange rates. If you use currency exchange booths at airports, rail and bus stations, hotels, stores, and privately run exchange firms, you'll typically get less favorable rates, but you may find the hours more convenient.

You can get good rates and avoid long lines at airport currency-exchange booths by getting a small amount of currency at **Thomas Cook Currency Services** (630 5th Ave., New York, NY 10111, tel. 212/757–6915 or 800/223–7373 for locations in major metropolitan areas throughout the United States) or **Ruesch International** (tel. 800/424–2923 for locations) before you depart.

Getting Money from Home

Cash Machines Many automated-teller machines (ATMs) are tied to international networks such as **Cirrus** and **Plus.** You can use your bank card at ATMs to withdraw money from an account and get cash advances on a credit-card account if your card has been programmed with a personal identification number, or PIN. Check in advance on limits on withdrawals and cash advances within specified periods. Ask whether your bank card or credit-card PIN will need to be reprogrammed for use in the area you'll be visiting. Four digits are commonly used overseas. Note that Discover is accepted only in the United States. On cash advances you are charged interest from the day you receive the money from ATMs as well as from tellers. Although transaction fees for ATM withdrawals abroad may be higher than fees for withdrawals at home, Cirrus and Plus exchange rates are excellent because they are based on wholesale rates offered only by major banks. They also may be referred to abroad as "a withdrawal from a credit account."

Plan ahead: Obtain ATM locations and the names of affiliated cash-machine networks before departure. For specific foreign Cirrus locations, call 800/424–7787; for foreign Plus locations, consult the Plus directory at your local bank.

Wiring Money You don't have to be a cardholder to send or receive a **MoneyGram from American Express** for up to $10,000. Go to a MoneyGram agent in retail and convenience stores and American Express travel offices, pay up to $1,000 with a credit card and anything over that in cash. You are allowed a free long-distance call to give the transaction code to your intended recipient, who needs only present identification and the reference number to the nearest MoneyGram agent to pick up the cash. MoneyGram agents are in more than 70 countries (call 800/926–9400 for locations). Fees range from 3% to 10%, depending on the amount and how you pay.

You can also use **Western Union.** To wire money, take either cash or a cashier's check to the nearest agent or call and use MasterCard or Visa. Money sent from the United States or Canada will be available for pickup at agent locations in 100 countries within minutes. Once the money is in the system, it can be picked up at *any* one of 25,000 locations (call 800/325–6000 for the one nearest you; 800/321–2923 in Canada). Fees range from 4% to 10%, depending on the amount you send.

Spanish Currency

The peseta is Spain's currency unit. Bills are 10,000, 5,000, 2,000, and 1,000. Coins are 500, 200, 100, 50, 25, 10, 5, and 1 peseta. Be careful not to mix up the 100- and 500-peseta coins—they are the same color and almost the same size. There are two types of 25 peseta coins, large silver ones and small bronze ones with a hole in the center. Five-peseta coins are always called *duros*, but watch out for the new microsized 1- and 5-peseta coins. At press time (spring 1994) the currency markets of Europe were highly unstable, with exchange rates of 142 pesetas to the U.S. dollar, 108 pesetas per Canadian dollar, and 213 pesetas to the pound sterling.

What It Will Cost

Spain's rush to catch up with the rest of Europe has kept prices climbing; annual inflation runs about 5%. But devaluations of the peseta have brought prices down substantially for foreigners, while hotels and restaurants have moderated their tariffs in order to attract more visitors. Still, Madrid and Barcelona are nearly as expensive as any international capital and harder on the pocketbook than many big cities in the United States and Great Britain.

Restaurants and clothing are among the most expensive items in Spain. World-famous Spanish leather jackets and shoes may be beautiful, but they are no bargain. Hotels are generally reasonably priced, and the government-run parador hotel chain is a good value.

Transportation is economical in Spain, and new competition with Iberia on domestic routes has brought airfares down. Train and bus travel are inexpensive. The price of gas throughout the country is also low; however, highway tolls along the Mediterranean coast are high.

Taxes Value-added tax (or sales tax) is called IVA in Spain. It is charged on services, such as hotels and restaurants, and many categories of consumer products. Restaurant menus will generally say at the bottom whether tax is included *(IVA incluido)* or not *(más 6% IVA)*. The highest category restaurants are required to charge 15% IVA. Five-star hotels also charge 15% tax, but all other hotels charge only 6% IVA. When in doubt as to whether tax is included in a price, ask, *Está incluido el IVA* (ee-vah)?

Sample Prices Coffee in a bar: 125 pesetas (standing), 150 pesetas (seated). Beer in a bar: 125 pesetas (standing), 150 pesetas (seated). Small glass of wine in a bar: 100 pesetas. Soft drink: 150–200 pesetas a bottle. Ham and cheese sandwich: 300–450 pesetas. One-mile taxi ride: 400 pesetas, but the meter keeps ticking in traffic jams. Local bus or subway ride: 150 pesetas. Movie-theater seat: 600 pesetas. Foreign newspaper: 225 pesetas.

Long-Distance Calling

AT&T, MCI, and Sprint have several services that make calling home or the office more affordable and convenient when you're on the road. Use one of them to avoid pricey hotel surcharges. **AT&T** Calling Card (tel. 800/225–5288) and the AT&T Universal Card (tel. 800/662–7759) give you access to the service. With AT&T's USA Direct (tel. 800/874–4000 for codes in the countries you'll be visiting) you can reach an AT&T operator with a local or toll-free call. **MCI's** Call USA (MCI Customer Service, tel. 800/444–4444) allows that service from 85 countries or from country to country via MCI WorldReach. From MCI ExpressInfo in the United States you can get 24-hour weather, news, and stock quotes. MCI PhoneCash (tel. 800/925–0029) is available through American Express and through several convenience stores and retailers nationwide. **Sprint** Express (tel. 800/793–1153) has a toll-free number travelers abroad can dial using the WorldTraveler Foncard to reach a Sprint operator in the United States. The Sprint operator can offer international directory assistance to 224 countries in the world. All three companies offer message delivery services to international travelers and have added debit cards so that you don't have to fiddle with change.

Passports and Visas

All visitors are required by law to carry their passports at all times. Visitors who are stopped by police and found not to be carrying their passports are sometimes jailed. If you are worried about losing your passport by chance or to pickpockets, make a photocopy to carry with you during your visit and leave the passport in the hotel safe.

If your passport is lost or stolen, report the loss immediately to the nearest embassy or consulate and to the local police. If you can provide the consular officer with the information contained in the passport, he or she will usually be able to issue you a new passport promptly. For this reason, keep a photocopy of the data page of your passport separate from your money and traveler's checks. Also leave a photocopy with a relative or friend at home.

U.S. Citizens All U.S. citizens, even infants, need a valid passport to enter Spain for stays of up to 90 days. You can pick up new and renewal application forms at any of the 13 U.S. Passport Agency offices and at some post offices and courthouses. Although passports are usually mailed within four weeks of your application's receipt, allow five weeks or more from April through summer. Call the Department of State Office of Passport Services' information line (tel. 202/647–0518) for details.

Canadian Citizens Canadian citizens need a valid passport to enter Spain for stays of up to 90 days. Application forms are available at 23 regional passport offices as well as post offices and travel agencies. Whether for a first or subsequent passport, you must apply in person. Children under 16 may be included on a parent's passport but must have their own to travel alone. Passports are valid for five years and are usually mailed within two weeks of an application's receipt. For more information in English or French, call the passport office (tel. 514/283–2152 or 800/567–6868).

U.K. Citizens Citizens of the United Kingdom need a valid passport to enter Spain for stays of up to 90 days. Applications for new and renewal passports are available from main post offices as well as at the six passport offices, located in Belfast, Glasgow, Liverpool, London, Newport, and Peterborough. You may apply in person at all passport offices, or by mail to all except the London office. Children under 16 may travel on an accompanying parent's passport. All passports are valid for 10 years. Allow a month for processing.

A British Visitor's Passport is valid for holidays and some business trips of up to three months to Spain and other countries. It can include both partners of a married couple. A British visitor's passport is valid for one year and will be issued on the same day that you apply. You must apply in person at a main post office.

Customs and Duties

On Arrival Limits on transportation of goods from one EC country to another have been eliminated. From other countries, visitors age 15 and over are permitted to bring into Spain up to 200 cigarettes or 50 cigars, up to one liter of alcohol over 22 proof, and up to two liters of wine. Dogs and cats are admitted, providing they have up-to-date vaccination records from the home country.

Returning Home
U.S. Customs If you've been out of the country for at least 48 hours and haven't already used the exemption, or any part of it, in the past 30 days, you may bring home $400 worth of foreign goods duty-free. So can each member of your family, regardless of age; and your exemptions may be pooled, so one of you can bring in more if another brings in less. A flat 10% duty applies to the next $1,000 of goods; above $1,400, the rate varies with the merchandise. (If the 48-hour or 30-day limits apply, your duty-free allowance drops to $25, which may not be pooled.) Please note that these are the *general* rules, applicable to most countries, including Spain.

Travelers 21 or older may bring back 1 liter of alcohol duty-free, provided the beverage laws of the state through which they reenter the United States allow it. In addition, 100 non-Cuban cigars and 200 cigarettes are allowed, regardless of your age. Antiques and works of art more than 100 years old are duty-free.

Gifts valued at less than $50 may be mailed to the United States duty-free, with a limit of one package per day per addressee, and do not count as part of your exemption (do not send alcohol or tobacco products or perfume valued at more than $5); mark the package "Unsolicited Gift" and write the nature of the gift and its retail value on the outside. Most reputable stores will handle the mailing for you.

For a copy of "Know Before You Go," a free brochure detailing what you may and may not bring back to the United States, rates of duty, and other pointers, contact the **U.S. Customs Service** (Box 7407, Washington, DC 20044, tel. 202/927–6724).

Canadian Customs Once per calendar year, when you've been out of Canada for at least seven days, you may bring in C$300 worth of goods duty-free. If you've been away less than seven days but more than 48 hours, the duty-free exemption drops to C$100 but can be claimed any number of times (as can a C$20 duty-free exemption for absences of 24 hours or more). You cannot combine the yearly and 48-hour exemptions, use the C$300 exemption only partially (to save the balance for a later trip), or pool exemptions with family members. Goods claimed under the C$300 exemption may follow you by mail; those claimed under the lesser exemptions must accompany you on your return.

Alcohol and tobacco products may be included in the yearly and 48-hour exemptions but not in the 24-hour exemption. If you meet the age requirements of the province through which you reenter Canada, you may bring in, duty-free, 1.14 liters (40 imperial ounces) of wine or liquor *or* two dozen 12-ounce cans or bottles of beer or ale. If you are 16 or older, you may bring in, duty-free, 200 cigarettes, 50 cigars or cigarillos, and 400 tobacco sticks or 400 grams of manufactured tobacco.

An unlimited number of gifts valued up to C$60 each may be mailed to Canada duty-free. These do not count as part of your exemption. Label the package "Unsolicited Gift—Value under $60." Alcohol and tobacco are excluded.

For more information, including details of duties on items that exceed your duty-free limit, ask the Revenue Canada Customs and Excise and Taxation Department (2265 St. Laurent Blvd. S, Ottawa, Ontario, K1G 4K3, tel. 613/957–0275) for a copy of the free brochure "I Declare/Je Déclare."

U.K. Customs If your journey was wholly within EC countries, you no longer need to pass through customs when you return to the United Kingdom. According to EC guidelines, you may bring in 800 cigarettes, 400 cigarillos, 200 cigars, and 1 kilogram of smoking tobacco, plus 10 liters of spirits, 20 liters of fortified wine, 90 liters of wine, and 110 liters of beer. If you exceed these limits, you may be required to prove that the goods are for your personal use or are gifts.

For further information or a copy of "A Guide for Travellers," which details standard customs procedures as well as what you may bring into the United Kingdom from abroad, contact HM Customs and Excise (Dorset House, Stamford St., London SE1 9PY, tel. 0171/928–3344).

Traveling with Cameras, Camcorders, and Laptops

Film and Cameras If your camera is new or if you haven't used it for a while, shoot and develop a few test rolls before you leave. Store film in a cool, dry place—never in the car's glove compartment or on the shelf under the rear window.

Airport security X-rays generally aren't harmful to film with ISO below 400. To protect your film, carry it with you in a clear plastic bag and ask for a hand inspection. Such requests are honored at U.S. airports but are up to the inspector abroad. Don't depend on a lead-lined bag to protect film in checked luggage—the airline may increase the radiation to see what's inside. Call the Kodak Information Center (tel. 800/242–2424) for details.

Camcorders Before your trip, put camcorders through their paces, invest in a skylight filter to protect the lens, and check all the batteries. Most newer camcorders are equipped with batteries that can be recharged with a universal or worldwide AC adapter charger (or multivoltage converter), usable whether the voltage is 110 or 220. All that's needed is the appropriate plug.

Videotape Videotape is not damaged by X-rays, but it may be harmed by the magnetic field of a walk-through metal detector, so ask for a hand-check. Airport security personnel may ask you to turn on the camcorder to prove that it's what it appears to be, so make sure the battery is charged. Note that rather than the National Television System Committee video standard (NTSC) used in the United States and Canada, Spain uses PAL/SECAM technology. You will not be able to view your tapes through the local TV set or view movies bought there in your home VCR. Blank tapes bought in Eastern Europe can be used for NTSC camcorder taping, but they are pricey.

Laptops Security X-rays do not harm hard-disk or floppy-disk storage, but you may request a hand-check, at which point you may be asked to turn on the computer to prove that it is what it appears to be. (Check your battery before departure.) Most airlines allow you to use your laptop aloft except during takeoff and landing (so as not to interfere with navigation equipment). For international travel, register your foreign-made laptop with U.S. Customs as you leave the country. If your laptop is U.S.-made, call the consulate of the country you'll be visiting to find out whether it should be registered with customs upon arrival. Before departure, find out about repair facilities at your destination, and don't forget any transformer or adapter plug you may need (*see* Electricity in What to Pack, *above*).

Language

Spanish is referred to as Castellano, or Castilian. Roughly half the people you come in contact with will speak some English. But they speak the British variety, so don't be surprised if you are told to queue (line up) or take the lift (elevator) to the loo (toilet). All your attempts at Spanish are genuinely appreciated, and Spaniards will not make fun of your mistakes. Try to use at least the following basic phrases: *por favor* (please), *gracias* (thank you), *buenos días* (hello—until 2 PM), *buenas tardes* (good afternoon—until 8 PM), *buenas noches* (hello—after dark), *adiós* (good-bye), *encantado* (pleased to meet you), *sí* (yes), *no* (same as English), *los servicios* (the toilets), *la cuenta* (bill/check), *habla inglés?* (do you speak English?), *no comprendo* (I don't understand). Many guided tours offered at museums and historic sites are in Spanish; ask about the language that will be spoken before signing up.

Staying Healthy

Two problems frequently encountered during Spanish summers are sunburn and sunstroke. On hot, sunny days, even people who are not normally bothered by strong sun should cover themselves with a long-sleeve shirt, a hat, and long pants or a beach wrap. These are essential for a day at the beach but are also advisable for a long day of touring. Carry some sun-block lotion for nose, ears, and other sensitive areas, such as eyelids or ankles. Be sure to drink enough liquids. Above all, limit your sun time for the first few days until you become accustomed to the heat.

No special shots are required before visiting Spain.

Finding a The **International Association for Medical Assistance to Travellers**
Doctor (IAMAT, 417 Center St., Lewiston, NY 14092, tel. 716/754–4883; 40 Regal Rd., Guelph, Ontario N1K 1B5; 57 Voirets, 1212 Grand-Lancy, Geneva, Switzerland) publishes a worldwide directory of English-speaking physicians whose qualifications meet IAMAT standards and who have agreed to treat members for a set fee. Membership is free.

Assistance Pretrip medical referrals, emergency evacuation or repatriation,
Companies 24-hour telephone hot lines for medical consultation, dispatch of medical personnel, relay of medical records, cash for emergencies, and other personal and legal assistance are among the services provided by several membership organizations specializing in medi-

cal assistance to travelers. Among them are **International SOS Assistance** (Box 11568, Philadelphia, PA 19116, tel. 215/244–1500 or 800/523–8930; Box 466, Pl. Bonaventure, Montréal, Québec H5A 1C1, tel. 514/874–7674 or 800/363–0263), **Medex Assistance Corporation** (Box 10623, Baltimore, MD 21285, tel. 410/296–2530 or 800/874–9125), **Near Services** (450 Prairie Ave., Suite 101, Calumet City, IL 60409, tel. 708/868–6700 or 800/654–6700), and **Travel Assistance International** (1133 15th St. NW, Suite 400, Washington, DC 20005, tel. 202/331–1609 or 800/821–2828). Because these companies will also sell you death-and-dismemberment, trip-cancellation, and other insurance coverage, there is some overlap with the travel-insurance policies discussed under Insurance, *below.*

Publications *The Safe Travel Book* by Peter Savage ($12.95; Lexington Books, 866 3rd Ave., New York, NY 10022, tel. 212/702–4771 or 800/257–5755, fax 800/562–1272) is packed with handy lists and phone numbers to make your trip smooth. *Traveler's Medical Resource* by William W. Forgey ($19.95; ICS Books, Inc., 1 Tower Plaza, 107 E. 89th Ave., Merrillville, IN 45410, tel. 800/541–7323) is also a good, authoritative guide to care overseas.

Insurance

For U.S. Residents Most tour operators, travel agents, and insurance agents sell specialized health-and-accident, flight, trip-cancellation, and luggage insurance as well as comprehensive policies with some or all of these features. Before you make any purchase, review your existing health and homeowner policies to find out whether they cover expenses incurred while traveling.

Health-and-Accident Insurance Specific policy provisions of supplemental health-and-accident insurance for travelers include reimbursement for from $1,000 to $150,000 worth of medical and/or dental expenses caused by an accident or illness during a trip. The personal-accident, or death-and-dismemberment, provision pays a lump sum to your beneficiaries if you die or to you if you lose a limb or your eyesight; the lump sum awarded can range from $15,000 to $500,000. The medical-assistance provision may reimburse you for the cost of referrals, evacuation, or repatriation and other services, or it may automatically enroll you as a member of a particular medical-assistance company (*see* Assistance Companies in Staying Healthy, *above*).

Flight Insurance Often bought on a last-minute impulse at the airport, flight insurance pays a lump sum when a plane crashes, either to a beneficiary if the insured dies or sometimes to a surviving passenger who loses eyesight or a limb. Like most impulse buys, flight insurance is expensive and basically unnecessary. It supplements the airlines' coverage described in the limits-of-liability paragraphs on your ticket. Charging an airline ticket to a major credit card often automatically entitles you to coverage and may also embrace travel by bus, train, and ship.

Baggage Insurance In the event of loss, damage, or theft on international flights, airlines' liability is $20 per kilogram for checked baggage (roughly about $640 per 70-pound bag) and $400 per passenger for unchecked baggage. On domestic flights, the ceiling is $1,250 per passenger. Excess-valuation insurance can be bought directly from the airline at check-in for about $10 per $1,000 worth of coverage. However, you cannot buy it at any price for the rather extensive list of excluded items shown on your airline ticket.

Trip Insurance **Trip-cancellation-and-interruption insurance** protects you in the event you are unable to undertake or finish your trip, especially if your airline ticket, cruise, or package tour does not allow changes or cancellations. The amount of coverage you purchase should equal the cost of your trip should you, a traveling companion, or a family member fall ill, forcing you to stay home, plus the nondiscounted one-way airline ticket you would need to buy if you had to return home early. Read the fine print carefully, especially sections defining "family member" and "preexisting medical conditions." **Default or bankruptcy insurance** protects you against a supplier's failure to deliver. Such policies often do not cover default by a travel agency, tour operator, airline, or cruise line if you bought your tour and the coverage directly from the firm in question. Tours packaged by one of the 33 members of the United States Tour Operators Association (USTOA, 211 E. 51 St., Suite 12B, New York, NY 10022, tel. 212/750–7371), which requires members to maintain $1 million each in an account to reimburse clients in case of default, are likely to present the fewest difficulties.

Comprehensive Companies supplying comprehensive policies with some or all of the
Policies above features include **Access America, Inc.** (Box 90315, Richmond, VA 23230, tel. 800/284–8300); **Carefree Travel Insurance** (Box 310, 120 Mineola Blvd., Mineola, NY 11501, tel. 516/294–0220 or 800/323–3149); **Tele-Trip** (Mutual of Omaha Plaza, Box 31762, Omaha, NE 68131, tel. 800/228–9792); **The Travelers Companies** (1 Tower Sq., Hartford, CT 06183, tel. 203/277–0111 or 800/243–3174); **Travel Guard International** (1145 Clark St., Stevens Point, WI 54481, tel. 715/345–0505 or 800/826–1300); and **Wallach and Company, Inc.** (107 W. Federal St., Box 480, Middleburg, VA 22117, tel. 703/687–3166 or 800/237–6615).

U.K. Most tour operators, travel agents, and insurance agents sell spe-
Residents cialized policies covering accident, medical expenses, personal liability, trip cancellation, and loss or theft of personal property. You can also buy an annual travel-insurance policy valid for every trip (usually of less than 90 days) you make during the year in which it's purchased. Make sure you will be covered if you have a preexisting medical condition or are pregnant.

For advice by phone or a free booklet, "Holiday Insurance," that sets out what to expect from a holiday-insurance policy and gives price guidelines, contact the Association of British Insurers (51 Gresham St., London EC2V 7HQ, tel. 0171/600–3333; 30 Gordon St., Glasgow G1 3PU, tel. 0141/226–3905; Scottish Providence Bldg., Donegall Sq. W, Belfast BT1 6JE, tel. 01232/249176; call for other locations).

Car Rentals

Spain's leading car-rental firm is **ATESA** (Orense 83, Madrid, tel. 91/571–2145; Plaza Carmen Benitez 7, Seville, tel. 95/441–9712). In addition, most major car-rental companies are represented in Spain, including **Avis** (tel. 800/331–1084, 800/879–2847 in Canada); **Budget** (tel. 800/527–0700); **Hertz** (tel. 800/654–3001, 800/263–0600 in Canada); and **National** (tel. 800/227–3876), the latter two known internationally as InterRent and Europcar, respectively.

In cities, unlimited-mileage rates range from $46 per day for an economy car to $125 for a large car; weekly unlimited-mileage rates range from $180 to $450. This does not include IVA tax, which in Spain is 15% on car rentals.

Requirements Your own driver's license is not acceptable. An International Driver's Permit, available from the American or Canadian Automobile Association, is necessary.

Extra Charges Picking up the car in one city and leaving it in another may entail substantial drop-off charges or one-way service fees. The cost of a collision or loss-damage waiver (*see below*) can be high, also. Some rental agencies will charge you extra if you return the car *before* the time specified on your contract. Ask before making unscheduled drop-offs. Be sure the rental agent agrees *in writing* to any changes in drop-off location or other items of your rental contract. Fill the tank when you turn in the vehicle to avoid being charged for refueling at what you'll swear is the most expensive pump in town. In Europe, manual transmissions are standard and air-conditioning is a rarity and often unnecessary. Asking for an automatic transmission or air-conditioning can significantly increase the cost of your rental.

Insurance and Collision-Damage Waiver Until recently, standard rental contracts included liability coverage (for damage to public property, injury to pedestrians, and so on) and coverage for the car against fire, theft, and collision damage with a deductible. Due to law changes in some states and rising liability costs, several car rental agencies have reduced the type of coverage they offer. Before you rent a car, find out exactly what coverage, if any, is provided by your personal auto insurer. Don't assume that you are covered. If you do want insurance from the rental company, secondary coverage may be the only type offered. You may already have secondary coverage if you charge the rental to a credit card. Only Diners Club (tel. 800/234–6377) provides primary coverage in the United States and worldwide.

In general if you have an accident, you are responsible for the automobile. Car rental companies may offer a collision damage waiver (CDW), which ranges in cost from $4 to $14 a day. You should decline the CDW only if you are certain you are covered through your personal insurer or credit card company.

Rail Passes

Spain Flexipasses give you three, five, or 10 days of travel during any one-month period; cost is $185, $265, and $470 for first class, $145, $225, and $345 for second class. Various rail/drive packages are also available. The **Spain Rail 'N Drive Pass** gives you three days of rail travel in Spain and three days' use of an Avis car with unlimited mileage in both Spain and Portugal; cost ranges from $325 for an economy car to $475 for a small automatic if you opt for first-class train travel, $279–$435 if you go second class ($265–$339 in first-class, $219–$295 in second, per person, for two adults traveling together). Prices include local tax and free drop-off. (None of the above rail passes are valid for the Andalusia Express nor the Pablo Casals, and you must pay extra, in local currency, to ride the AVE, Talgo, and some other trains.)

These passes must be purchased before you reach Spain. Apply through your travel agent, or **Rail Europe** (226–230 Westchester Ave., White Plains, NY 10604, tel. 914/682–5172 or 800/848–7245 from the East and 800/848-7245 from the West).

Seat Reservations Don't make the mistake of assuming that your rail pass guarantees you seats on the trains you want to ride. Seat reservations are required on some trains, particularly high-speed trains, and are a good idea on trains that may be crowded. You will also need reservations for overnight sleeping accommodations. Rail Europe can help you determine if you need reservations and can make them for you (about $10 each, less if you purchase them in Europe at the time of travel).

Student and Youth Travel

Travel Agencies
Council Travel Services (CTS), a subsidiary of the nonprofit Council on International Educational Exchange (CIEE), specializes in low-cost travel arrangements abroad for students and is the exclusive U.S. agent for several discount cards. Newly available from CTS are domestic air passes for bargain travel within the United States. CIEE's twice-yearly *Student Travels* magazine is available at the CTS office at CIEE headquarters (205 E. 42nd St., 16th Floor, New York, NY 10017, tel. 212/661–1450) and in Boston (tel. 617/266–1926), Miami (tel. 305/670–9261), Los Angeles (tel. 310/208–3551) and at 43 branches in college towns nationwide (free in person, $1 by mail). **Campus Connections** (1100 E. Marlton Pike, Cherry Hill, NJ 08034, tel. 800/428–3235) specializes in discounted accommodations and airline fares for students. The **Educational Travel Centre** (438 N. Frances St., Madison, WI 53703, tel. 608/256–5551) offers low-cost domestic and international airline tickets, mostly for flights departing from Chicago, and rail passes. Other travel agencies catering to students include **TMI Student Travel** (1146 Pleasant St., Watertown, MA 02172, tel. 617/661–8187 or 800/245–3672), and **Travel Cuts** (187 College St., Toronto, Ontario M5T 1P7, tel. 416/979–2406).

Discount Cards
For discounts on transportation and on museum and attractions admissions, buy the **International Student Identity Card** (ISIC) if you're a bona fide student or the **International Youth Card** (IYC) if you're under 26. In the United States the ISIC and IYC cards cost $16 each and include basic travel accident and illness coverage and a toll-free travel assistance hotline. Apply to **CIEE** (*see* address *above*, tel. 212/661–1414; the application is in *Student Travels*). In Canada the cards are available for $15 each from **Travel Cuts** (*see above*). In the United Kingdom they cost £5 and £4 respectively at student unions and student travel companies, including Council Travel's London office (28A Poland St., London W1V 3DB, tel. 0171/437–7767).

Hostelling
There are some 55 youth hostels *(albergues juveniles)* throughout Spain, and more open during the summer months. But because of the abundance of unsupervised cheap lodging at pensions, hostels are not as popular in Spain as in other European countries. A youth hostel card is needed. Spanish hostels are listed in the international YHA directory, or you can contact the **Red Nacional de Albergues Juveniles** (Ortega y Gasset 71–3A, 28006 Madrid, tel. 91/347–7700).

A **Hostelling International** (HI) membership card is the key to more than 5,000 hostels in 70 countries; the sex-segregated, dormitory-style sleeping quarters, including some for families, go for $7 to $20 a night per person. Membership is available in the United States through **Hostelling International-American Youth Hostels** (HI-AYH, 733 15th St. NW, Suite 840, Washington, DC 20005, tel. 202/783–6161), the U.S. link in the worldwide chain, and costs $25 for adults 18 to 54, $10 for those under 18, $15 for those 55 and over, and $35 for families. Volume 1 of the *AYH Guide to Budget Accommodation* lists hostels in Europe and the Mediterranean ($13.95, including postage). HI membership is available in Canada through **Hostelling International-Canada** (205 Catherine St., Suite 400, Ottawa, Ontario K2P 1C3, tel. 613/748–5638) for $26.75, and in the United Kingdom through the **Youth Hostel Association of England and Wales** (Trevelyan House, 8 St. Stephen's Hill, St. Albans, Hertfordshire AL1 2DY, tel. 01727/855215) for £9.

Tour Operators Contiki (300 Plaza Alicante #900, Garden Grove, CA 92640, tel. 714/740–0808 or 800/266–8454) specializes in package tours for travelers from 18 to 35.

Traveling with Children

Spaniards love children, and bringing them along on your trip should not be a problem. You will see children accompanying their parents everywhere, including bars and restaurants. Shopkeepers will shower your child with *caramelos* (sweets), and even the coldest waiters tend to be friendlier when you have a youngster with you. But although you will not be shunted into a remote corner when you bring children into a Spanish restaurant, you won't find high chairs or special kids' menus. Children are expected to eat what their parents do, and it is perfectly acceptable to ask for an extra plate and share your food. Museum admissions and bus and metro rides are generally free for children up to age five. Be prepared for late bedtimes. Especially in summer, it is surprisingly common to see under-fives playing cheerfully outdoors until midnight. Disposable diapers (*pañales*), formula (*papillas*), and bottled baby foods are readily available at supermarkets and pharmacies.

Publications **Family Travel Times,** published 10 times a year by Travel With Your
Newsletter Children (TWYCH, 45 W. 18th St., New York, NY 10011, tel. 212/206–0688; annual subscription $55), covers destinations, types of vacations, and modes of travel. TWYCH also publishes *Cruising with Children* ($22) and *Skiing with Children* ($29).

Books *Traveling with Children—And Enjoying It,* by Arlene K. Butler ($11.95 plus $3 shipping per book; Globe Pequot Press, Box 833, 6 Business Park Rd., Old Saybrook, CT 06475, tel. 800/243–0495, or 800/962–0973 in CT) helps you plan your trip with children, from toddlers to teens. *Innocents Abroad: Traveling with Kids in Europe,* by Valerie Wolf Deutsch and Laura Sutherland ($15.95 or $4.95 paperback; Penguin USA, 120 Woodbine St., Bergenfield, NJ 07621, tel. 800/253–6476), covers child- and teen-friendly activities, food, and transportation.

Getting There On international flights, the fare for infants under age 2 not occupy-
Air Fares ing a seat is generally either free or 10% of the accompanying adult's fare; children ages 2 through 11 usually pay from half to two-thirds of the adult fare. On domestic flights, children under 2 not occupying a seat travel free, and older children currently travel on the "lowest applicable" adult fare.

Baggage In general, infants paying 10% of the adult fare are allowed one carry-on bag, not to exceed 70 pounds or 45 inches (length + width + height), and a collapsible stroller; check with the airline before departure, because you may be allowed less if the flight is full. The adult baggage allowance applies for children paying half or more of the adult fare.

Safety Seats The FAA recommends the use of safety seats aloft and details approved models in the free leaflet "**Child/Infant Safety Seats Recommended for Use in Aircraft**" (available from the Federal Aviation Administration, APA–200, 800 Independence Ave. SW, Washington, DC 20591, tel. 202/267–3479); information hotline, tel. 800/322–7873). Airline policy varies. U.S. carriers allow FAA-approved models bearing a sticker declaring their FAA approval. Because these seats are strapped into regular passenger seats, airlines may require that a ticket be bought for an infant who would otherwise ride free.

Facilities Aloft Some airlines provide other services for children, such as children's meals and freestanding bassinets (only to those with seats at the bulkhead, where there's enough legroom). Make your request when reserving. Biennially the February issue of *Family Travel Times* details children's services on three dozen airlines ($12; *see above*). "Kids and Teens in Flight" (free from the U.S. Department of Transportation's Office of Consumer Affairs (R-25, Washington, DC 20590, tel. 202/366-2220) offers tips for children flying alone.

Lodging Spanish hotels have no trouble providing a crib or cot for children who share a room with their parents, but there is almost always a small extra charge. The **Novotel** hotel chain (tel. 800/221-4542) allows up to two children to stay free in their parents' room. Many of the hotels include playgrounds.

Baby-Sitting While there is no such thing as a baby-sitting agency in Spain, reli-
Services able child minders can be located through your hotel. With a few hours' notice, the concierge or reception desk can find a baby-sitter, usually a moonlighting maid who will charge about 800 pesetas an hour.

Hints for Travelers with Disabilities

Unfortunately, Spain has done little to make traveling easy for visitors with disabilities. Only the newest museums, such as the Reina Sofia and the Thyssen-Bornemisza museum in Madrid, have wheelchair entrances or elevators. Most of the churches, castles, and monasteries on a tourist's itinerary involve quite a bit of walking and climbing uneven terrain.

Organizations Several organizations provide travel information for people with disabilities, usually for a membership fee, and some publish newsletters and bulletins. Among them are the **Information Center for Individuals with Disabilities** (Fort Point Pl., 27-43 Wormwood St., Boston, MA 02210, tel. 617/727-5540 or 800/462-5015 in MA between 11 AM and 4 PM, or leave message; TTY 617/345-9743); **Mobility International USA** (Box 10767, Eugene, OR 97440, tel. and TTY 503/343-1284, fax 503/343-6812), the U.S. branch of an international organization based in Britain (*see below*) that has affiliates in 30 countries; **MossRehab Hospital Travel Information Service** (tel. 215/456-9603, TTY 215/456-9602); the **Travel Industry and Disabled Exchange** (TIDE, 5435 Donna Ave., Tarzana, CA 91356, tel. 818/344-3640, fax 818/344-0078); and **Travelin' Talk** (Box 3534, Clarksville, TN 37043, tel. 615/552-6670, fax 615/552-1182).

In the United Important information sources include the **Royal Association for**
Kingdom **Disability and Rehabilitation** (RADAR, 12 City Forum, 250 City Rd., London EC1V 8AF, tel. 0171/250-3222), which publishes travel information for people with disabilities in Britain, and **Mobility International** (228 Borough High St., London SE1 1JX, tel. 0171/403-5688), an international clearinghouse of travel information for people with disabilities.

Travel **Flying Wheels Travel** (143 W. Bridge St., Box 382, Owatonna, MN
Agency 55060, tel. 507/451-5005 or 800/535-6790) is a travel agency specializing in domestic and worldwide cruises, tours, and independent travel itineraries for people with mobility problems.

Publications Two free publications are available from the U.S. Consumer Information Center (Pueblo, CO 81009): "New Horizons for the Air Traveler with a Disability" (include Dept. 608Y in the address), a U.S. Department of Transportation booklet describing changes resulting from the 1986 Air Carrier Access Act and from the 1990 Americans with Disabilities Act, and the Airport Operators Council's *Access Travel: Airports* (Dept. 5804), which describes facilities and services for people with disabilities at more than 500 airports worldwide.

Travelin' Talk Directory (*see* Organizations, *above*) was published in 1993. This 500-page resource book ($35 check or money order with a money-back guarantee) is packed with information for travelers with disabilities. Twin Peaks Press (Box 129, Vancouver, WA 98666, tel. 206/694–2462 or 800/637–2256) publishes the *Directory of Travel Agencies for the Disabled* ($19.95), listing more than 370 agencies worldwide. Add $2 for shipping.

Hints for Older Travelers

In Spain seniors are called *Tercer Edad* (literally "third age"). Older travelers should have no problems visiting Spain provided they do not try to cram too much sightseeing into one day, especially in the scorching months of July and August. Discounts on admissions and transportation for seniors are not common, however, and the RENFE Gold Card for half-price train tickets is available only to Spanish citizens and legal foreign residents over 60.

Organizations The **American Association of Retired Persons** (AARP, 601 E St. NW, Washington, DC 20049, tel. 202/434–2277) provides independent travelers who are members of the AARP (open to those age 50 or older; $8 per person or couple annually) with the Purchase Privilege Program, which offers discounts on lodging, car rentals, and sightseeing. AARP also arranges group tours, cruises, and apartment living through AARP Travel Experience from American Express (400 Pinnacle Way, Suite 450, Norcross, GA 30071, tel. 800/927–0111 or 800/745–4567).

Two other organizations offer discounts on lodgings, car rentals, and other travel products, along with such nontravel perks as magazines and newsletters: the **National Council of Senior Citizens** (1331 F St. NW, Washington, DC 20004, tel. 202/347–8800 (membership $12 annually) and **Mature Outlook** (6001 N. Clark St., Chicago, IL 60660, tel. 800/336–6330; $9.95 annually).

Note: Mention your senior-citizen identification card when booking hotel reservations for reduced rates, not when checking out. At restaurants, show your card before you're seated; discounts may be limited to certain menus, days, or hours. If you are renting a car, ask about promotional rates that might improve on your senior-citizen discount.

Educational The nonprofit **Elderhostel** (75 Federal St., 3rd Floor, Boston, MA
Travel 02110, tel. 617/426–7788) has offered inexpensive study programs for people 60 and older since 1975. Held at more than 1,800 educational and cultural institutions, courses cover everything from marine science to Greek myths and cowboy poetry. Participants generally attend lectures in the morning and spend the afternoon sightseeing or on field trips; they live in dormitory-type lodgings. Unique home-stay programs are offered in a few countries. Fees for the two- to three-week international trips—including room, board, tuition, and transportation from the United States—range from $1,800 to $4,500.

Interhostel (University of New Hampshire, 6 Garrison Ave., Durham, NH 03824, tel. 603/862–1147 or 800/733–9753) caters to a slightly younger clientele—50 and over—and runs programs in some 25 countries. The idea is similar: Lectures and field trips mix with sightseeing, and participants stay in dormitories at cooperating educational institutions or in modest hotels. Programs usually last two weeks and cost $1,500–$2,100, excluding airfare.

Publications *The 50 + Traveler's Guidebook: Where to Go, Where to Stay, What to Do* by Anita Williams and Merrimac Dillon ($12.95; St. Martin's Press, 175 5th Ave., New York, NY 10010) is available in bookstores and offers many useful tips. "The Mature Traveler" (Box 50820, Reno, NV 89513, tel. 702/786–7419; $29.95), a monthly newsletter, contains many travel deals.

Hints for Gay and Lesbian Travelers

Organizations The **International Gay Travel Association** (Box 4974, Key West, FL 33041, tel. 800/448–8550), which has 700 members, will provide you with names of travel agents and tour operators who specialize in gay travel. The **Gay & Lesbian Visitors Center of New York Inc.** (135 W. 20th St., 3rd Floor, New York, NY 10011, tel. 212/463–9030 or 800/ 395–2315; $100 annually) mails a monthly newsletter to its members with information about domestic and international destinations.

Travel Agencies and Tour Operators The dominant travel agency in the market is **Above and Beyond** (3568 Sacramento St., San Francisco, CA 94118, tel. 415/922–2683 or 800/ 397–2681). Tour operator **Olympus Vacations** (8424 Santa Monica Blvd., #721, West Hollywood, CA 90069, tel. 310/657–2220) offers all-gay-and-lesbian resort holidays. **Skylink Women's Travel** (746 Ashland Ave., Santa Monica, CA 90405, tel. 310/452–0506 or 800/ 225–5759) handles individual travel for lesbians all over the world and conducts two international and five domestic group trips annually.

Publications The premier international travel magazine for gays and lesbians is **Our World** (1104 N. Nova Rd., Suite 251, Daytona Beach, FL 32117, tel. 904/441–5367; $35 for 10 issues). **Out & About** (tel. 203/789–8518 or 800/929–2268; $49 for 10 issues, full refund if you aren't satisfied) is a 16-page monthly newsletter with extensive information on resorts, hotels, and airlines that are gay-friendly.

Further Reading

Spain's people and history are explained through the metaphors of their monuments and landscapes in Jan Morris's brilliant series of essays entitled *Spain;* James A. Michener fills us in on all the anecdotes that make sightseeing worthwhile in *Iberia: Spanish Travels and Reflections;* and Ted Walker has more of a vagabond approach to travel in his book *In Spain.* Madrid-based journalist John Hooper examines the post-Franco era in *The Spaniards.*

Ernest Hemingway is the writer most responsible for embellishing the image of Spain. Read *The Sun Also Rises,* also known as *Fiesta,* for a vicarious visit to the Running of the Bulls in Pamplona. *For Whom the Bell Tolls* depicts the physical and psychological horrors of the Spanish civil war, and *Death in the Afternoon* contains a convincing argument on bullfighting.

H. V. Morton *(A Stranger in Spain),* George Orwell *(Homage to Catalonia),* V. S. Pritchett *(The Spanish Temper),* and Washington

Irving (the romantic and mystical *Tales of the Alhambra*) have all paid their respects to Spain.

Among Spanish writers, the story of the errant knight *Don Quixote*, by Miguel de Cervantes, will always be Spain's towering classic. The disturbing drama of Spain's repressed women is told in Federico García Lorca's play *Blood Wedding*.

For more modern fare try translations of the realism-drenched novels of Galician Camilo José Cela, the 1989 recipient of the Nobel Prize for literature. *The Beehive* and *The Family of Pascual Duarte* are his best-known works. *The Story of Spain*, by Mark Williams, is a fascinating account of the role Spain has played in world events throughout the centuries.

Gourmet Janet Mendel Searl's *Cooking in Spain* goes beyond the recipes to offer mouth-watering explanations of the country's regional specialties; Penelope Casas's *The Food and Wine of Spain* and *Tapas* both capture the flavor of Spanish life in essays and recipes; *404 Spanish Wines*, by Frank Snell, includes information on wine-growing regions; Author Colman Andrews's contagious enthusiasm for that region's foods is revealed in *Catalan Cuisine: Europe's Last Great Culinary Secret*.

Arriving and Departing

All transatlantic flights arriving in Spain from the United States and Canada pass through Madrid. Some stop briefly to let off passengers, while others require you to change planes to get to a farther destination in Spain.

From North America by Plane

Flights are either nonstop, direct, or connecting. A **nonstop** flight requires no change of plane and makes no stops. A **direct** flight stops at least once and can involve a change of plane, although the flight number remains the same; if the first leg is late, the second waits. This is not the case with a **connecting** flight, which involves a different plane and a different flight number.

Airports and Airlines Madrid's airport is called **Barajas** (tel. 91/305–8343), Barcelona's is **El Prat de Llobregat** (tel. 93/478–5000).

The seven airlines that fly nonstop from North America are **Iberia** (tel. 800/772–4642), from New York, Montreal, Miami; **TWA** (tel. 800/892–4141), from New York; **Continental** (tel. 800/231–0856), from Newark, New Jersey; **American Airlines** (tel. 800/433–7300), from Dallas/Ft. Worth and Miami; **United Airlines** (tel. 800/241–6522), from Washington, D.C.; **Delta** (800/221–1212), from Atlanta; and **AeroMexico** (tel. 800/237–6639), from Miami. Two of the best-known charters for flights to Spain are **Air Europa** (tel. 718/244–6016) and **Spanair** (tel. 212/695–8660).

If you are arriving early in the morning on an overnight flight, be sure to let your hotel know in advance so it can have a room ready and you can get a nap.

Flying Time to Madrid From New York: 7 hours. From Dallas/Ft. Worth: 10½ hours. From Los Angeles (including one stop): 14½ hours.

Cutting Costs The Sunday travel section of most newspapers is a good source of deals. When booking, particularly through an unfamiliar company, call the Better Business Bureau and your local or state Consumer

Protection Bureau to find out whether any complaints have been registered against the company, pay with a credit card if you can, and consider trip-cancellation and default insurance (*see* Insurance, *above*). A helpful resource is *Airfare Secrets Exposed*, by Sharon Tyler and Matthew Wonder ($16.95; Universal Information Publishing), available in bookstores.

Promotional Airfares Less expensive fares, called promotional or discount fares, are round-trip and involve restrictions, which vary according to the route and season. You must usually buy the ticket—commonly called an APEX (advance purchase excursion) when it's for international travel—in advance (seven, 14, or 21 days are usual), although some of the major airlines have added no-frills, cheap flights to compete with new bargain airlines on certain routes.

With the major airlines, the cheaper fares generally require minimum and maximum stays (for instance, over a Saturday night or at least seven and no more than 30 days). Airlines generally allow some return date changes for a $25 to $50 fee, but most low-fare tickets are nonrefundable. Only a death in the family would prompt the airline to return any of your money if you cancel a nonrefundable ticket. However, you can apply an unused nonrefundable ticket toward a new ticket, again with a small fee. The lowest fare is subject to availability, and only a small percentage of the plane's total seats will be sold at that price. Contact the U.S. Department of Transportation's Office of Consumer Affairs (I–25, Washington, DC 20590, tel. 202/366–2220) for a copy of "Fly-Rights: A Guide to Air Travel in the U.S." *The Official Frequent Flyer Guidebook*, by Randy Petersen ($14.99, plus $3 shipping and handling; 4715-C Town Center Dr., Colorado Springs, CO 80916, tel. 719/597–8899 or 800/487–8893), yields valuable hints on getting the most for your air travel dollars. Also new and helpful is *202 Tips Even the Best Business Travelers May Not Know*, by Christopher McGinnis, president of the Travel Skills Group ($10 in bookstores; Box 52927, Atlanta, GA 30355, tel. 404/659–2855).

Consolidators Consolidators or bulk-fare operators—"bucket shops"—buy blocks of seats on scheduled flights that airlines anticipate they won't be able to sell. They pay wholesale prices, add a markup, and resell the seats to travel agents or directly to the public at prices that still undercut the airline's promotional or discount fares (higher than a charter ticket but lower than an APEX ticket, and usually without the advance-purchase restriction). Moreover, some consolidators sometimes give you your money back. Carefully read the fine print detailing penalties for changes and cancellations. If you doubt the reliability of a company, call the airline once you've made your booking and confirm that you do, indeed, have a reservation on the flight.

The biggest U.S. consolidator, C.L. Thomson Express, sells only to travel agents. Well-established consolidators selling to the public include **UniTravel** (Box 12485, St. Louis, MO 63132, tel. 314/569–0900 or 800/325–2222); **Council Charter** (205 E. 42nd St., New York, NY 10017, tel. 212/661–0311 or 800/800–8222); and **Travac** (989 6th Ave., New York, NY 10018, tel. 212/563–3303 or 800/872–8800).

Discount Travel Clubs Travel clubs offer members unsold space on airplanes, cruise ships, and package tours at as much as 50% below regular prices. Membership may include a regular bulletin or access to a toll-free hotline giving details of available trips departing from three or four days to several months in the future. Most also offer 50% discounts off hotel rack rates, but double-check with the hotel to make sure it isn't offering a better promotional rate independent of the club. Clubs include **Discount Travel International** (114 Forrest Ave., Suite 203, Narberth, PA 19072, tel. 215/668–7184; $45 annually, single or family), **Entertainment Travel Editions** (Box 1014, Trumbull, CT 06611, tel. 800/445–4137; $28–$48 annually), **Great American Traveler** (Box 27965, Salt Lake City, UT 84127, tel. 800/548–2812; $29.95 annually), **Moment's Notice Discount Travel Club** (425 Madison Ave., New York, NY 10017, tel. 212/486–0503; $45 annually, single or family), **Privilege Card** (3391 Peachtree Rd. NE, Suite 110, Atlanta, GA 30326, tel. 404/262–0222 or 800/236–9732; domestic annual membership $49.95, international, $74.95), **Travelers Advantage** (CUC Travel Service, 49 Music Sq. W, Nashville, TN 37203, tel. 800/548–1116; $49 annually, single or family), and **Worldwide Discount Travel Club** (1674 Meridian Ave., Miami Beach, FL 33139, tel. 305/534–2082; $50 annually for family, $40 single).

Publications The newsletter "Travel Smart" (40 Beechdale Rd., Dobbs Ferry, NY 10522, tel. 800/327–3633; $44 a year) has a wealth of travel deals in each monthly issue. The monthly "Consumer Reports Travel Letter" (Consumers Union, 101 Truman Ave., Yonkers, NY 10703, tel. 800/234–1970) is filled with information on travel savings and indispensable consumer tips.

Enjoying the Fly at night if you're able to sleep on a plane. Because the air aloft is
Flight dry, drink plenty of fluids while on board. Drinking alcohol contributes to jet lag, as do heavy meals. Bulkhead seats, in the front row of each cabin—usually reserved for people who have disabilities, are elderly, or are traveling with babies—offer more legroom, but trays attach awkwardly to seat armrests, and all possessions must be stowed overhead.

Smoking Since February 1990, smoking has been banned on all domestic flights of less than six hours' duration; the ban also applies to domestic segments of international flights aboard U.S. and foreign carriers. On U.S. carriers flying to Spain and other destinations abroad, a seat in a no-smoking section must be provided for every passenger who requests one, and the section must be enlarged to accommodate such passengers if necessary, as long as they have complied with the airline's deadline for check-in and seat assignment. If smoking bothers you, request a seat far from the smoking section. Smoking has been banned on all flights within the Iberian Peninsula.

From the U.K. by Plane, Train, Car, and Bus

By Plane It's important to distinguish between scheduled services to Spain, operated chiefly by **Iberia** and **British Airways**, and inexpensive charter flights, operated by a whole range of companies, that serve the holiday airports in the summer. If you're looking for bargains, don't mind traveling at inconvenient times, and are prepared for delays—up to 48 hours at peak periods—then consider a charter flight. But if you value reliability—and don't mind paying for it—you're better off with a scheduled flight. There are up to seven flights a day to Madrid from London, and up to six to Barcelona. Flying time is between 2 and 2½ hours. The lowest fares require a Saturday night stayover. For reservations and information: **British Airways** (tel. 0171/897–4000), **Iberia** (tel. 0171/437–5622).

By Train Train services to Spain are not as frequent, fast, or inexpensive as airplane travel.

To reach Spain from Britain, you have to change trains (and rail stations) in Paris. It's worth paying extra for a "TALGO" express or for the "Puerta del Sol" express to avoid having to change trains again at the Spanish border. Journey time to Paris is around six hours; to Madrid from Paris, an additional 13 hours. Allow at least two hours in Paris for changing trains.

International overnight trains run from Madrid to Lisbon (11½ hours) and Barcelona to Paris (11½ hours). A daytime trip is offered from Barcelona to Grenoble and Geneva (10 hours).

Eurotrain (52 Grosvenor Gardens, London SW1W OAG, tel. 0171/730–3402) and **Transalpino** (71–75 Buckingham Palace Rd., London SW1W ORE, tel. 0171/834–9656) both offer excellent deals for those under 26. Otherwise, book through **British Rail Travel Centers** (tel. 0171/834–2345).

By Car Potentially the cheapest route to Spain by car, though not the fastest, is by cross-Channel ferry to France and then overland to Spain. The drawbacks are that the shortest, and thus the cheapest, ferry crossings (Dover–Calais or Folkestone–Boulogne) leave you with the greatest amount of driving, which can be not only tiring but also expensive, depending on whether you take toll autoroutes through France and how many nights you spend en route. Even the longer ferry crossings leave you with a significant amount of driving. Cherbourg, for example, with ferries from Portsmouth, is 980 km (610 mi) from the Spanish border.

An alternative is to put your car on the train in France, at either Calais or Boulogne, and travel overnight to Narbonne, 80 km (50 mi) from Spain's northeast border, or Biarritz, right on Spain's northwest border. Though fast and restful, this option is significantly more expensive. Similarly, direct ferry links between Britain and Spain are also expensive, but they get you there in 24 hours with no strain, weather permitting. Brittany Ferries runs between Plymouth and Santander, while P&O European Ferries operates from Plymouth to Bilbao.

For reservations and information: **Brittany Ferries** (tel. 01752/221–321), **Hover-Speed** (tel. 0171/554–7061), **P&O European Ferries** (tel. 0181/575–8555), **Sealink** (tel. 01223/47047), **SNCF** (for Motorail, tel. 0171/409–3518).

By Bus The **Eurolines/National Express** consortium runs regular bus services to more than 45 destinations in Spain. Journey times are around 32 hours to Madrid from London and around 26 hours to Barcelona. There's a daily bus to Barcelona at peak periods and never fewer than two a week the rest of the year. There are two buses a week to Madrid year-round. Fares are reasonable. For reservations and information: **Eurolines/National Express** (tel. 0171/730–0202).

Staying in Madrid and Barcelona

Getting Around

By Plane **Iberia** (tel. 901/333–111) and its sister carrier, **Aviaco,** are the main airlines offering domestic service. Between Madrid and Barcelona, Iberia operates the *Puente Aereo* (Air Bridge) commuter service. Flights leave every half-hour or hour, depending on the time of day, and no advance booking is needed; just show up at the airport, buy a ticket, and take the next flight out. On certain days of the week, Iberia offers *minifares*, which can save you 40% on domestic flights.

Tickets must be purchased in advance, and you must stay over Saturday night.

Two independent airlines, **Air Europa** (tel. 91/305–5130) and **Spanair** (tel. 902/131–415), began operations in 1994; both offer a number of domestic routes, including Madrid–Barcelona, at prices about one-third less than Iberia.

By Train In 1992 Spain launched its first high-speed train, the AVE, which travels between Madrid and Seville in less than three hours. However, the rest of the government-run railroad, RENFE, remains below par by European standards. Train travel can be tediously slow, and most long-distance runs are made at night. While overnight trains have comfortable sleeper cars, first-class fares that include a sleeping compartment are about the same as those for air travel.

For most journeys, however, trains are the most economical way to go. First- and second-class seats are reasonably priced, and you can get a bunk in a compartment with five other people for a supplement of about $25. The most comfortable train is called a TALGO, and has a special inverted suspension system designed to give a faster and smoother ride on winding rails. Food in the dining cars and bars is overpriced and uninspired.

Most Spaniards buy train tickets in advance by standing in long lines at the station. But the overworked clerks rarely speak English, so you are better off going to a travel agency that displays the blue and yellow RENFE sign; the price is the same.

Fares Those planning extensive train travel during their stay should weigh the benefits of buying a *tarjeta tourista*, which allows unlimited travel during a 15-day or 30-day period. Large families are also eligible for substantial discounts, but there are no special fares for foreign senior citizens. Another option is to consider traveling on *valles* (literally, "valleys"), a special category of cheaper trains that leave at unpopular times, usually early in the morning.

If you are under 26 and have not invested in a Eurail Youthpass or any of the other rail passes, inquire about discount travel fares under a *Billet International Jeune* (BIJ) scheme. The special one-trip tariff is offered by **EuroTrain International,** with offices in London, Dublin, Paris, Madrid, Lisbon, Rome, Zurich, Athens, Brussels, Budapest, Hannover, Leiden, Vienna, and Tangier. You can purchase a EuroTrain ticket at one of these offices, or through travel agent networks, mainline rail stations, and specialist youth travel operators.

Smoking RENFE provides nonsmoking cars on many short runs and all long-distance service; ask for a seat or bunk in these areas when you reserve. But be prepared for second-hand smoke: Many Spaniards happily ignore all posted signs.

By Bus An array of private companies operates Spain's buses, providing service that ranges from knee-crunching basic to luxurious. Some buses have television and free drinks. Fares are lower than for rail travel. If you want to reach a town not served by train, you can be sure a bus will go there. Spanish towns don't usually have a central bus depot, so ask at the tourist office where to pick up a bus to your destination.

Bus tours are a popular way to see large cities and the surrounding sights. Among the largest operators, most with tours in English, are **Julia Tours** (Gran Vía 68, Madrid, tel. 91/571–5300); **Pullmantur** (Plaza de Oriente 8, Madrid, tel. 91/541–1805); **Marsans** (Gran Vía

59, Madrid, tel. 91/547–7300). In most cases you can book bus tours through your hotel.

By Car Driving is the best way to see rural areas and get off the beaten track. Roads are classified as follows: A for *autopista* (tollroad or *peaje*); N for *nacional* (main roads that are either divided highways or two lanes); and C for *comarcal* (local roads that crisscross the countryside).

Road Conditions Spain's highway system was overhauled in 1992 and the improvement is startling. It now includes some 6,000 km (3,600 mi) of superhighways. Still, however, you find some stretches of major national highways that are two lanes wide, where traffic often backs up behind heavy trucks. Autopista tolls are steep.

Most Spanish cities have notoriously long morning and evening rush hours, which can try any driver's patience. Traffic jams *(atascos)* are especially bad in and surrounding Barcelona and Madrid, where the morning rush hour can last until noon! Evening rush hour runs from 7 PM to 9 PM.

Rules of the Road Residents of EU countries can use their national driver's license in Spain; others should have an International Driving Permit (*see* Car Rentals in Before You Go, *above*), although this rule is rarely enforced. Driving is on the right, and horns are banned in cities, but that doesn't keep Spaniards from blasting away. Children under 10 may not ride in the front seats, and seat belts are compulsory everywhere. Speed limits are 60 km per hour (37 mph) in cities, 100 km per hour (62 mph) on N roads, 120 km per hour (74 mph) on the autopista, and 90 km per hour (56 mph) unless otherwise signposted on other roads.

Gas Gas stations are plentiful. Prices, decontrolled in 1993, were 101 pesetas a liter for *normal* (regular; 92 octane) and 106 pesetas a liter for *super* (97 octane) at press time. Many small town service stations do not sell unleaded gas. Credit cards are frequently accepted, especially along main routes.

Breakdowns The large car-rental companies, Hertz and Avis, have 24-hour breakdown service. If you are a member of an automobile club (AAA, CAA, or AA), you can get help from the Spanish auto club RACE (Jose Abascal 10, Madrid, tel. 91/447–3200; emergency assistance, 91/593–3333).

Telephones

Pay Phones There are three types of pay phones in Spain, all of them bright green. The most common kind has a digital readout, so you can see your money ticking away. You need at least 15 pesetas for a local call, 50 pesetas to call another province. Simply insert coins and wait for a dial tone. (At older models, you must line coins up in a groove on top of the dial and they drop down as needed.) Neither model accepts the new micro-size 5 and 10 peseta coins, nor the small 25 peseta coins.

Newer pay phones work on special telephone credit cards, which can be purchased at any tobacco shop for 1,000 or 2,000 pesetas.

Long-Distance Calls To call other provinces from within Spain, both from pay and private phones, dial the area code first. Large cities such as Madrid (91) and Barcelona (93) have a two-digit area code followed by a seven-digit local number. A massive overhaul of the telephone system aims to install this pattern throughout Spain, but less-populated regions still have a three-digit area code followed by a six-digit local number.

All provincial codes begin with a 9, but you don't need to use the 9 when dialing from outside Spain.

International Calls
International calls are awkward from public pay phones and can be expensive from hotels, which often add a surcharge. The best way to make them is to go to the local telephone office. Every town has one, and big cities have several. When the call is connected, you will be sent to a quiet cubicle, and you will be charged according to the meter. If the price is 500 pesetas or more, you can pay with Visa or MasterCard.

In Madrid the main telephone office is on Gran Vía 28. There is another at the main post office and a third on Paseo Recoletos 43, just off Plaza Colón. In Barcelona calls can be placed from the office on Carrer de Fontanella 4, off Plaça de Catalunya.

To make an international call yourself, dial 07 and wait for a loud tone. Then dial the country code (1 for the United States and Canada, 44 for the United Kingdom), followed by the area code and number.

It is worthwhile to sign up for a U.S. long-distance service before you travel. For example, you can save about half the cost of phone calls from Spain to the states by using **AT&T USA Direct** (access tel. 900–99–0011), **Sprint** (access tel. 900–99–0013), or **MCI** (access tel. 900–99–0014). Simply dial the number from any phone in Spain and you will be connected to an English-speaking operator who will place the call. Collect calls are also cheaper and more convenient this way. **British Telecom** (access tel. 900–99–0044) has a similar service for its customers to ring the U.K.

Operators and Information
For general information in Spain, dial 003; the international information and assistance operator is at 025. Information on hotels, transportation, museum hours, and the like is dispensed by friendly multi-lingual operators on the **Tourist Information Line** (tel. 901–300–600) daily 10–2.

Mail

Postal Rates
Airmail letters to the United States and Canada cost 90 pesetas up to 15 grams. Letters to the United Kingdom and other countries in the European Union cost 45 pesetas up to 20 grams. Letters within Spain are 27 pesetas. Postcards are charged the same rate as letters. Stamps can be bought at post offices and government-run tobacco shops.

Receiving Mail
Because mail delivery in Spain can often be slow and unreliable, it is best to have your mail sent to **American Express** or **Thomas Cook** (call 800/528–4800 for a list of foreign American Express offices). Mail-holding service is free if you are a card member. An alternative is to have mail held at a Spanish post office; have it addressed to **Lista de Correos** (general delivery) in a town you will be visiting. Postal addresses should include the name of the province in parentheses, e.g., Marbella (Málaga).

Tipping

Pride keeps Spaniards from acknowledging tips, but waiters and other service people are poorly paid, and you can be sure your contribution will be appreciated. On the other hand, if you run into some bad or surly service, don't feel obligated to leave a tip.

Restaurant checks may or may not include service, but no more than 10% of the bill is necessary for a tip, and if you eat *tapas* or sandwiches at a bar, leave less, enough to round out the bill to the nearest 100. Cocktail waiters get 25–50 pesetas a drink, depending on the bar.

Taxi drivers get about 25 pesetas, but more for long rides or extra help with luggage, although there is an official surcharge for airport runs and baggage.

Hotel porters are tipped 50 pesetas a bag; 50 pesetas also goes to someone who brings you room service. A doorman who calls you a taxi gets 25 pesetas. If you stay in a hotel for more than two nights, tip the maid about 100 pesetas per night. A concierge should be tipped for any additional help he or she gives you.

Tour guides should be tipped about 200 pesetas, ushers in theaters or bullfights 25–50 pesetas, barbers 100 pesetas, and ladies' hairdressers at least 200 for a wash and set. Washroom attendants are tipped 5–10 pesetas.

Opening and Closing Times

Public Holidays January 1 (New Year's Day), January 6 (Epiphany), March 19 (St. Joseph), April 14 (Good Friday), April 17 (Easter Monday—Barcelona and Palma de Mallorca), May 1 (Labor Day), August 15 (Assumption), October 12 (International Hispanic Day–Columbus Day), November 1 (All Saints Day), December 6 (Constitution), December 8 (Immaculate Conception—except Barcelona), December 25 (Christmas), and December 26 (Boxing Day—Barcelona and Palma de Mallorca).

In addition, each city and town has its own holidays honoring political events and patron saints. Madrid is closed May 2 (Madrid Day), May 15 (San Isídro), and November 9 (Almudena). Barcelona celebrates April 23 (St. George), September 11 (Catalunya Day), and September 24 (Merced).

If a public holiday falls on a Tuesday or Thursday, many businesses also close on the Monday or Friday in between for a long weekend called a *puente* (bridge).

Banks Banks are generally open weekdays 8:30 to 2, Saturdays 8:30 to 1, but in the summer most banks close at 1 PM weekdays and do not open on Saturday. Money exchanges at airports and train stations stay open later. Traveler's checks can also be cashed at the Corte Inglés department stores until 9 PM.

Museums Most museums are open from 9:30 to 2 and from 4 to 7, and are closed one day a week, usually Mondays, but opening hours vary widely, so check before you set off. A few big museums, such as the Prado, the Reina Sofía Museum in Madrid, and the Picasso Museum in Barcelona, do not close at midday.

Shops One of the most inconvenient things about Spain is that almost all shops close at midday for at least three hours, except for the two big department store chains (Corte Inglés and Gallerías Preciados). Generally store hours are from 10 to 1:30 and 5 to 8. Shops are closed all day Sunday, and in Madrid and several other places they are also closed Saturday afternoons.

Shopping

Ceramics and leather goods are what most tourists shop for in Spain. The best selection of leather clothing, purses, and shoes can be found in Madrid, although shoes are generally made in Alicante and the Balearic Islands.

Madrid has begun to earn an international reputation for high fashion. Clothes are pricey. Search out Calle Almirante off Paseo Recoletos, if only for window shopping.

If you're buying a gift for a child, duck into any stationery shop and you will find a wide selection of unusual pen and pencil boxes, the likes of which can't be bought in the States.

Tax Refunds A number of shops, particularly large stores and boutiques in holiday resorts, offer a refund of the 15% IVA sales tax on large purchases. The purchase must be a single item worth more than $500. You show your passport, fill out a form, and the store then mails you the refund at your home.

Galerías Preciados department stores issue foreign shoppers a card good for a 10% discount on all nonsale merchandise.

Dining

Cuisine Seafood and roast meats are the national specialties; foods are lightly seasoned. Salads are delicious and are usually served topped with canned tuna and olives. If you get tired of adventurous dining, order an *ensalada mixta* (mixed salad) and a *solomillo* (filet mignon).

Spaniards eat paella, the delicious seafood and rice dish, exclusively at midday and preferably at a beachside restaurant, but it is served to tourists at dinnertime as well.

Lunch usually consists of the first plate, which is a salad, soup, vegetable, or smoked fish or cured meat; the second plate, almost always meat or fish; and dessert, which can be ice cream, yogurt, or flan, but is more typically a piece of fresh fruit. All this is accompanied by bread (no butter) and washed down with a bottle of wine. In big cities some businessmen now grab a quick sandwich instead of stopping for the traditional three-course lunch, but not many.

Restaurants are required by law to offer a *menú del día* at lunch that includes all the above at a price that is 80% of what each course would cost separately. Restaurants that specialize in a menú del día will post it at the door; in other establishments you have to ask to see the menú del día, and then it is often a couple of unappetizing choices designed to get you to order from the regular menu.

Supper is another three courses, sometimes with lighter fare replacing the meat course. Some restaurants may offer a menú del día, but it is usually leftover lunch.

Breakfast in Spain is usually coffee and a roll; in Madrid, it's *chocolate* and *churros* (strips of fried dough dipped in a cup of thick hot cocoa). Spanish coffee is strong espresso taken straight *(café solo)* or with hot milk *(café con leche);* if you prefer weaker coffee, ask for *café américano.*

Mealtimes The hardest thing to get used to about Spanish meals is not the food but the hours. Mealtimes are late. Lunch, considered the main meal of the day, is eaten between 2 and 4 PM. Supper is served anytime between 9 and midnight.

Restaurants that cater to tourists in coastal resorts may serve meals earlier, but Spanish restaurants generally open for lunch at 1:30 and dinner at 9. Foreigners are usually the first to arrive, so at least there's never a wait for a table.

You will enjoy your trip more if you can adapt to Spanish mealtimes. But there are tricks you can use to get around eating two big meals a day. Eat a big lunch, then just a snack for supper at a tapas bar. Eat a sandwich at a bar or fast-food restaurant for lunch and then a full dinner. Order just a salad course at lunch; restaurants have no trouble accepting this, but if you're dining with others who are eating more, be sure to tell the waiter when you want your salad served.

Precautions Tap water is perfectly safe throughout Spain, but mineral water is routinely ordered with meals. If you want a pitcher of tap water, ask for *una jarra de agua*.

Ratings The government rates restaurants from five forks (deluxe) down to one fork (basic). We use four categories ($$$$, $$$, $$, $) to indicate average prices in pesetas (ptas) for a three-course meal excluding wine.

Lodging

The government has spent decades buying up old castles and historic buildings and converting them into outstanding lodging for its parador hotel chain. The rest of Spain's hotels tend to be newish high rises, although there is a growing trend toward the restoration of historic buildings. By law, prices must be posted at the reception desk and should indicate whether tax is included (IVA is 6%, 15% for 5-star hotels). Breakfast is not included in the price of a room in Spain.

Hotels Hotels are rated by the government with one to five stars. While quality is a factor, the ratings also indicate how many extra facilities the hotel offers. You may find a three-star hotel just as good as a four-star hotel, but without a swimming pool, for example.

The major private hotel groups in Spain include the upscale **Melia** chain and the moderately priced **Tryp** and **Sol** chains. Dozens of reasonably priced beachside high rises along the coast cater to package tours. The new **Estancias de España** (Velázquez 111, 4–D, 28006 Madrid, tel. 91/561–0170, fax 91/561–0172) is an association of 20 independently owned hotels located in restored palaces, monasteries, mills and post houses, generally in rural Spain; a free directory is available.

High season rates prevail not only in summer, but also during Easter week and local fiesta periods.

Paradors There are about 100 of these. Some are in castles on a hill with sweeping views. Others are in historic monasteries or convents filled with art treasures. Still others are in modern buildings on Spain's choicest beachfront property. Prices are reasonable, considering that most paradors are four- and five-star hotels. Paradors are immaculate and tastefully furnished, often with antiques or reproductions. All have restaurants that serve some regional specialties. You can stop for a meal or a drink at a parador and look around without spending the night. Breakfast, however, is an expensive buffet, and you'll do better to go down the street for a cup of coffee and a roll.

Because paradors are extremely popular with foreigners and Spaniards alike, make reservations well in advance. You can contact the central reservations office (**Paradores de España,** Central de Reservas, Requena 3, Madrid 28013, tel. 91/559–0069, fax 91/559–3233); in the United States, **Marketing Ahead** (433 5th Ave., New York, NY 10016, tel. 212/686–9213); in the United Kingdom, **Keytel International** (402 Edgeware Rd., London W2 1ED, tel. 0171/402–8182).

Credit Cards

The following credit card abbreviations have been used: AE, American Express; DC, Diners Club; MC, MasterCard; V, Visa. It's a good idea to call ahead to check current credit card policies.

2 Portrait of Spain

Spain's Food and Wine

*By Michael
Jacobs*

The cuisine of Spain is among the most varied and sophisticated in Europe. Favored by a wealth of natural produce almost unrivaled, Spain has traditionally been an agricultural country, famous since ancient times for its extensive wheat fields, vineyards, and olive groves and for pig and cattle raising. A recent medical report has even concluded that the Spaniards eat more healthily than any other Western nation, largely because they insist on fresh produce and avoid canned and convenience foods.

The geographic variety of the peninsula accounts, of course, for the extremely varied nature of Spain's produce: For instance, the snowcapped mountains of the Sierra Nevada have Nordic cultures on their upper slopes, while those lower down yield tropical fruits unique to Europe, such as custard apples. Furthermore, with both an Atlantic and a Mediterranean coastline, Spain boasts an exceptional range of fish and seafood.

Another major influence on Spanish cuisine has been the 7½ centuries of Moorish presence in the peninsula. The Moors gave the local cooking an exotic quality by using new ingredients, such as saffron, almonds, and peppers; they introduced the art of making sweets and pastries and created refreshing dishes such as *ajo blanco* that still remain popular. The Moors produced one of the world's pioneering gastronomes, Ziryab, an Arab who worked in 10th-century Córdoba and brought over to Europe the new Arab fashion for eating a regular sequence of dishes, beginning with soup and ending with dessert.

Whether inherited from the Moors or not, the Spanish love of food stretches back at least several centuries. A famous poem by the 16th-century Seville writer Baltasar del Alcázar expresses this feeling:

> There are three things
> That hold my heart Love's captive
> My fair Inés, cured ham,
> And aubergines and cheese

Spaniards, when traveling around their country, often seem to prefer hunting down local gastronomic specialties to visiting museums and monuments. They tend to assume that foreigners do not have the same interest in food as they do, largely because so many of these foreigners are not adventurous in their tastes and refuse to adapt to Spain's idiosyncratic eating times and traditions. You are more likely to find outstanding food in some remote and dirty village bar where olive stones and shrimp heads are spat out onto the floor than in many of the luxury restaurants: The Spaniards aren't as snobbish about eating as, say, the French are. But if you decide to have lunch before 2 PM or to dine before 10, the only restaurants that you will probably find open are those that cater to bland international tastes.

The most Spanish of culinary traditions is undoubtedly that of the *tapa* (bar snack). Many people who dismiss Spanish food as unimaginative will make an exception of the tapa, without realizing that these snacks are miniature versions of dishes that you can find in restaurants or in Spanish homes. The tradition originated in Andalucía, where a combination of heat and poverty made it impractical to sit down to a heavy meal in a restaurant. Today tapas are generally taken as appetizers before lunch or supper, but in the south they are still often regarded as a meal in themselves. The eating of tapas makes you aware of the variety of Spanish food and also prevents you from getting too drunk, especially if you decide to go on the Spanish equivalent of a bar crawl, a *tapeo*. In some of the more old-fashioned bars, a tapa of the barman's choice is automatically presented to you when you order a drink. Having to choose a tapa yourself is not always easy, for the barman often recites at great speed a seemingly interminable list. The timid, baffled tourist usually ends up pointing to some familiar tapa that is standing on the counter.

The Spaniards' love of tasting small quantities of many dishes is evident also in their habits in restaurants, where they normally share food and order dishes *para picar* (to nibble at). If you go to a restaurant in a group, a selection of *raciones* (larger versions of tapas) makes a popular starter.

Soups in Spain tend not to be smooth and creamy, as they are in France, but watery, highly spiced, and very garlicky. One of the most common hot soups is a *sopa de ajo* (garlic soup), which consists of water, oil, garlic, paprika, stale bread, and cured ham. This is far more appetizing than it sounds, as is the famous gazpacho, a cold blend of water, bread, garlic, tomatoes, and peppers. Most people today make gazpacho in a blender, but it is at its best when prepared by hand in a terra-cotta mortar, the ingredients slowly pounded with a pestle. There are several variations on gazpacho, including *salmorejo*, which comes from Córdoba and has a denser texture. Particularly good is the *ajo blanco*, the basis of which is almonds rather than tomatoes: Served always with peeled muscatel grapes or slices of honeydew melon, this dish encapsulates the Moorish love of combining sweet and savory flavors.

The Spanish egg dish best known abroad is the *tortilla* (not the same as the Mexican tortilla—instead it's an omelet of onions and potatoes), which is generally eaten cold. *Huevos flamencos* ("Gypsy eggs") is a traditional Seville dish now found in all parts of Spain, consisting of eggs fried in a terra-cotta dish with cured ham, tomatoes, and a selection of green vegetables. The exact ingredients vary as much as does Gypsy cooking itself, which tends cleverly to incorporate whatever is at hand.

The Spaniards—and the Andalusians and Galicians, in particular—are known for the vast quantities of fish and seafood they consume. Some of the finest seafood can be found in western Andalucía and in Galicia, the former being renowned for shrimp, prawns, and crayfish, the latter for its oysters, lobsters, and crabs, and the much sought after if also revolting-looking *percebes* (goose barnacles). Another specialty of the Galician coast is scallops chopped up with breadcrumbs, onions, parsley, and peppers and served in their shells (the same shells that are worn by pilgrims on their way to Santiago de Compostela). *Changurro*, a stuffed king crab, is a specialty of the Basque country, where you will also find one of Spain's most interesting fish dishes, *bacalao al pil-pil* (cod fried in garlic and covered in a green sauce made from the gelatin of the fish). A fish dish now common all over Spain is *trucha a la Navarra* (trout wrapped in pieces of bacon). In Andalucía most fish is deep-fried in batter—which is why the place is sometimes disparagingly referred to by outsiders as the land of the fried fish, an unattractive image. You, in fact, need considerable art, as well as spanking-fresh fish, to be able to fry the fish as well as they do here and achieve the requisite texture of crispness on the outside and succulence inside. The *chancetes* (whitebait) and *sardinas* (sardines) are especially good in Málaga, while along the Cádiz coast, you should try the *salmonetes* (red mullet) and *acedías* (miniature soles). *Adobo*, also delicious, is fried fish marinated in wine.

The cold meats and sausage products of Spain are renowned—in particular, the cured hams of Trevélez and Jabugo, the *chorizo* (spicy paprika sausage), and the *morcilla* (blood sausages) of Granada and Burgos, the latter sometimes incorporating nuts. Meat, when served hot, is usually unaccompanied by a sauce or vegetables and presented rare. The great meat-eating center of Spain is Castile, which is famous for its *cochinillo* (suckling pig), a specialty of Segovia, and *cordero* (lamb), both of which are roasted in wood or clay ovens. The most sophisticated and elaborate poultry dishes in Spain are prepared in the Catalan district of Gerona and include chicken with lobster and turkey stuffed with raisins, pine nuts, and *butifarras* (spicy Catalan sausages).

Fish, meat, and seafood come together in *paella*, a saffron-flavored rice dish that many consider to be the most typical of Spanish dishes. Originating in Valencia, paella, in fact, dates no earlier than the late 19th century. The one Spanish dish that can truly claim to be the most national and traditional is the meat stew referred to by the people of Madrid as *cocido*, by the Andalusians as *potaje*, and by the Catalans as *escudella*. Despite the slight regional variations, the three basic ingredients remain the same—meats, legumes, and vegetables. The dish is usually served in three courses, beginning with the broth in which everything is cooked and finishing with the meats, which Spaniards sometimes shred and mix together on their plates to form what they call *pringa*.

The range and quality of Spanish cheeses is impressive, but most of them are little known and can be bought only in the area where they are made. The hard cheeses of La Mancha are best well matured: A good *Manchego viejo* is almost the equal of an Italian Parmesan. If you find it, you should try *Cabrales*, an exquisite sheep's cheese that is rather like a melting Roquefort.

Spaniards do not usually finish a meal with a dessert. They tend to bake the many almond- and honey-based sweets and pastries of Moorish derivation, such as *polvorones*, around Christmas or Easter time. Ever since St. Teresa devised *yemas* (egg-yolk sweets), Spanish convents have specialized in all kinds of sweet products. The yemas were once distributed free to the poor, but their production has now become a profitable industry for the nuns. The correct procedure for buying anything from a convent is to ring the bell and then address the nun (who is usually hidden behind a rotating drum) with the words *Ave María Purísima*. This religious formality over with, you can then proceed to order your yemas, *bizcochos* (sponge biscuits), *tocinos de cielo* (an excellent variant of crème caramel), or whatever else appears on the list pinned up in the convent's entrance hall.

Spain claims to be more extensively covered with vineyards than is any other country in the world. Until recently, the quality of Spanish wines was considered by foreigners to be barely equal to the quantity, and Spanish "plonk" was thought suitable only for parties where people would be too drunk to notice. The Spaniards themselves, as unpretentious in their drinking as in their eating habits, did not help matters with their love of wine washed down with *gaseosa* (carbonated lemonade) and their tendency to buy wine from great barrels simply marked *tinto* (red) or *blanco* (white), along with a figure indicating the alcohol content. Recently, increased tourism has led to the enormous promotion of Spanish wines, which are now very much in fashion. Villages with excellent wine that has yet to be commercialized still do exist.

The cheap variety of Spanish wines comes mainly from Valdepeñas, in the middle of the dreary plains of La Mancha, Spain's largest wine-growing area. On the other end of the scale are the celebrated red wines of Rioja, which have a full-bodied woody flavor resulting from their having matured for up to eight years in casks made of American oak (the oldest and best of these wines are labeled *Reserva*). The technique of aging the wine in this way was introduced by French vintners from Bordeaux and Burgundy, who moved to the Rioja area in the last century, hoping to escape the phylloxera epidemic that was destroying the vines in their own country; curiously, however, there are few places today in France where the aging process is as long as it is here. Among the better Riojas are those of Imperial, Marqués de Murrieta, and Marqués de Riscal. Marqués de Riscal, in fact, has recently moved into the nearby Rueda district, where it has marketed one of Spain's most distinguished white wines. Sparkling white wines are the specialty of Catalunya (the most renowned being Codorniu and Freixenet), which is also the Spanish area with the greatest variety of wine production.

The one Spanish wine that has always been popular with foreigners is sherry. The English have dominated the sherry trade in Jerez de la Frontera since the 16th century, and most of the famous labels are foreign (for instance, Domecq, Harvey, Sandeman). The classic dry sherry is the *fino;* amontillado is deeper in color and taste, and *oloroso* is really a sweet dessert wine. Another fortified wine from the area is Manzanilla, which is made in the delightful coastal town of Sanlúcar de Barrameda and is dependent for its production on the cool sea breezes there; this wine, with a faint tang of the sea, does not travel well, and there are even those who believe that it tastes better in the lower part of Sanlúcar than in the upper town. Sherry and Manzanilla tend to be thought of as aperitif wines, and indeed they are the ideal accompaniment to tapas; to eat a Sanlúcar prawn with a glass of Manzanilla is many Spaniards' idea of paradise. Spaniards tend also to drink sherry and Manzanilla when sitting down to a meal, a custom that has yet to catch on outside the country. In England, sherry still has the genteel associations of an Oxford college, but the Spaniards have a more robust attitude toward it. You will probably never think of sherry in the same way again if you attend the Seville *Feria*, where reputedly more sherry and Manzanilla are drunk in a week than in the whole of Spain in a year. Manzanilla, incidentally, has a reputation for not giving a hangover, and some make the dubious claim that it is an excellent cure for gout.

Some of Spain's finest brandies, such as Osborne, Terry, Duque de Alba, and Carlos III, also come from Jerez. Málaga has a sweet dessert wine that enjoyed a vogue with the English in the last century (look for the label Scholtz). *Aguardientes* (aquavits) are manufactured throughout Spain, famous brands being from Chinchón, near Madrid. A sweet and popular liquor called *Ponche Caballero* comes in a silver-coated bottle that looks like an amateur explosive. Sangría, which is usually drunk by tourists, should consist of fruits, wine, brandy, and Cointreau, but is usually served as a watered-down combination of wine and lemonade with the odd piece of orange thrown in. If you truly wish to appear a tourist, you should try drinking wine from a *porrón*, a glass vessel from which you pour the wine into your mouth from a distance of at least one foot: A raincoat is recommended.

You are truly initiated into Spanish ways after your first night spent drinking until dawn. Ideally, this experience is followed by a snack of *churros* (doughnut fritters) dipped into hot chocolate; the more hardened souls will be ordering the morning's glass of aguardiente. After a few hours' sleep, you will have a proper breakfast (around 11 o'clock), consisting, if you are brave, of toast rubbed in garlic or covered in *manteca colorada* (spicy pig's fat). Soon it will be time for the midday tapas. And so a typical Spanish day continues.

3 Madrid

By Mark
Potok and
Deborah
Luhrman

At the heart of Spain, Madrid's pulsing energy and openness make it Europe's most lively capital. Its people—called Madrileños—are a joyful lot, famous for their seeming ability to defy the need for sleep. Life here is lived in the crowded streets and in the noisy cafés, where endless rounds of socializing last long into the night. The publicness of Madrid's lifestyle makes it especially easy for visitors to get involved, and its allure is hard to resist.

Madrid's other chief attraction is its unsurpassed collection of paintings by some of the world's great artists, among them: Goya, El Greco, Velázquez, Picasso, and Dalí. Nowhere else will you find such a concentration of masterpieces as in the three museums—the Prado, the Reina Sofía, and the Thyssen-Bornemisza—that make up Madrid's so-called golden triangle of art.

The bright blue sky, as immortalized in Velázquez' paintings, is probably the first thing you'll notice about Madrid. Despite 20th-century pollution, that same color sky is still much in evidence thanks to breezes that sweep down from the Guadarrama mountains, blowing away the urban smog.

The city's skyline has its share of soaring modern skyscrapers but the more typical Madrid towers of red brick crowned by gray slate roofs and spires far outnumber them. This Habsburg-era architecture, built in the 1500s and 1600s by Spain's Austrian kings who made Madrid capital of the realm, gives parts of town a timeless, Old World feel.

Monumental neoclassical structures like the Prado Museum, the Royal Palace, and the Puerta de Alcalá arch make up Madrid's other historic face. These are the sights most visited by tourists and most were built in the 1700s during the reign of Bourbon monarch Charles III, who, inspired by the enlightened ideas of the age, also created Retiro Park, and the broad, leafy boulevard called Paseo del Prado.

Modern-day Madrid sprawls northward in block after block of dreary high-rise brick apartment buildings and office towers. A swelling population of 3.2 million is also moving into surrounding villages and new suburbs, creating tremendous traffic problems in and around the capital.

While these new quarters and many of Madrid's crumbling old residential neighborhoods may seem unappealing to the visitor, don't be put off by first impressions. The city's attractiveness has mostly to do with its people and the electricity they generate—whether at play in the bars and discotheques or at work in the advertising, television, and film industries headquartered here.

Situated on a plateau 646 meters (2,120 feet) above sea level, Madrid is the highest capital in Europe. It can also be one of the world's hottest cities in summer, and freezing cold in winter. Spring and summer are the most delightful times to visit when a balmy evening has virtually everyone in town lingering at an outdoor café, but each season has its own charms; in winter steamy café windows beckon and the famous blue skies are especially crisp and bright. That's when Madrid, as the local bumper stickers will tell you, is the next best place to heaven.

The sophistication of Madrid stands in vivid contrast to the ancient ways of the historic villages close to the capital. Less than an hour away from the downtown skyscrapers you can find villages where farm fields are still plowed by mule. Like city dwellers the world over, Madrileños like to visit the countryside, and getaways to the dozens of Castilian hamlets nearby, and excursions to Toledo, El

Escorial, and Segovia are a favorite pastime of locals, as well as being regular stops on the tourist trail.

Essential Information

Arriving and Departing by Plane

Airports and Airlines Madrid is served by **Barajas Airport,** 12 km (7 mi) east of the city; it's a rather grim-looking facility, although the national terminal was recently renovated. Major carriers, including American, Delta, TWA, and United, provide regular service to the United States. Most connections are through Miami, Washington, or New York, but American offers daily direct flights to and from Dallas–Fort Worth International Airport (reserve well in advance because they're very popular). Many carriers serve London and other European capitals daily, but if you shop around at Madrid travel agencies, you'll generally find better deals than those available abroad (especially to and from Great Britain). For more information on getting to Madrid by air, *see* Arriving and Departing in Chapter 1. For general information and information on flight delays, call the airport (tel. 91/305–8343/44/45).

Between the Airport and Downtown For a mere 300 pesetas, there's a convenient **bus** to the central Plaza Colón, where taxis wait to take you to your hotel. The buses run between 5:40 AM and 2 AM, leaving every 15 minutes—slightly less often very early or late in the day. Be sure to watch your belongings, as the underground Plaza Colón bus station is one of the favorite haunts of purse snatchers and con artists. **Taxis** are usually waiting outside the airport terminal near the clearly marked bus stop. Expect to pay up to 2,000 pesetas, or even more in heavy traffic, plus small holiday, late-night, and luggage surcharges. Make sure the driver works on the meter—off-the-meter "deals" almost always cost more.

Arriving and Departing by Car, Train, and Bus

By Car Felipe II made Madrid the capital of Spain because it was at the geographic center of his peninsular domains, and today many of the nation's highways radiate out from it like the spokes of a wheel. Originating at Kilometer Zero, marked by a brass plaque on the sidewalk of the central Puerta del Sol, these highways include A6 (Segovia, Salamanca, Galicia); A1 (Burgos and the Basque Country); the N II (Guadalajara, Barcelona, France); the N III (Cuenca, Valencia, the Mediterranean Coast); the A4 (Aranjuez, La Mancha, Granada, Seville); N401 (Toledo); and the N V (Talavera de la Reina, Portugal). The city is surrounded by M30, the inner ring road, and M40, the outer ring road, from which most of these highways are easily picked up.

By Train Madrid has three train stations: Chamartín, Atocha, and Norte. **Chamartín** Station, near the northern tip of the Paseo Castellana, serves trains heading for points north, including Barcelona, France, San Sebastián, Burgos, León, Oviedo, La Coruña, Segovia, Salamanca, and Portugal. The **Atocha** Station, at the southern end of the Paseo del Prado, was renovated in honor of the inauguration of high-speed AVE train service in 1992, and serves points south and east, including Seville, Malaga, Córdoba, Valencia, Castellon, and Toledo. The **Norte** Station is used primarily as a terminal for local trains serving Madrid's western suburbs, including El Escorial. For schedules and reservations call RENFE (tel. 91/563–0202, in Spanish only) or go to the information counter in any of the train stations.

Reservations can be made by phone, and tickets can be charged on a credit card and delivered to your hotel. Most major travel agencies can also provide information and tickets.

By Bus Madrid has no central bus station, and, in general, buses are less popular than trains (though they can be faster). Most of southern Spain is served by the **Estación del Sur** (Canarias 17, tel. 91/468–4200), while buses for much of the rest of the peninsula, including Cuenca, Extremadura, Salamanca, and Valencia, depart from the **Auto-Rés Station** (Plaza Conde de Casal 6, tel. 91/551–7200). There are several other smaller stations, however, so inquire at travel agencies for the one for your destination.

Other bus companies of interest include **La Sepulvedana** (Paseo de la Florida 11, near the Norte Station, tel. 91/527–9537), serving Segovia, Ávila, and La Granja; **Herranz** (departures from Fernandez de los Ríos s/n, metro: Moncloa, tel. 91/543–3645 or 91/543–8167), for the Escorial and Valle de los Caidos; **Continental Auto** (Alenza 20, metro: Ríos Rosas, tel. 91/533–0400), serving Cantabria and the Basque region; and **La Veloz** (Mediterraneo 49, metro: Conde de Casal, tel. 91/409–7602), with service to Chinchón.

Getting Around

Madrid has a distinctly different feel depending on the neighborhood—from winding medieval streets to superchic shopping boulevards, regal formal parks to seedy red-light districts. While you will probably want to start out in the old city, where the majority of attractions are clustered, further adventures are likely to call you to other parts of town.

By Metro The metro is quick, frequent, and, at 125 pesetas no matter how far you travel, cheap. Vastly cheaper is the 10-ride *billete de diez*, which costs 600 pesetas and has the added merit of being accepted by automatic turnstiles (lines at ticket booths can be long). The system is open from 6 AM to 1:30 AM, although a few entrances close earlier. Ten metro lines crisscross the city, and there are system maps in every station. Note the end station of the line you need, and just follow the signs to the correct corridor. Exits are marked *salida*. Crime is still rare on the system.

By Bus Red city buses run between 6 AM and midnight and cost 125 pesetas per ride. Signs listing stops by street name are located at every stop but are hard to comprehend if you don't know the city well. Pick up a free route map from EMT kiosks on the Plaza de Cibeles or the Puerta del Sol, where you can also buy a 10-ride ticket (*bonobus*, 600 pesetas). If you speak Spanish, you can call for information (tel. 91/401–9900).

Drivers will make change for you, generally up to a 1,000-peseta note. If you've bought a 10-ride ticket, step up just behind the driver and insert it in the ticket-punching machine you see there until you hear the mechanism make a ding.

By Taxi Taxis are one of the few truly good deals in Madrid. Meters start at 150 pesetas and add 70 pesetas a kilometer thereafter; numerous supplemental charges, however, mean your total cost often bears little resemblance to what you see on the meter. There's a 150-peseta supplement on Sundays and holidays, and between 11 PM and 6 AM; 125 pesetas to sports stadiums and the bullring; and 300 pesetas to or from the airport, plus 50 pesetas per suitcase.

Taxi stands are numerous, and taxis are easily hailed in the street—except when it rains, when they're exceedingly hard to come by. Free

Madrid Metro

KEY
- **1** Metro Terminals
- ○ Metro Stations
- ▭ Transfer Stations
- — Railway Lines
- • Train Stations

cabs will display a *libre* sign during the day, a green light at night. Generally, a tip of about 25 pesetas is right for shorter in-city rides, while you may want to go as high as 10% for a trip to the airport. Radio-dispatched taxis can be ordered from **Tele-Taxi** (tel. 91/445–9008), **Radioteléfono Taxi** (tel. 91/547–8200), or **Radio Taxi Independiente** (tel. 91/447–5180).

By Motorbike Motorbikes, scooters, and motorcycles can be rented by the day or week at **Moto Alquiler** (Conde Duque 13, tel. 91/542–0657). If driving in a strange city doesn't bother you, this is a fast and pleasant way to see the city. You'll need your passport, your driver's license, and either a cash deposit or a credit card.

By Car Driving automobiles in Madrid is best avoided by all but the most adventurous. Parking is nightmarish, traffic extremely heavy almost all the time, and the city's drivers can be frightening. An exception may be August, when the streets are largely emptied by the mass exodus of Madrileños on vacation.

Important Addresses and Numbers

Tourist Information There are four provincial tourist offices in Madrid, but the best is on the ground floor of the Torre Madrid building, on the **Plaza España** (Princesa 1, tel. 91/541–2325; open weekdays 9 AM–7 PM, Sat. 9:30–1:30, closed Sun. and holidays). Others are at **Barajas Airport** (tel. 91/305–8656; open weekdays 8 AM–8 PM, Sat. 9–2); the **Chamartín railroad station** (tel. 91/315–9976; open weekdays 8–8, Sat. 9–2); and **Duque de Medinaceli 2** (tel. 91/429–4951; open weekdays 9–6, Sat. 9–1). The city tourism office on the Plaza Mayor (tel. 91/366–5477; open weekdays 10–8) is good for little save a few pamphlets.

Embassies **United States** (Serrano 75, tel. 91/577–4000), **Canada** (Nuñez de Balboa 35, tel. 91/431–4300), and **United Kingdom** (Fernando el Santo 16, tel. 91/319–0200).

Emergencies **Police** (tel. 091), **ambulance** (tel. 91/522–2222 or 91/588–4400), and English-speaking **doctors** (Conde de Aranda 7, tel. 91/435–1823). Major **hospitals** include La Paz (tel. 91/358–2600) and 12 de Octubre (tel. 91/390–8000).

English-Language Bookstores **Turner's English Bookshop** (Génova 3, tel. 91/319–0926) has a very large collection of English-language books. It also offers a useful bulletin board exchange. **Booksellers** (José Abascal 48, tel. 91/442–8104) also has a large English-language selection.

Late-Night Pharmacies Forty percent of all pharmacies are required by law to be open 24 hours a day, on a rotating basis. Listings of those pharmacies are found in all major daily newspapers.

Travel Agencies Travel agencies, found almost everywhere in Madrid, are generally the best bet for obtaining deals, tickets, and information without hassles. Some major agencies: **American Express,** located next door to the Cortés, the parliament building on Génova (Plaza de las Cortés 2, tel. 91/322–5500); **Wagons-Lits** (Paseo de la Castellana, tel. 91/563–1202); and **Pullmantur,** across the street from the Royal Palace (Plaza de Oriente 8, tel. 91/541–1807).

Guided Tours

Orientation Standard city tours, in English or Spanish, can be arranged by your hotel; most include **Madrid Artístico** (Royal Palace and Prado Museum included), **Madrid Panorámico** (half-day tour for first-time visitors), **Madrid de Noche** (combinations include a flamenco or a nightclub show), and **Panorámico y Toros** (on Sundays, a brief city overview followed by a bullfight). **Trapsatur** (Saw Bernardo 23, tel. 91/542–6666) runs the *Madridvision* tourist bus, which makes a one-hour sightseeing circuit of the city with recorded commentary in English. No advance reservation is needed. Buses leave from the front of the Prado Museum every 1½ hours, beginning at 10:45 Monday–Saturday, 10:30 on Sunday. A round-trip ticket costs 500 pesetas, while a day pass, which allows you to get on and off at various attractions, is 1,000 pesetas.

Personal Guides Contact the **Asociación Profesional de Informadores** (Ferraz 82, tel. 91/542–1214 or 91/541–1221) if you wish to hire a personal guide to take you around the city.

Exploring Madrid

Madrid is a compact city, and most of the things visitors want to see are concentrated in a downtown area barely a mile across, stretching between the Royal Palace and Retiro Park. Broad avenues, twisting medieval alleys, grand museums, stately gardens, and tiny tiled taverns are all jumbled together in an area easily explored on foot.

In fact, the texture of Madrid is so rich that walking is the only way to experience those special moments—peeking in on a guitar maker at work or watching a child dip churros into a steamy cup of chocolate—whose images linger long after the holiday photos have faded.

This Exploring section is divided into five tours: the first is the longest (covering about 2 miles) and is designed to help you get your bearings on a leisurely walk across town, stopping at the Plaza Mayor and strolling up the leafy Paseo del Prado; the second tour takes in Madrid's famous museum mile, said to have more masterpieces per meter than anywhere else in the world; the third tour focuses on regal Madrid, with stops at the royal convent, the sumptuous royal palace, the Almudena cathedral, and the king's gardens; the fourth tour winds through the narrow streets of medieval Madrid, tracing the city's history from its beginnings as an Arab fortress; and our fifth tour explores the humble but vibrant neighborhoods known as *castizo* or "authentic" Madrid, where Miguel de Cervantes once lived and where today poets, musicians, and average people still do.

Highlights for First-time Visitors

Centro de Arte Reina Sofía (*see* Tour 2)
Paseo del Prado (*see* Tour 1)
Plaza de Paja (*see* Tour 4)
Plaza Mayor (*see* Tour 1)
Prado Museum (*see* Tour 2)
Retiro Park (*see* Tour 1)
Royal Palace (*see* Tour 3)
Tapas bars (*see* Tour 4)

Tour 1: Introduction to the City

Numbers in the margin correspond to points of interest on the Madrid map.

❶ Begin at the stately **Plaza de Oriente** in front of the Royal Palace, where you'll find yourself surrounded by stone statues of all the Spanish kings from Ataulfo to Fernando VI. These massive sculptures were meant to be mounted on the railing atop the palace,

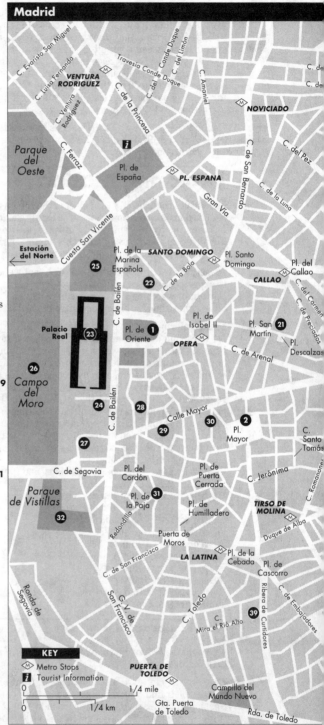

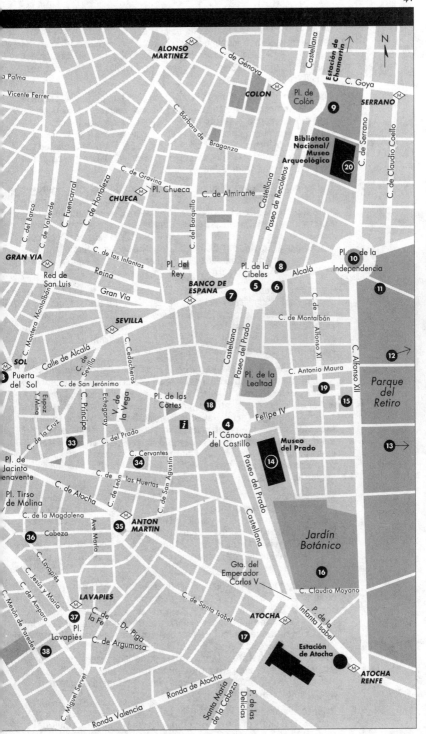

where there are now stone urns. But Queen Isabel de Farnesio, one of the first royals to inhabit the palace, had them taken off because she was afraid their enormous weight would bring the roof down. At least that's what she *said*. Palace insiders reported the Queen wanted the statues removed because her own likeness had not been placed front and center.

The statue of King Felipe IV in the center of the plaza was the first equestrian bronze ever to be cast of a horse rearing up. This action pose comes from a painting of the king by Velázquez by which the monarch was so smitten that in 1641 he commissioned an Italian artist, Pietro de Tacca, to turn it into a sculpture. De Tacca enlisted the help of the scientist Galileo to figure out the feat of engineering that keeps the statue from falling over.

In the minds of most Madrileños, the Plaza de Oriente is forever linked with Francisco Franco. The *generalissimo* liked to make speeches from the roof of the Royal Palace to his thousands of followers crammed into the plaza below. Even now, on the November anniversary of Franco's death, the plaza fills with his supporters, most of whom are old-timers, although lately the occasion has also drawn Nazi flag-waving skinheads from other European countries in a chilling pro-fascist tribute.

Turn away from the palace and walk to the right (south) of the **Teatro Real** (Royal Theater) on calle Carlos III. Built in about 1850, the neoclassical theater was once the center of Madrid's cultural society. It has been closed for renovations and was set to reopen as the city's opera house by the end of 1995. From the front of the theater continue straight up Calle Arenal for four blocks.

Just past the 14th-century church of San Ginés, one of the oldest in Madrid, turn right onto the narrow **San Ginés passageway** that runs alongside the church. Wooden stalls selling used books and prints of old Madrid are built into the church wall. Across the way is Joy Eslava, one of Madrid's late-night discotheques. Where the passageway jogs to the right is the **Chocolatería San Ginés,** a Madrid institution known for its chocolate and churros, and the final stop on many a night owl's bar crawl. Continue along the passageway past a couple more old-fashioned cafés, then cross the traffic-clogged Calle

2 Mayor and climb the short hill into the **Plaza Mayor.**

This arcaded square is the heart of Madrid. Austere, grand—and surprisingly quiet compared to the rest of the city—the Plaza Mayor has seen it all: *autos da fe* (public burnings of heretics); the canonization of saints; criminal executions; royal marriages, such as that of Princess Maria and the King of Hungary in 1629; bullfights (until 1847); masked balls; fireworks displays; and all manner of events and celebrations.

Measuring 110 by 90 m (360 by 300 ft), this is one of the largest public squares in Europe, and considered by many to be one of the most beautiful. It was designed by Juan de Herrera, the architect to Felipe II and the same man who designed the forbidding El Escorial monastery outside Madrid. Construction of the plaza lasted just two years and was completed in 1620 during the reign of Felipe III, whose **equestrian statue** stands in the center. The inauguration ceremonies included celebrating the canonization of four Spanish saints: Teresa of Ávila, Ignatius of Loyola, Isidro (Madrid's male patron saint), and Francis Xavier.

Prior to becoming the Plaza Mayor, this space was occupied by a city market, and many of the surrounding streets retain the names of the trades and foodstuffs once ensconced there. Nearby is *Calle de Cuchilleros* (Knife Makers' Street), *Calle de Lechuga* (Lettuce Street), *Calle de Fresa* (Strawberry Street), and *Calle de Botoneros* (Button Makers' Street). The oldest building on the plaza is the one with the brightly painted murals and the gray spires, *Casa de la Panadería* (the bakery) in honor of the bread shop it was built on top of. Opposite it is the *Casa de la Carniceria* (the butcher shop) which now houses a police station.

The plaza is closed to motorized traffic, making this a pleasant place to sit in the sun or while away a warm summer evening at one of the sidewalk cafés, watching alfresco portrait artists, street musicians, and Madrileños from all walks of life. At Christmas the plaza fills with stalls selling trees, ornaments, and nativity scenes, as well as all types of practical jokes and tricks to be used on December 28, the *Dia de los Inocentes*, a Spanish version of April Fool's Day.

Leave the Plaza Mayor through the arch in the northeast corner to the right of the *Casa de la Panadería* onto *Calle de la Sal* (Salt Street) and follow this pedestrian walkway back down to Calle Mayor. A right turn will bring you to the **Puerta del Sol.**

Always crowded with people and exhaust fumes, this busy square is Madrid's traffic nerve center. The city's main subway interchange is located below, and buses fan out through the city from here. A brass plaque in the sidewalk on the south side of the plaza marks **Kilometer 0,** the spot from which all distances in Spain are measured. The restored 1756 French neoclassic building by the marker now houses government offices, but during the Franco period it was used as a political prison and is still known as the "house of screams." Across the square is a bronze statue of Madrid's official symbol, a bear and a *madroño* (strawberry) tree.

Head east on Carrera San Jeronimo, past the jumble of shops and cafés. At number 8 peek into the ground-floor delicatessen of **Lhardy,** one of Madrid's oldest and most traditional restaurants. Shoppers stop in here on cold winter mornings for steamy cups of *caldo* (chicken broth). As you continue down Carrera San Jeronimo, be sure to have a look at the beautifully tiled and decorated tops of buildings, especially at the corner of Calle Sevilla. The big white granite building on the left with the lions out in front is the **Congress,** the lower house of Spain's parliament.

Past the Palace Hotel and the boutique-filled Galeria del Prado shopping center is the Plaza Canovas del Castillo with its **Fuente de Neptuno** (Neptune's fountain). This plaza is the hub of Madrid's so-called "golden triangle of art," made up of the red brick Prado Museum spreading out along the east side of the boulevard, the Thyssen-Bornemisza Museum across the plaza, and five blocks to the south, the Reina Sofia Museum.

Leaving the museums until later (*see* Tour 2, *below*), continue north along the wide, landscaped walkway that runs down the center of the Paseo del Prado to the Plaza de la Cibeles, which is home to the **Fuente de la Cibeles.** Sybil, the wife of Saturn, is depicted atop this fountain driving a chariot drawn by lions. Even more than the officially designated bear and the strawberry tree, this monument, beautifully lit at night, has come to symbolize Madrid—so much so that during the civil war, patriotic citizens risked life and limb sandbagging it as Nationalist aircraft bombed the city.

On the southeast side of the plaza is the ornate **Palacio de Comunicaciónes,** otherwise known as the main post office, and the place to go for all your postal and telecommunications needs. *Open for stamps weekdays 9 AM–10 PM, Sat. 9–8, Sun. 10–1; open for telephone, telex, telegrams, and fax weekdays 8 AM–midnight, weekends 8 AM–10 PM.*

7 Across the Paseo del Prado from the post office is the massive 1884 **Banco de España** (Spain's equivalent of the U.S. Federal Reserve) that takes up the entire city block, and where it's said the nation's gold reserves are held in great vaults that stretch under the traffic circle all the way to the fountain. If you want to risk dodging traffic to reach the median strip in front of the bank, you can get a fine photo of the fountain and the palaces with the monumental Puerta de Alcalá arch in the background.

8 Continuing north up the boulevard, the first building on the right is the **Casa de las Americas,** a cultural center and art gallery focusing on Latin America. It opened in 1992 in the allegedly haunted Palacio de Linares, which was built by a man who made his fortune in the New World and returned to a life of incestuous love and strange deaths. *Paseo Recoletos 2, tel. 91/576–3590. Admission: Palace tour 300 ptas.; art gallery, free. Palace tours Mon.–Sat. 9–11:30; art gallery open daily 11–8.*

To the left behind the trees is the red brick neoclassical **Palacio de Buenavista,** which now serves as a headquarters for the army, but was built in 1747 by the duchess of Alba, whose clothed and unclothed portraits by Goya hang in the Prado Museum (*see* Tour 2, *below*).

The grand mansions that once lined the paseo have been replaced with modern high-rise buildings or converted to other purposes, such as the elegant yellow **Banco Argentaria** (formerly Banco Hipotecario), on the right. This was the home of the Marquis of Salamanca who, at the turn of the 20th century, built the exclusive shopping and residential neighborhood that bears his name.

Time Out To rest your feet and sip a cup of coffee or a beer, pull up a chair on the shady terrace or inside the air-conditioned, stained-glass bar of **El Espejo** (Paseo Recoletos 31, tel. 91/308–2347. Open daily 10 AM–2 AM), located right in the center of the paseo, and decorated in the style of Belle-Epoque Paris.

9 Two more blocks north is the modern **Plaza Colón.** Named for Christopher Columbus, a statue of the explorer (identical to one in the port of Barcelona), looks west from atop a high tower in the middle of the square. Behind Plaza Colón is **Calle Serrano,** the city's number-one shopping street. Turn right onto Serrano for some window shopping. The big gray building on the right side of the street is Spain's **archaeology museum** (*see* Tour 2, *below*). Four blocks south **10** along Serrano brings you to the **Puerta de Alcalá,** a triumphal arch built by Carlos III in 1778 to mark the spot of the former city gates. Bomb damage inflicted on the arch during the civil war is still visible.

11 This plaza is also the main entrance to **Parque del Retiro** (Retiro Park). Once royalty's private playground, Retiro is a vast expanse of green that includes formal gardens, fountains, lakes (complete with rentable rowboats), exhibition halls, children's play areas, and a puppet theater. It is especially lively here on weekends, when it fills with street musicians, jugglers, clowns, gypsy fortune tellers, and sidewalk painters, along with hundreds of Spanish families out for a walk. During May the park hosts a month-long book fair, and in summer flamenco concerts often take place here.

If you head straight towards the center of the park, you'll find the
⑫ Estanque (lake), presided over by a grandiose equestrian statue of King Alfonso XII, erected by his mother. One of the best of the many cafés within the park is behind the lake, just north of the statue. Or if you're feeling more energetic, you can rent a boat and work up an appetite rowing around the lake.

⑬ The 19th-century **Palacio de Cristal** (Crystal Palace), southeast of the lake, was built to house a collection of exotic plants from the Philippines, a Spanish possession at the time. This airy marvel of steel and glass sits on a base of decorative tile, and now occasionally hosts exhibitions of sculpture. A small lake with ducks and swans is next door. A 10-minute walk south brings you to the **Rosaleda** (rose garden), an English garden design bursting with color and heavy with the scent of flowers for most of the summer. Nearby look for a statue called the **Ángel Caído** (fallen angel), which Madrileños claim is the only one in the world depicting the prince of darkness before—during, actually—his fall from grace.

Tour 2: Museum Mile

⑭ This tour starts at the **Museo del Prado** (Prado Museum), which for many visitors is Madrid's chief attraction. It was commissioned in 1785 by King Carlos III, and was originally meant to be a natural science museum. The king, popularly remembered as "Madrid's best mayor," intended the museum, the adjoining botanical gardens, and the elegant Paseo del Prado to serve as a center of scientific enlightenment for his subjects. By the time the building was completed in 1819, its purpose had been changed to exhibiting the vast collection of art gathered by Spanish royalty since the time of Ferdinand and Isabella.

Painting represents one of Spain's greatest contributions to world culture, and the jewels of the Prado are the works of the nation's three great masters: Francisco Goya, Diego Velázquez, and El Greco. The museum also contains masterpieces of Flemish and Italian artists, collected when those lands were part of the Spanish Empire. The museum benefitted greatly from anticlerical laws in 1836, which forced monasteries, convents, and churches to turn over many of their art treasures so that they could be enjoyed by the general public.

The visit begins on the **upper floor** (primera planta) of the museum, where you enter through a series of halls dedicated to **Renaissance painters.** While many visitors hurry through these rooms to get to the Spanish canvases, don't miss the *Portrait of Emperor Charles V* by Titian, and Raphael's exquisite *Portrait of a Cardinal.*

Next comes a hall filled with the passionately spiritual works of **El Greco** (Doménikos Theotokópoulos, 1541–1614). This Greek-born artist, who lived and worked in Toledo, is known for his mystical, elongated faces. His style was quite shocking to a public accustomed to strict, representational realism; and as he intended his art to provoke emotion, El Greco is sometimes called the world's first "modern" painter. *The Resurrection* and the *Adoration of the Shepherds*, considered two of his greatest paintings, are on view here.

Straight ahead and to the left are the rooms dedicated to **Velázquez** (1599–1660). The artist's meticulous brushwork is visible in numerous portraits of kings and queens. Be sure to look for the magnificent painting *Las Hilanderas* (The Spinners)—evidence of the artist's talent for painting light. One hall is reserved exclusively for the Prado's most famous canvas, Velázquez's *Las Meninas* (the Maids of Honor). It combines a self portrait of the artist at work with a mirror reflection of the king and queen in an astounding interplay of space and perspectives. Picasso was obsessed with this work and painted numerous copies of it in his own abstract style, which can be seen in the Picasso Museum in Barcelona.

The south end of this floor is reserved for **Goya** (1746–1828), whose works span a staggering range of tone, from bucolic to horrific. Among his early masterpieces are numerous portraits of the family of King Carlos IV, to whom he was court painter. A glance at their unflattering and imbecilic expressions, especially in the painting *The Family of Carlos IV*, reveals the loathing Goya developed for these self-indulgent and reactionary rulers. His famous side-by-side canvases, *The Clothed Maja* and *The Nude Maja*, represent the young duchess of Alba, whom Goya adored and frequently painted. It is not known whether she ever returned his affection. Adjacent rooms house a series of bucolic scenes of Spaniards at play, painted by Goya as designs for tapestries.

His paintings take on political purpose starting in 1808, when the population of Madrid rose up against occupying French troops. The *2nd of May* portrays the insurrection at the Puerta del Sol, and the even more terrifying companion piece *3rd of May*, depicts the nighttime executions of patriots who had rebelled the day before. The garish lighting effects of this work typifies the romantic style, which favors drama over detail, and makes it one of the most powerful indictments of violence ever committed to canvas.

Downstairs you'll find the extreme of Goya's range in a hall that features his "black paintings," dark, disturbing works completed late in his life that reflect the inner turmoil he suffered after losing his hearing and his deep embitterment over the bloody War of Independence. The rest of the ground floor is taken up with Flemish paintings including the bizarre masterpiece *Garden of Earthly Delights* by Hieronymous Bosch. *Paseo del Prado s/n, tel. 91/420–2836. Admission: 400 pesetas. Open Tues.–Sat. 9–7, Sun. 9–2; closed Mon.*

⑮ The **Casón del Buen Retiro** (Calle Alfonso XII, s/n) is a museum annex five-minutes' walk from the Prado that can be entered on the same ticket. This building, once a ballroom, and the formal gardens in nearby Retiro Park are all that remains of Madrid's second royal palace complex, which until the early 19th century occupied the entire neighborhood. On exhibit here are 19th-century Spanish painting and sculpture, including works by Sorolla and Rusiñol.

⑯ Just south of the Prado is the entrance to the **Jardín Botánico** (Botanical Gardens), a pleasant place to stroll or sit under the trees. True to the wishes of King Carlos III, the garden holds an array of plants, flowers, and cacti from around the world. *Plaza de Murillo 2, tel. 91/585–4700. Admission: 100 pesetas, children under 10 free. Open daily, summer 10–8, winter 10–6.*

Time Out Instead of eating in the Prado's so-so basement cafeteria, head across the paseo and up one block on Calle Lope de Vega to the tiny Plaza de Jesus, where you'll find **La Dolores** (Pl. de Jesus 4), one of Madrid's most atmospheric old tiled bars, and the perfect place for a beer or glass of wine and a plate of olives.

At the south end of the Paseo del Prado, on the traffic-clogged Glorieta del Emperador Carlos V, you'll come to an immense building of painted tiles and winged statues that currently houses the **Ministerio de Agricultura** (Agriculture Ministry). The Prado is trying to acquire this building in order to display some of its art that remains in storage for lack of space. Across the street is the **Atocha train station,** thoroughly restored in 1992. The high-speed train to Seville leaves from here, as do local trains to Toledo and long-distance trains to points south.

On the far side of the traffic circle you'll see Madrid's modern art museum, the **Centro de Arte Reina Sofía.** Often called "the Sofidu," after Paris's Pompidou modern art center, the museum is housed in a converted hospital, whose classic granite austerity is somewhat relieved (or ruined, depending upon who you ask) by the two transparent glass elevator shafts that have been added to the facade.

Like the Prado, the collection focuses on three great Spanish artists, this time modern masters: Pablo Picasso, Salvador Dalí, and Joan Miró. Take the elevator to the second floor to see the permanent collections; the other floors house visiting exhibits.

The first rooms are dedicated to the beginnings of Spain's modern art movement and contain paintings completed around the turn of the century. The focal point is Picasso's 1901 *Woman in Blue*—hardly beautiful, but surprisingly representational compared to his later works.

Moving on to the **Cubist collection,** which includes nine works by Juan Gris, be sure to see the splintered, blue-gray *Self-Portrait* by Dalí, in which he painted his favorite things, a morning newspaper and a pack of cigarettes. The other highlight here is Picasso's *Musical Instruments on a Table,* one of many variations on this theme created by the Spanish-born artist.

The museum's showpiece is Picasso's famous *Guernica,* which occupies the center hall and is surrounded by dozens of studies for individual figures within it. It depicts the horror of the Nazi Condor Legion's bombing of the ancient Basque town of Guernica in 1937, which helped bring Spanish dictator Francisco Franco to power. The work, in many ways a 20th-century version of Goya's *3rd of May,* is something of a national shrine, as evidenced by the solemnity of Spaniards viewing it. The painting was not brought into Spain until 1981. Picasso, an ardent anti-fascist, refused to allow it to enter the country while Franco was alive.

The room in front of *Guernica* contains a collection of **surrealist** works, including six canvases by Miró, known for his childlike graphicism. On the opposite side of *Guernica* is a hall dedicated to the surrealist **Salvador Dalí,** and hung with paintings bequeathed to the government in the artist's will. Although Dalí is perhaps best known for works of a somewhat whimsical tone, many of these canvases are dark and haunting, and bursting with symbolism. Among the best known are *The Great Masturbator* (1929) and *The Enigma of Hitler* (1939), with its broken, dripping telephone.

The rest of the museum is devoted to more recent art, including the massive, gravity-defying sculpture *Toki Egin* by Eduardo Chillida, considered Spain's greatest living sculptor, and five textural paintings by Barcelona artist Antoni Tàpies, who incorporates materials such as wrinkled sheets or straw into his works. *Santa Isabel 52, tel. 91/467–5062. Admission: 400 pesetas. Open Mon. and Wed.–Sat. 10–9, Sun. 10–2:30; closed Tues.*

To complete the triangle, head back north on the Paseo del Prado to the third and newest art center, the **Museo Thyssen-Bornemísza,** which opened in 1992 in the Villahermosa Palace—elegantly renovated to include lots of airy space and natural light. This ambitious collection of 800 paintings attempts to trace the history of Western art with examples from all the important movements beginning with 13th-century Italy.

The artworks were gathered over the past 70 years by industrialist Baron Hans Heinrich Thyssen-Bornemisza and his father. At the urging of his Spanish wife, a former Miss Spain, the baron agreed to donate the collection to Spain. While the museum itself is beautiful and its Impressionist paintings are the only ones on exhibit in the country, critics have characterized the collection as the minor works of major artists and the major works of minor artists.

Among the museum's gems are the *Portrait of Henry VIII* by Hans Holbein (purchased from Princess Diana's grandfather, who used the money to buy a new Bugatti sports car). American artists are also well represented. Look for the Gilbert Stuart portrait of George Washington's black cook, and note how much the composition and rendering resembles the artist's famous painting of the founding father himself. Two halls are devoted to the Impressionists and Postimpressionists, including many works by Pissarro, and a few each by Renoir, Monet, Degas, Van Gogh, and Cézanne.

Of 20th-century art, the baron shows a weakness for terror-filled (albeit dynamic and colorful) German Expressionism, but there are also soothing paintings by Georgia O'Keefe and Andrew Wyeth. *Paseo del Prado 8, tel. 91/420–3944. Admission: 600 pesetas, children under 12 free. Open Tues.–Sun. 10–7; closed Mon.*

⑲ Also along the "museum mile" is the **Museo del Ejército** (Army Museum), located in the pink palace just behind the Ritz Hotel, and displaying arms and armor. Among the 27,000 items on view are a sword allegedly belonging to Spanish hero El Cid, suits of armor, bizarre-looking pistols with barrels capable of holding scores of bullets, Moorish tents, and a cross carried by Christopher Columbus. This is an unusually entertaining museum of its genre. *Mendez Nuñez 1, tel. 91/522–8977. Admission: 50 pesetas. Open Tues.–Sun. 10–2.*

The nearby **Museo Naval** (Navy Museum) has on display the first map of the New World, drawn by cartographer Juan de la Cosa in 1500. Scale models of ships through the ages and lush reproductions of two ships' cabins are also on exhibit. *Calle de Montalbán 2, tel. 91/521–0419. Admission: 50 pesetas. Open Tues.–Sun. 10:30–1:30.*

⑳ About six blocks north on the paseo you'll come to the **Biblioteca Nacional** (National Library). The back side of this neoclassical building is the **Museo Arqueológico** (Archeology Museum). The biggest attraction here is a replica of the prehistoric Altamira cave paintings, located underground in the garden. Inside the museum, look for the *Dama de Elche*, a bust of a wealthy woman of the 4th-century Iberian culture. Notice how her headgear is a rough precursor to the mantillas and hair combs still associated with traditional Spanish costumes. Be sure to see the ancient Visigothic votive crowns discovered in 1859 near Toledo and believed to date back to the 8th century. *Calle Serrano 13, tel. 91/577–7912. Admission: 200 pesetas. Open Tues.–Sat. 9:30–8:30, Sun. 9:30–2:30; closed Mon.*

Tour 3: Regal Madrid

㉑ Our tour of royal Madrid begins at the **Convento de las Descalzas Reales** (Convent of the Royal Barefoot Nuns), just two blocks northwest of the Puerta del Sol. The 16th-century convent was restricted for 200 years to women of royal blood, and its plain brick-and-stone facade hides a treasure trove of riches. Inside there are paintings by Zurbarán, Titian, and Breughel the Elder, as well as a hall of sumptuous tapestries crafted from drawings by Rubens. The convent was founded in 1559 by Juana of Austria, whose daughter shut herself up here rather than endure marriage to Felipe II. A handful of nuns (not necessarily royal) still live here, cultivating their own vegetables in the convent's garden. Unfortunately you must visit as part of a tour, which is conducted only in Spanish. *Plaza de las Descalzas Reales 3, tel. 91/559-7404. Admission: 350 pesetas. Open Tues.–Thurs. and Sat. 10:30–12:30 and 4–5:30; Fri. 10:30–12:30; Sun. 11–1:30; closed Mon.*

From here, walk two blocks down to Calle Arenal. Turn right and follow the street around the right side of the royal theater, heading ㉒ up Calle Arrieta to the **Convento de la Encarnación** (Convent of the Incarnation), which can be entered on the same ticket as the Convent of Descalzas Reales. Once connected to the Royal Palace by an underground passageway, this Augustinian convent was founded in 1611 by the wife of Felipe III. It houses many artistic treasures, but the convent's biggest attraction is the reliquary chamber where among the sacred bones is a vial containing the dried blood of St. Pantaleón, which is said to liquify every year on July 27th. *Plaza de la Encarnación 1, tel. 91/547-0510. Admission: 350 pesetas. Open Wed. and Sat. 10:30–1 and 4–5:30, Sun. 4–5:30.*

Behind the convent is the restored **Palacio del Senado,** yellow, neoclassical headquarters for Spain's upper house of parliament. Just north of here you'll find the unappealing *Plaza de España*, which has been taken over by trinket vendors and homeless immigrants.

Time Out Stop for a drink or a snack in the Royal Palace neighborhood at the **Taberna del Alabardero** (Felipe V 6). Named for a regiment of the king's guards, this cozy bar stocks a dozen types of tapas. Try the garlicky *patatas à la pobre* (poor man's potatoes).

㉓ Now head across the Plaza del Oriente to the entrance of the **Palacio Real** (Royal Palace). Standing on the same strategic spot where Madrid's first Alcazar or Arab fortress was built in the 9th century, the Royal Palace was commissioned in the early 1700s by the first of Spain's Bourbon rulers, Felipe V. But before building began, the old fortress-palace burned to the ground in a terrible fire on Christmas Eve 1734, and the king decided to use its site instead.

Before entering, take time to walk around the graceful **Patio de Armas** and admire the classical French architecture. It's clear that King Felipe was inspired by his childhood days spent with his grandfather, Louis XIV, at Versailles. Look for the stone statues of Inca Prince Atahualpa and Aztec King Montezuma, perhaps the only tributes in Spain to these pre-Columbian American rulers. Notice how the steep bluff drops down to the Manzanares River to the west. On a clear day this vantage point also commands a good view of the mountain passes leading into Madrid from Old Castile and it becomes obvious as to why the Moors picked this particular spot for a fortress.

Inside, the palace's 2,800 rooms compete with each other for over-the-top opulence. A nearly two-hour guided tour in English winds a mile-long path through the palace. Highlights include: the **Salón de Gasparini,** King Carlos III's private apartments, a riot of Rococo decoration, with swirling inlaid floors, curlicued ceramic wall and ceiling decoration all glistening in the light of a two-ton crystal chandelier; the **Salón del Trono,** an exceedingly grand throne room that contains the royal seats of King Juan Carlos and Queen Sofia; and the **banquet hall,** which is the palace's largest room and seats up to 140 people for state dinners. No monarch has lived here since 1931, when Alfonso XIII was hounded out of the country by a populace fed up with centuries of royal oppression. The current king and queen live in the far simpler Zarzuela Palace on the outskirts of Madrid, using this Royal Palace only for state functions and official occasions, such as the first Middle East peace talks in 1991.

Within the palace you can also visit the **Biblioteca Real** (Royal Library), which has a first edition of Cervantes' *Don Quixote;* the **Museo de Música** (Music Museum), where the five stringed instruments by Stradivarius make up the world's largest collection; the **Armería Real** (Royal Armory), with its vast array of historic suits of armor and some frightening medieval torture implements; and the **Real Oficina de Farmacía** (Royal Pharmacy), boasting an assortment of vials and flasks used for concocting the king's medicines. *Calle Bailén s/n, tel. 91/559-7404. Admission: 500 pesetas for entire complex, 350 pesetas for palace alone. Open Mon.–Sat. 9:30–5, Sun. 9–2; closed during official receptions.*

㉔ Adjoining the palace to the south is the **Catedral de la Almudena,** which, after 110 years of construction, was consecrated by Pope John Paul II in 1993. The first stone was laid in 1883 by King Alfonso XII, and at the time it was planned as a Gothic-style structure of needles and spires, but as time ran long and money ran short the design was simplified by Fernando Chueca Goltia to become the more austere classical building you see today. The cathedral houses the remains of Madrid's male patron saint, St. Isidro, and a wooden statue of Madrid's female patron saint, the Virgin of Almudena, which was said to have been discovered following the Christian reconquest of Madrid in 1085. Legend has it that a divinely inspired woman named Maria led authorities to a secret spot in the old wall of the Alcazar (which in arabic can also be called *almudeyna*), where the statue was found framed by two lit candles inside a grain storage vault. That wall is part of the cathedral's foundation. *Calle de Bailén s/n, tel. 91/548-3514. Admission free. Open daily 10–1:30 and 6–8.*

㉕ Walking north past the palace, explore the formal **Jardínes Sabatini** (Sabatini Gardens). Crawling with stray cats, the gardens are a pleasant place for a rest and a good spot from which to watch the sunset. Below the gardens, but accessible only by walking around to ㉖ an entrance on the far side, is the **Campo del Moro.** This park's clusters of shady trees, winding paths, and long lawn that leads up to the palace offer a prime spot for photographing the building. Even without considering the riches inside, the palace's immense size (twice as large as Buckingham Palace) is awe-inspiring.

Tour 4: Medieval Madrid

Madrid's historic quarters are not so readily apparent as the ancient neighborhoods that characterize Toledo, Segovia, and Ávila. Nor are they so grand. But the visitor who takes time to explore the quiet, winding streets of medieval Madrid will be rewarded with an impression of the city that is light-years away from today's traffic-clogged avenues.

Our tour starts where the city began, on Calle Cuesta de la Vega at the ruins of the **Arab Wall,** which protected a fortress built on this site in the 8th century by Emir Mohammed I. In addition to being an excellent defensive position, the site had plentiful water and was called *Mayrit*, which is Arabic for "water source" and the likely origin of the city's name. All that remains of the Arab *medina* or early city that formed within the walls of the fortress is this neighborhood's crazy-quilt of streets and plazas, which likely follow the same layout as they did more than 1,100 years ago. The park Emir Mohammed I, alongside the wall, is a venue for summertime concerts and plays.

Walking uphill across Calle Bailén, head up Calle Mayor for three short blocks and turn left onto the tiny Calle San Nicolás, where you'll see the red-brick *mudéjar* tower of the **Iglesia de San Nicolás de las Servitas** (Church of St. Nicholas). The tower is one of the oldest buildings in Madrid and there's some debate over whether it once formed part of an Arab mosque. More likely it was built after the Christian reconquest of Madrid in 1085, but the brickwork and horseshoe arches are clear evidence that it was crafted by either Moorish workers or Spaniards well versed in the style. Inside the church are exhibits detailing the Islamic history of early Madrid. *Pl. de San Nicolás, tel. 91/559–4064. Admission: free. Open daily 5:30–6:30 or by appointment.*

Back on Calle Mayor continue two blocks uphill to the **Plaza de la Villa,** a medieval-looking complex of buildings that is now Madrid's city hall. Once called the Plaza de San Salvador for a church that used to stand here, this site has been the meeting place for the town council since the Middle Ages. The oldest building is the one with the *mudéjar* tower on the east side of the plaza, known as the **Casa de los Lujanes.** Built as a family home in the late 15th century, the Lujanes' crest can be seen over the main doorway. Directly across the plaza is the **Casa de la Villa,** built in 1629. This brick-and-stone building is a classic example of Madrid design with its clean lines and spire-topped corner towers. It is joined by an overhead walkway to the **Casa de Cisneros,** commissioned in 1537 by the nephew of Cardinal Cisneros, and one of Madrid's rare examples of the flamboyant Plateresque style, which has been likened to splashing water—liquid exuberance wrought in stone. *Buildings are open to the public for guided tours in Spanish Mon. 5 PM.*

The narrow picturesque streets behind the Plaza de la Villa are also worth exploring. Head three more blocks up Calle Mayor and turn right onto **Cava de San Miguel.** With the Plaza Mayor on your left and the iron-and-glass San Miguel market on your right, walk downhill past the row of ancient tapas bars built right into the retaining wall of the plaza above. Each one specializes in something different: Mesón de Champiñones has mushrooms, Mesón de Boquerones serves anchovies, Mesón de Tortilla cooks up excellent Spanish omelettes, and so on. Madrileños and tourists flock here each evening to sample the food and sing along with raucous musicians, who delight in playing foreign tunes for tourists.

About halfway down the street is the oldest of the taverns, the **Cuevas de Luis Candelas,** named for a 19th-century Madrid version of Robin Hood who was famous for his ingenious ways of tricking the rich out of their money and jewels. Farther down on the left is Casa

Botín (*see* Dining, *below*), Madrid's oldest restaurant and a favorite haunt of Ernest Hemingway. This curving street was once a moat just outside the walls of old Madrid. The plaza with the bright murals at the intersection of Calle Segovia is called the **Puerta Cerrada** (Closed Gate) for the entrance to the city that once stood here.

Turn right onto Calle Segovia, one of the main streets of Madrid during the Middle Ages. The first street on the left, Costanilla del Nuncio, is a ramp with steps that lead up to the **Palacio de la Nunciatura** (Palace of the Nunciat). Although it's not open to the public, you can peek inside the Renaissance garden of this mansion that once housed the Pope's ambassadors to Spain, and is now the official residence of the Archbishop of Madrid.

Time Out The **Café del Nuncio** (Costanilla del Nuncio s/n) on the corner of Calle Segovia is a relaxing Old World–style spot for coffee or a beer where classical music plays in the background.

Continue down Calle Segovia another block to the Plaza Cruz Verde and turn left up another ramp street, Costanilla de San Andrés, which leads to the heart of the old city. Halfway up the hill, look left down the narrow Calle Principe Anglona for a good view of the *mudéjar* tower of the **church of San Pedro el Viejo,** which, after San Nicolás, is one of the city's oldest. The brick tower is believed to have been built in 1354 following the Christian reconquest of Algeciras, in southern Spain. Be sure to notice the tiny defensive slits designed to accommodate crossbows.

㉛ At the top of the hill is the **Plaza de Paja,** the most important square of medieval Madrid. Although a few upscale restaurants have moved in, the quiet plaza remains unpaved and atmospheric. The jewel of this square is the **Capilla del Obispo** (Bishop's Chapel) built between 1520 and 1530. This was where peasants deposited their tithes called *diezmas,* literally one-tenth of their crop. Reference to this is made by the stacks of wheat shown on the ceramic tiles on the chapel. Architecturally, the chapel marks a transition from the blockish Gothic period—the basic shape of this structure—to the Renaissance, as evidenced by its decorations. Try to get inside to see the intricately carved polychrome altarpiece by Francisco Giralta, featuring scenes from the life of Christ. Opening hours of the chapel are erratic; the best time to visit is during Mass or on feast days.

The chapel forms part of the complex of the **church of San Andres,** whose dome was raised to house the remains of Madrid's male patron saint San Isidro Labrador. Isidro was a peasant who worked fields belonging to the Vargas family. The 16th-century **Vargas** palace forms the eastern side of the Plaza de Paja. According to legend, Isidro actually worked little, but thanks to many hours spent in prayer had the best-tended fields. When Señor Vargas came out to investigate the phenomenon, Isidro made a spring of sweet water spurt from the ground to quench his master's thirst. Because Saint Isidro's power had to do with water, in times of drought his remains were paraded through the city to bring rain (even as recently as the turn of the century). His bones now reside in another church.

Walk west from the Plaza de Paja on Calle de la Redondilla for one block to the **Plaza Moreria,** which is really no more than a wide spot in the street. This neighborhood was once the home of Moors who had chosen to stay in Madrid after the Christian reconquest. Although most of the buildings date from the 18th and 19th centuries, the steep, narrow streets and twisting alleyways are reminiscent of the much older *medina.*

Climb the stairway and cross Calle Bailén near the **viaduct,** a metal bridge that spans a ravine 31 meters (100 ft) above Calle Segovia. The viaduct has won grisly fame as the preferred spot in Madrid for suicides.

32 On the opposite side of the street is the neighborhood of **Las Vistillas,** named for the pleasant park on the bluffs that overlooks Madrid's western edge. A great place to watch the sun go down or catch a cool breeze on a sweltering summer's night, the best thing to do here is find an empty outdoor table and order a drink and some tapas.

Tour 5: Castizo Madrid

Castizo is a Spanish word that means "authentic," and while there are few "sights" in the usual sense on this tour, our walk wanders through some of the most traditional and lively neighborhoods of Madrid.

33 Begin at the **Plaza Santa Ana,** the heart of the theater district in the 17th century—the Golden Age of Spanish Literature—and today the center of Madrid's thriving nightlife. In the plaza is a statue of playwright Pedro Calderón de la Barca on a base depicting scenes from his works. His likeness faces the **Teatro Español,** which is adorned with the names of Spain's greatest playwrights. The theater, rebuilt in 1980 following a fire, stands in the same spot in which plays were performed as early as the 16th century, at that time in a rowdy outdoor setting called a *corral.* These makeshift theaters were usually installed in a vacant lot between two apartment buildings and families with balconies overlooking the action rented out seats to wealthy patrons of the arts. On the opposite side of the plaza is the ceramic tile facade of the **Casa de Guadalajara,** one of the most beautiful buildings in Madrid and currently a popular nightspot. On the same side of the plaza stands the recently refurbished **Hotel Victoria,** now an upscale establishment but once a rundown residence frequented by famous and not-so-famous bullfighters, including Manolete.

To the side of the hotel is the diminutive **Plaza del Angel,** home of one of the city's best jazz clubs, the Café Central. Back on Plaza Santa Ana is one of Madrid's most famous cafés, the **Cervecería Alemana.** Another Hemingway haunt, the café's marble-topped tables still attract struggling writers, poets, and beer-lovers.

Walk east on the street where the Alemana sits, Calle del Prado, for two blocks and turn right onto Calle León, named for a lion kept here **34** long ago by a resident Moor. At the corner of **Calle Cervantes** you'll see a plaque marking the house where the author of *Don Quixote* lived and died. Miguel de Cervantes's 1605 epic story of the man with the impossible dream is said to be the world's second most-widely translated and read book, after the Bible.

The **home of Lope de Vega,** a contemporary of Cervantes, is at number 11 Calle Cervantes, and has been turned into a museum that shows how a typical home of the period was furnished. Considered the Shakespeare of Spanish literature, Lope de Vega (1562–1635) wrote some 1,800 plays and enjoyed huge success during his lifetime. *Tel. 91/429–9216. Admission: 200 pesetas. Open Mon.–Fri. 9:30–2:30, Sat. 10–1:30; closed Sun.*

Continuing down Calle León one block, turn left onto Calle Huertas, the premier street of bars in bar-besotted Madrid. One block down Huertas turn right onto **Calle Amor de Dios,** the center of the city's flamenco community. Look for the music shops and guitar makers. At number 4 Calle Amor de Dios is a flamenco dancing school that attracts students from around the world. If you stop and listen, you may hear the staccato sound of stamping heels.

Amor de Dios ends at busy Calle Atocha. The ugly modern church you see across the street is **San Nicolás.** The burning of this church in 1936 is vividly described by writer Arturo Barea in his autobiographical *The Forge.* Like many other churches during that turbulent period, the original building here fell victim to the wrath of working-class crowds who felt themselves to be the victims of centuries of clerical oppression. Next door is the **Pasaje Doré,** home to a colorful assortment of market stalls typical of most Madrid neighborhoods. At the end of the market turn left for a look at the **Cine Doré,** a rare example of Art Nouveau architecture in Madrid. The theater shows movies from the Spanish National Film Archives.

Cross the street and walk down Calle de la Rosa, which turns into Calle de la Cabeza. This is the beginning of the **Barrio Lavapiés**—the old *judería* (Jewish Quarter). Today it remains one of the most typical or *castizo* of all working-class Madrid neighborhoods, although there are some recent signs of creeping gentrification. Don't be surprised to see graffiti reading "Yuppies No!"

Jews as well as Moors were forced to live outside the city walls in old Madrid, and this was one of the suburbs they founded. For a chilling reminder of the depth of Catholic Spain's intolerance, stop at the southeast corner of Calle Cabeza and Calle Lavapiés. Here, unmarked by any historical plaque, is the former **Cárcel de la Inquisición** (Inquisition Jail). Today a lumber warehouse, in this little building, Jews, Moors, and others designated as unrepentant heathens and sinners suffered the many tortures devised by the merciless inquisitors.

Walk down the long hill traced by Calle Lavapiés until you reach the **Plaza Lavapiés,** the heart of this historic neighborhood. To the left is the *Calle de la Fe* (Street of Faith), which was called Calle Synagogue up until the expulsion of the Jews in 1492. At the top of this narrow way is the **Church of San Pedro el Real,** built on the site of the razed synagogue. Legend has it that Jews and Moors who accepted baptism over exile were forced to walk up this street barefoot to be baptized in the church, as a demonstration of the sincerity of their newfound faith.

Leave the plaza heading southwest on Calle Sombrerete two blocks until you reach the intersection of Calle Mesón de Paredes. On the corner you'll see a lovingly preserved example of popular Madrid architecture called the **Corrala.** Life in this type of balconied apartment building is lived very publicly, with laundry flapping in the breeze, babies crying, and old ladies dressed in black gossiping over the railings. In the past, common kitchen and bathroom facilities in the patio were shared among neighbors. This building is not unlike the *corrales* that were used as the city's early theater venues and there is a plaque to remind us that the setting for the famous 19th-century *zarzuela* or light opera called *La Revoltosa* was a *corrala* like this one. In summer, city-sponsored musical theater events are occasionally held here. The ruins across the street were once the Escalopios de San Fernando—another church and parochial school that fell victim to anti-Catholic sentiments in this neighborhood during the civil war.

Time Out Drop in at Madrid's oldest bar, the **Taberna de Antonio Sanchez** (Mesón de Paredes 13), for a glass of wine and some tapas or just a peek inside. The dark walls lined with bullfighting paintings, zinc bar, and pulley system used to lift casks of wine from the cellar look much the same as they did when the place was first opened in 1830. Meals are also served in a dining room in back. Specialties include *rabo de buey* (bull's tail stew) and *morcillo al horno* (a beef stew).

Continue west on Calle de los Abades, crossing Calle de Embajadores into the neighborhood known as **"El Rastro."** Filled with tiny shops selling antiques and all types of used stuff (some of it junk), the rastro becomes an overcrowded flea market on Sunday mornings from 10 to 2. The best time for exploring is any other morning, when a little browsing and bargaining are likely to turn up such treasures as old iron grillwork, marble tabletops, or gilt picture frames. The main street of the rastro is Ribera de Curtidores and the best streets for shopping are the ones to the west.

Excursion: El Escorial and the Valley of the Fallen

Numbers in the margin correspond to points of interest on the Madrid Excursions map.

Felipe II was certainly one of history's most deeply religious and forbidding monarchs—not to mention one of its most powerful—and the great granite monastery he had constructed in a remarkable 21 years (1563–84) offers enduring testimony to that austere character. Severe, rectilinear, and unforgiving, the **Real Monasterio de San Lorenzo de El Escorial** (El Escorial Monastery) stands 50 km (31 mi) from Madrid on the slopes of the Guadarrama Mountains, one of the most massive yet simple examples of architecture on the Iberian Peninsula.

Felipe built the monastery in the village of San Lorenzo de El Escorial to commemorate Spain's crushing victory over the French at Saint-Quentin on August 10, 1557, and as a final resting place for his all-powerful father, the emperor Carlos V. The vast rectangle it traces, along with 16 courts, is modeled on the red-hot grille upon which San Lorenzo was martyred—appropriate, given that August 10 was the saint's day (it's also said that Felipe's troops accidentally destroyed a church dedicated to the saint during the battle, and he sought to make amends). A Spanish psychohistorian recently theorized that it is actually shaped like a prone woman, an unintended emblem of Felipe's sexual repression. Perhaps most surprising is not the fact that this thesis was put forward by a serious academic, but that it provoked several heady newspaper articles and other commentary.

El Escorial can be easily reached by car, train, bus, or organized tour; simply inquire at a travel agency or the appropriate station. While the building and its adjuncts—a palace, museum, church, and more—can take hours or even days to tour, you should be able to include a visit to the Valley of the Fallen, where General Franco is buried, in a day trip. At the monastery, be prepared for the mobs of tourists who visit daily, especially during the summer.

The Escorial was begun by Juan Bautista de Toledo but finished in 1584 by Juan de Herrera, who was to give his name to a major Spanish architectural school. It was completed just in time for Felipe to die here, gangrenous and in great pain from the gout that had plagued him for years, in the tiny, sparsely furnished bedroom that resembled a monk's cell more than the resting place of a great mon-

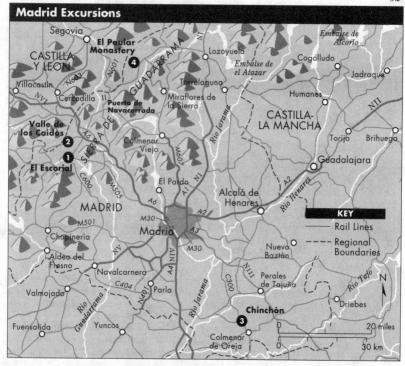

Madrid Excursions

arch. It is in this bedroom—which looks out, through a private entrance, into the royal chapel—that one most appreciates the Spartan nature of this man. Later, Bourbon kings, such as Carlos III and Carlos IV, had clearly different tastes, and their apartments, connected to Felipe's by the Hall of Battles, are far more luxurious.

Perhaps the most interesting spot in the entire Escorial is the **Royal Pantheon,** which contains the body of every king since Carlos I save three—Felipe V (buried at La Granja palace), Ferdinand VI (in Madrid), and Amadeus of Savoy (in Italy). The body of Alfonso XIII, who died in Rome in 1941, was brought to the Escorial only in January 1980. The bodies of the rulers lie in 26 sumptuous marble and bronze sarcophagi that line the walls (three of which are empty, awaiting future rulers). Only those queens who bore sons later crowned lie in the same crypt; the others, along with royal sons and daughters who never ruled, lie nearby in the **Pantheon of the Infantes.** Many of the child infantes are in a single, circular tomb made of Carrara marble.

Another highlight is the uncharacteristically lavish and beautiful **Library,** with 40,000 rare manuscripts, codices, and ancient books including St. Teresa of Ávila's diary and the gold-lettered, illuminated *Codex Aureus*. **Tapestries** woven from cartoons by Goya, Rubens, and El Greco cover almost every inch of wall space in huge sections of the building, and extraordinary canvases by Velázquez, El Greco, David, Ribera, Tintoretto, Rubens, and other masters have been collected from around the monastery and are now displayed in the New Museums. In the **Basilica,** don't miss the fresco over the choir depicting heaven or Titian's fresco of *The Martyrdom*

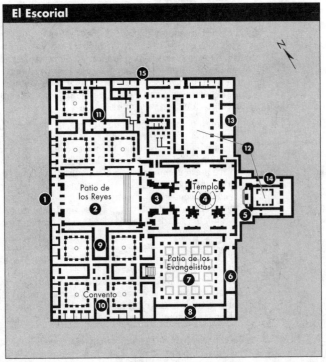

El Escorial

of St. Lawrence, showing the saint being roasted alive. *San Lorenzo de El Escorial, tel. 91/890–5905. Admission: 800 pesetas. Open Apr.–Sept., Tues.–Sun. 10–6; Oct.–Mar., Tues.–Sun. 10–5; closed Mon.*

Time Out Many Madrileños consider El Escorial the perfect place for a huge weekend lunch. Topping the list of favorite eating spots is the outdoor terrace of **Charoles** (Floridablanca 24, tel. 91/890–5975, reservations advised), where imaginative seasonal specialties round out a menu of Spanish favorites like *bacalao al pil-pil* (spicy cod) and grilled *chultetón* (steak).

2 Just a few miles north of El Escorial on C600 is the **Valle de los Caídos** (Valley of the Fallen). You'll drive through a pine-studded state park to this massive basilica, which is carved out inside a hill of solid granite and commands magnificent views to the east. Topped with a cross nearly 150 m (500 ft) high, this is the tomb of both Franco and José Antonio Primo de Rivera, founder of the Spanish Falange. It was built with the forced labor of Republican prisoners after the civil war and dedicated rather disingenuously to *all* those who died in the three-year conflict. The inside of this gigantic hall is more reminiscent of the palace of the Wizard of Oz than of anything else, with every footstep resounding loudly off its stone walls. Tapestries of the Apocalypse add to the generally terrifying flavor of the place. *Tel. 91/890–5611. Admission: 600 pesetas, 300 pesetas for funicular to top of the hill. Open Apr.–Sept., daily 10–7; Oct.–Mar., daily 10–6.*

Excursion: Chinchón

❸ The picturesque village of **Chinchón** lies only 54 km (28 mi) southeast of Madrid, off the N III highway to Valencia on the C300 local road; yet it seems a good four centuries away in time, a true Castilian town. It's an ideal place for a day trip and lunch at one of its many rustic restaurants—the only down side being that swarms of Madrileños have the very same idea, so it's often difficult to find a table for lunch on weekends.

The high point of Chinchón is its charming Plaza Mayor, an uneven circle of ancient three- and four-story houses embellished with wooden balconies resting on granite columns. It's reminiscent of an open-air Elizabethan theater, but with a Spanish flavor. In fact, the entire plaza is converted to a bull ring from time to time, with temporary bleachers erected in the center and seats on the privately owned balconies being rented out for a splendid view of the festivities. (It should be noted that these fights are rare, and tickets hard to come by, as they are snatched up by Spanish tourists as soon as they go on sale.)

Time Out Two of the best and most popular restaurants on Chinchon's arcaded plaza are **Mesón de la Virreina** (Plaza Mayor 21, tel. 91/894–0015) and **Café de la Iberia** (Plaza Mayor 17, tel. 91/894–0998). Both have balconies for dining outside and it's a good idea to call and reserve an outdoor table ahead of time. The food in each is hearty Castilian fare such as roast lamb and suckling pig or thick steaks.

On the way back to Madrid, you'll pass through the valley of Jarama, just at the point where C300 joins the main highway. This is the scene of one of the bloodiest battles in which the Abraham Lincoln Brigade, American volunteers fighting with the Republicans against Franco in the Spanish Civil War, played a major role (immortalized by folksinger Pete Seeger, who sang, "There's a valley in Spain called Jarama . . ."). Until just a few years ago, you could find bones and rusty military hardware in the fields here; today, there are still a number of clearly discernible trenches.

Excursion: The Valley of Lozoya and the El Paular Monastery

Behind the great meseta where Madrid sits, the Guadarrama Mountains rise like a dark, jagged shield that separates New and Old Castile. The mountains, snowcapped for much of the year, are indeed rough-hewn in many spots, particularly so on their northern face, but there is a dramatic exception—the **Valley of Lozoya.**

About 100 km (62 mi) north of the capital, this valley of pine, poplar, and babbling brooks is a cool and green retreat from the often searing heat of the plain. In it, Madrileños often take a day for a picnic or a simple driving tour, rarely joined by foreign tourists, to whom the area is virtually unknown.

A car is required for visiting this place, but the drive will be a pleasant one. Take the A6 motorway northwest from the city, exiting at signs for the Navacerrada Pass on the N601 highway. As you climb toward the 6,100-ft mountain pass, you'll come to a road bearing off to the left toward Cercedilla. This little village, also reachable by train from Madrid, is a favorite spot for mountain hikers. Just above the town an old Roman road leads up to the ridge of the Guadarrama, where an ancient fountain, known as Fuenfría, long provided the spring water that fed the Roman aqueduct of Segovia (*see* Chapter 4, Around Madrid). The path traced by this cobble road is very close to the route Hemingway had his hero Robert Jordan take in his novel of the civil war, *For Whom the Bell Tolls;* eventually it will take you near the bridge that Jordan blew up in the novel.

If you continue past the Cercedilla road, you'll come to a ski resort at the highest point of the Navacerrada Pass. Take a right here on the C604 and you'll follow the ridge of the mountains for a few miles before descending into the Lozoya Valley.

❹ The **El Paular Monastery** will loom up on your left as you approach the valley floor. This was the first Carthusian monastery in Castile, built by King Juan I in 1390, but it has been badly neglected since the Disentailment of 1836. Fewer than a dozen Benedictine monks still live here, eating and praying exactly as their predecessors did centuries ago. One of them gives tours—as well as abundant advice on the state of your soul—at noon, 1, and 5.

The monastery is physically connected to the Santa María del Paular hotel (reserve in advance: tel. 91/869–1011, fax 91/869–1006). This hotel is tastefully furnished and charming, but very expensive and not as grand as similarly priced paradors.

The valley is filled with spots to picnic along the Lozoya River, including several campgrounds. Afterward, take the C604 north a few kilometers to Rascafria, where you turn right on a smaller road marked for Miraflores de la Sierra. In that town you'll turn right again, following signs for Colmenar Viejo, where you pick up a short expressway back to Madrid.

What to See and Do with Children

Spaniards love children. Take a baby into a restaurant, and chances are he or she will be whisked away by a waiter wanting to show the little darling off to the kitchen staff (don't worry; the child is in good hands). Walk into almost any park, and a swing set and other child-oriented amenities will be waiting. There's hardly a bar or restaurant that would look askance at you for bringing a child of any age with you, whatever the time of day or night.

Park Attractions That said, there are a few attractions of special interest for those of lesser years. A leading candidate is the **Parque de Atracciones,** a large amusement park in the Casa de Campo, a sprawling park northwest of the city. *Metro: Batán; bus No. 33 from Plaza de Isabel II. Admission and 2 rides: 600 pesetas. All-ride ticket: 1,375 pesetas, 800 pesetas children 7 and under. Open weekends noon–10.*

The Casa de Campo also has a large, well-laid-out **zoo,** with most of the animals allowed to roam free behind deep trenches. Most popular are the pandas donated by the People's Republic of China, but there are many other animals, too. There's also a dolphinarium with regular performances. *Metro: Lago; bus No. 33. Admission: 730 pesetas adults, 490 pesetas children under 8; admission with dolphin show: 940 pesetas adult, 695 pesetas children. Open Mon.–Fri. 10–7:30.*

Children love the **cable car** (*see* Off the Beaten Track, *below*) that takes you from just above the Rosaleda gardens in the Parque del Oeste to the center of Casa de Campo. Be warned, however, that it's at least a mile from where the cable car drops you off to both the zoo and the amusement park, and you'll have to ask directions.

Museums Another favorite with children—this one located downtown—is the **Wax Museum.** Along with such world figures as Mikhail Gorbachev and President Kennedy, there are grisly reconstructions of famous Spanish crimes. The complete line of Spanish royalty is intriguing for adults, too; if you read Spanish the plaques that accompany them provide a marvelous history lesson. *Paseo de Recoletos 41. Admission: 750 pesetas adults, 500 pesetas children. Open daily 10:30–2 and 4–9.*

While not properly a museum, the **planetarium** is a perennial children's favorite. *Parque de Tierno Galván, tel. 91/467–3898. Metro: Méndez Alvaro. Admission: 275 pesetas. Shows Tues.–Fri. 5:30 and 6:45; weekends 11:30, 12:45, 5:30, 6:45, and 8.*

Boating Rowboats can be rented at **El Estanque,** the lake in the center of Retiro Park, where you'll paddle around with scores of other parents and children. Or you can rent similar watercraft in the larger lake in Casa de Campo, near the Lago metro stop.

Puppet Shows Retiro Park is also the location of an outdoor puppet theater for children, featuring slapstick routines that even non-Spanish speakers will enjoy. Shows take place on Saturday at 1 PM and on Sunday at 1, 6, and 7. Free admission. The theater is located near the Puerta de Alcalá gate.

Off the Beaten Track

For a visit to the parks of northwest Madrid and the university, follow Calle Ferraz (the extension of Bailén) north from the Plaza de España. Atop a hill in the first park area to your left, you'll see the **Templo de Debod** (Debod Temple), an authentic 4th-century BC Egyptian temple donated to the Spanish in recognition of their engineering help during the construction of the Aswan Dam. It sits near the site of the former Montaña barracks, where Madrileños bloodily crushed the beginnings of a Francoist uprising in 1936.

If you continue down Pintor Rosales, the street that follows the upper edge of the park, you'll come to the **teleférico** (cable car; in the Rosaleda Gardens, tel. 91/541–7440; 445 pesetas; open Apr.–Sept., daily noon–sundown; Oct.–Mar., weekends noon–sundown) that will carry you high over the Manzanares River and out into **Casa de Campo** (*see* What to See and Do with Children, *above*), which contains a zoo, an amusement park, a convention center, major outdoor concerts, and a half-dozen cafés. Pintor Rosales ends at Paseo de Moret, where you'll turn right to climb up the hill that follows the hilly **Parque del Oeste** (West Park), a perfect place for a picnic. At the top of the hill you'll come into the Moncloa traffic circle.

For a panoramic view of Madrid from 92 meters (304 ft) up, ride the elevator to the top of the modernistic **Faro de Moncloa** (Moncloa Lighthouse). From this landmark's vantage point, the city's gray slate roofs and Habsburg spires look like pictures from a storybook. *Intersection of Avenida Reyes Católicos and Arco de la Victoria. Admission: 200 pesetas. Open Tues.–Sun. 10:30–1:45 and 2:30–7:15.*

The **Royal Tapestry Factory** has been in operation continuously since 1721, laboriously crafting rugs and tapestries for Spain's royal family. Here you can see the artisans working with modern methods and demonstrating traditional tapestry-making techniques. While most of the output of this workshop is on display in palaces throughout the country, there is also a exhibition of tapestries and the drawings on which they were based. *Fuenterrabia 2, tel. 91/551-3400. Admission: 50 pesetas. Open Mon.–Fri. 9–12:30, closed Aug.*

If you're in the mood for museums, head up Alcalá from the Puerta del Sol to the **Academia de Bellas Artes de San Fernando.** Designed by Churriguera in the early 18th century, the waning years of the Baroque period, this little visited museum is Madrid's second great showcase of painting and the other plastic arts. The same building houses the **Instituto de Calcografía,** where limited-edition prints from original plates engraved by Spanish artists—including Goya—are sold. *Alcalá 13, tel. 91/532-1249. Admission: 200 pesetas. Open Tues.–Fri. 9–7, Sat.–Mon. 9–2:30.*

Behind an elaborately sculpted stone portal, the **Museo Municipal** (Municipal Museum) offers a carefully selected collection of historical artifacts, including a huge, remarkably detailed wooden model of the city exactly as it was in 1830. Take a look at the riotous Carnaval posters of the creative 1930s; then compare them to those that came later, the bland and soulless official "art" of the Franco era. *Fuencarral 78, tel. 91/522-5732. Open Tues.–Sat. 10–2 and 5–9; Sun. 10–2.*

The Municipal Museum stands at the entrance to the area known as **Malasaña** (named after a heroine executed by the French). This neighborhood, in the narrow streets directly across from the museum, is filled with music clubs and is where much of the city's famed cultural reawakening was centered in the years following Franco's death. Today, the clubs and bars are still fascinating, often offering such intriguing fare as a kind of flamenco-jazz fusion, but drug use is rampant.

Around the corner from the Municipal Museum lies another museum that's not often visited by foreigners but makes for an offbeat adventure: the **Museo Romántico** (Romantic Museum). The Marquís of Vega Inclán established this museum in 1920 as a tribute to the movement that swept Europe in the 19th century, a literary current that brought scores of writers and artists to Spain to chronicle the "rustic" life that had already disappeared in neighboring lands. Note the *Satire of Romantic Suicide,* a painting by Leonardo Alenea, for an amusingly sarcastic view of these ideas. *San Mateo 13, tel. 91/448-1071. Admission: 200 pesetas. Open Tues.–Sat. 9–2:45, Sun. 9–1:45.*

Shopping

Beyond the popular Lladro porcelains, castanets, and bullfight posters, Madrid offers a great selection of gift items and unique souvenirs. In recent years Spain has achieved recognition as one of the world's top design centers. You'll have no trouble finding traditional crafts such as ceramics, guitars, and leather goods, but don't stop there. Madrid is famous for contemporary furniture and decorator items, as well as chic clothing, shoes, and jewelry. Most major credit cards are accepted at all shops.

Shopping Districts

Madrid has two main centers of shopping. The first is around the **Puerta del Sol** (*see* Tour 1, *above*) in the center of town and includes the two major department stores and a large number of midline shops in the streets nearby. The second area, far more elegant and expensive, is in the northwest Salamanca district, bounded, roughly, by Serrano, Goya, and Conde de Peñalver. In 1989, the Mercado Puerta de Toledo (Ronda de Toledo 1) opened south of the city center and has since become another major shopping area. It is a government-subsidized, ultraslick mall of dozens of shops that market only the most upscale goods, at prices to match. Another new, attractive mall also opened in 1989 underneath the Palace Hotel on the Paseo del Prado. Stores in this elegant, two-story complex include fine shops for books, gourmet foods, clothing, leather goods, art, and more.

Flea Market

On Sundays, Calle de Ribera de Curtidores, the main thoroughfare of **El Rastro** (*see* Tour 5, *above*), is closed to traffic and absolutely jammed with outdoor booths selling all manner of objects. The crowds grow so thick that day that it takes a while to advance just a few feet amid the hawkers and the gawkers. A word of warning: Hang on to your purse and wallet, and be especially careful if you choose to bring a camera—pickpockets abound. The flea market sprawls into most of the surrounding streets, with certain areas specializing in one product or another. Many of the goods sold here are wildly overpriced.

But what goods! You'll find everything from antique furniture to exotic parrots and cuddly puppies; from pirated cassette tapes of flamenco music to keychains emblazoned with symbols of the old anarchist trade union, the CNT; there are paintings, colorful Gypsy oxen yokes, heraldic iron gates, new and used clothes, and even hashish for sale.

Off the Ribera are two *galerías*, courtyards where small shops offer higher-quality, higher-priced antiques and other goods. The whole spectacle shuts down around 2 PM.

Department Stores

Non-Spanish-speaking visitors will find the department stores surprisingly good, and an easy way to shop. **Corte Inglés** is the better of the two chains, with a wider range of higher quality goods. There are four stores: on Calle de Preciados, just off the Puerta del Sol; at the corner of Goya and Alcalá; on Raimundo Fernández Villaverde, just west of the Castellana; and at the corner of Princesa and Alberto Aguilera. **Galerías Preciados** is this chain's main competitor. Its main store is on Plaza del Callao, just off Gran Vía and a few steps from the Puerta del Sol Corte Inglés. Another branch is at Calle Arapiles near the Glorieta de Quevedo, and a third is on Goya, corner of Peñalver, and a fourth is on Calle Serrano. Both chains offer interpreters and shipping services.

Specialty Stores

Ceramics The best of these is probably **Antigua Casa Talavera** (Isabel la Católica 2). Despite its name, the finest ware sold here is from Manises, near Valencia, although the blue-and-white Talavera is first-rate as well. Another good bet is **Cerámica El Alfar** (Claudio Coello 112). Distinctive, modern Spanish ceramics are made in Galicia, and an excellent selection of breakfast sets, coffee pots, and *objets d'art* can be found at **Sargadelos** (Zurbano 46).

Costume Chunky necklaces and dangling earrings can be found in abundance
Jewelry at **Del Pino** (Serrano 48) and **Musgo** (Hermosilla 36). Original crea-

tions with African and Indian motifs are crafted in silver and bronze by one of Spain's hottest designers, **Joaquín Berao**, at his own shop/studio (Conde de Xiquena 13). The gift shop of the **Prado Museum** is the source of classically styled jewelry, many of the pieces copied from the museum's paintings.

Crafts Contemporary handicrafts from all over Spain are sold at **El Arco** (Plaza Mayor 9), which has a good selection of modern ceramics, hand-blown glassware, jewelry, and leather items, as well as a whimsical collection of pendulum clocks. The best decorator furniture, lamps, and rugs are displayed stylishly at **Artespaña** (Hermosilla 14), a store run by the government to encourage Spanish craftsmanship.

Fans These quintessentially Spanish objects can be found in all variations at the **Casa de Diego** (Puerta del Sol 12).

Guitars Some of Spain's best guitar makers are in Madrid. Founded in 1882, the firm **José Ramirez** (Concepción Jerónimo 2) exports guitars around the world (prices start at 15,000 pesetas). The shop includes a museum of antique instruments. Another good place to look is the workshop of **Conde Hermanos** (Felipe II 2), where three generations of the same family have been building and selling guitars since 1917.

Hats There are two first-rate hat shops on the Plaza Mayor, offering everything from the Guardia Civil tricornered patent leather hat to the berets worn by the guardia's oft-time enemy, the Basques. These berets are much wider than those worn by the French Basques and make excellent gifts.

Leather Goods Leather goods are another fine Spanish tradition, but you'll find that, for the most part, deals are few and far between. You'll still pay in the neighborhood of $400 and up for a first-class man's leather jacket, for instance, but it will probably outrank anything you would find back home in quality. **Loewe** (Gran Vía 8 and Serrano 26 and 34) is the best-known leather shop for men and women, but it's outrageously expensive. You can find top leather goods and clothes at the more reasonable **Duna** (Lagasca 7). Designer leather purses and accessories at reasonable prices can also be found at **Piamonte** (Piamonte 16). Bargain hunters should check out the *muestrarios* or shoe showrooms just west of the market on Calle Augusto Figueroa, where you can find samples and one-of-a-kind pairs for half price or less. **Caligae** (Augusto Figueroa 27) shods Madrid's dress-for-less crowd with the avant-garde designs of Parisian Stephane Kélian.

Men's and Women's Clothing Many of the leading fashion designers' outlets are concentrated in the Salamanca district, particularly along Calle Serrano. Take a stroll along that street between Diego de León and Jorge Juan for a gander at a wide array of these shops, or head straight to some of the leading design shops: **Adolfo Domínguez** (Serrano 96), the best-known contemporary Spanish designer for men and women; **Ascot** (Serrano 88), featuring Maria Teresa de Vega's garments for women; **Irene Prada** (Columela 3), clothes by a woman who has dressed some members of the British royal family; or **Sybilla** (Jorge Juan 8), a women's shop.

Miscellaneous Excellent **cutlery** is sold at **Simon** (Espoz y Mina 12). For **kitchenware** try a shop that also offers world-renowned cooking classes, **Alambique** (Encarnación 2). **Books on Madrid,** all of them in Spanish, are the specialty at **La Librería** (Señores de Luzón 8). **Musical instruments** are sold at **Garrido-Bailén** (Bailén 19). A marvelous array of adult and children's **games** can be found at **Naipe** (Meléndez Valdes

55). The shop at the **Municipal Museum** (Fuencarral 78) sells gifts for children, such as wooden toys and puzzles.

Sports

Spectator Sports

Bullfighting For better or for worse, bullfighting is a spectacle, not a sport. Nevertheless, for those not turned off by the death of six bulls each Sunday afternoon from April to early November, it has all the elements of any major stadium event. Nowhere in the world is bullfighting better than at Madrid's **Las Ventas** (formally called the Plaza de Toros Monumental, Calle Alcalá 231; metro: Las Ventas). The city's *afición*, the sophisticated audience that follows the bulls intensely, is more critical in Madrid than anywhere, and you'll be amazed at how confusing their reactions to the fights are; cheers and hoots are difficult at first to distinguish, and it takes years to understand what has prompted the wrath of this most difficult-to-please audience. Tickets may be purchased at the ring or, for a 20% surcharge, at the agencies on Calle Victoria, just off the Puerta del Sol. Most fights start in the late afternoon, and the best of all—the world's top venue of bullfighting—come during the three weeks of consecutive daily fights in May marking the festival of San Isídro. Tickets can be tough to get through normal channels, but they'll always be available from scalpers in the Calle Victoria and at the stadium. You can bargain, but even Spaniards pay prices of perhaps 10 times the face value, up to 10,000 pesetas or even more.

Soccer Spain's number-one sport is soccer, or *fútbol*, as it's known locally. Madrid has two teams, both of them among Europe's best, and two stadia to match. The 130,000-spectator **Santiago Bernabeu Stadium** (Paseo de la Castellana 140) is home to the more popular Real Madrid, while the **Vicente Calderón Stadium** (Paseo de Melancólicos s/n), located on the outskirts of town, is where Atlético Madrid defends. Generally you'll have to stand in line at the stadia to get tickets, but for many major games tickets are available at agencies inside the Galerías Preciados and Corte Inglés department stores (*see* Shopping, *above*).

Participant Sports

Horseback Riding On the other side of Casa de Campo, **Club El Trebol** (tel. 91/711–8512) rents both animals and equipment to the public at reasonable prices.

Jogging The best bet is **Retiro Park,** where one path makes the circumference of the entire park, and numerous others weave their way under trees and through formal gardens. **Casa de Campo** is crisscrossed by numerous less shady trails.

Swimming Madrid has devised a perfect antidote to the sometimes intense dry heat of the summer months—a superb system of clean, popular, and well-run municipal swimming pools (about 350 pesetas for adults; there are several reduced-price multiple-ticket options). There are pools in most neighborhoods, but the biggest and best is in the **Casa de Campo** (take the metro to the Lago stop and walk up the hill a few yards to the entrance). **La Elipa** (Av. de la Paz s/n) has a nude sunbathing area. More expensive, and fitted with a comfortable, treeshaded restaurant by the pool, is the private **Piscina El Lago** (Av. de Valladolid 37), a trendy young people's hangout.

Tennis **Club de Tenis Chamartín** (Federico Salmon 2, tel. 91/345–2500), with 28 courts, is open to the public. There are also public courts in the **Casa de Campo** and on the Avenida de Vírgen del Puerto, behind the Palacio Real (ask for details at the tourist office).

Dining

Unlike most regions of Spain, Madrid does not really have a native cuisine. But, as capital of the realm and home of the king, Madrid has attracted generations of courtiers, foreign diplomats, politicians, and tradesmen, all of whom brought their own styles of and tastes in cooking, whether from another region of Spain, or from abroad.

The roast meats of Castile and the seafood dishes of the Cantabrian coast are just as at home in Madrid as they are in their native lands. Basque cooking, Spain's haute cuisine, is the specialty of Madrid's best restaurants, and seafood houses take advantage of the capital's abundant supply fish and shellfish, trucked in nightly from the coast. Spaniards joke that Madrid is Spain's biggest seaport.

The only truly local dishes are *cocido a la Madrileño* (garbanzo bean stew) and *callos a la Madrileño* (stewed tripe). Given half a chance, Madrileños will spend hours waxing lyrically over the mouth-watering merits of both. *Cocido* is a delicious and hearty winter meal consisting of garbanzo beans, vegetables, potatoes, sausages, and pork. The best *cocidos* are slowly simmered in earthenware crocks over open fires, and served as a complete meal in several courses, first the broth which comes with angel hair pasta, then the beans and vegetables, and finally the meat. *Cocido* can be found in the most elegant restaurants, such as Lhardy and at the Ritz hotel, as well as the most humble eateries, and is usually offered as a midday selection on Monday or Wednesday. *Callos*, on the other hand, is a much simpler concoction of veal tripe stewed with tomatoes, onions, and garlic, and is served in *tascas* or taverns.

Although the countryside near the capital produces some wines, they are not very good. The house wine in nearly all Madrid restaurants is a sturdy, uncomplicated *Valdepeñas* from La Mancha. A traditional anise-flavored liqueur called *Anís* is manufactured just outside the village of Chinchón.

Madrileños tend to eat their meals even later than other Spaniards. Restaurants generally open for lunch at 1:30 and fill up by 3. Dinnertime begins at 9, but reservations for 11 are common. A meal in Madrid is usually a lengthy (up to three hours) and rather formal affair, even at inexpensive places. Restaurants are at their best at midday, when most places offer a *menu del día* (daily special) consisting of two courses, dessert, wine, and coffee.

Dinner, on the other hand, can present something of a problem if you don't want to eat such a big meal so late. One solution is to take your evening meal at one of Madrid's many foreign restaurants. Good-quality Italian, Mexican, Russian, Argentine, and American places abound, and on the whole tend to be less formal, more lively, and open earlier.

The other alternative is to make a dinner of *tapas* and Madrid offers some of the best *tapa* bars in Spain. A *tapa* is a bit of food that usually comes free with a drink; it might be a few olives, a mussel in vinaigrette, a sardine, or spicy potatoes. A larger plate of the same sort food called a *ración* can also be ordered, and is meant to be eaten with toothpicks and shared among friends. While a *tapa* bar crawl is fun and filling, it isn't necessarily a way to save money and usually ends up costing the same, if not more, than a sit-down, three-course meal. Dress in most Madrid restaurants and *tapas* bars is stylish, but casual. The more expensive places tend to be a bit more formal, and men generally wear jackets and ties, and women wear skirts.

Highly recommended restaurants are indicated by a star ★.

Category	Cost*
$$$$	over 6,000 ptas
$$$	4,000–6,000 ptas
$$	1,800–4,000 ptas
$	under 1,800 ptas

*per person, excluding drinks, service, tip, and tax

$$$$ **Horcher.** Housed in a luxurious mansion at the edge of Retiro Park,
★ this classic restaurant is renowned for its hearty but elegant fare served with impeccable style. Specialties include the types of game dishes favored by Spanish aristocracy. Try the wild boar, venison, or roast wild duck with almond croquettes. The star appetizer is lobster salad with truffles. Offerings like Stroganoff with mustard, pork chops with sauerkraut, and *baumkuchen*, a chocolate-covered fruit and cake dessert, reflect the restaurant's Germanic roots (the Horcher family operated a restaurant in Berlin at the turn of the century). The intimate dining room is decorated with antique Austrian porcelains and rust brocade fabric on the walls. A wide selection of French and German wines rounds out the menu. *Alfonso XII 6, tel. 91/532–3596. Reservations required. Jacket and tie advised. AE, DC, MC, V. Closed Sun.*

Lhardy. Serving Madrid specialties from the same central city locale for more than 150 years, Lhardy's dark wood paneling, brass chandeliers, and red velvet chairs look pretty much the same as they have since day one. The menu features international fare, but most diners come for the traditional *cocido madrileño* (garbanzo beans with sausage, pork, and vegetables) and *callos madrileño* (stewed tripe). Sea bass in champagne sauce, game, and dessert soufflés are also very well prepared. The dining rooms are upstairs, and the ground-floor entryway doubles as a delicatessen and stand-up coffee bar that, on chilly winter mornings, is filled with shivering souls sipping *caldo* (chicken broth) ladled steaming hot from silver urns. *Carrera de San Jerónimo 8, tel. 91/521–3385. Reservations advised. Jacket and tie recommended. AE, DC, MC, V. Closed Sun. evening and holidays.*

Viridiana. The trendiest of Madrid's gourmet restaurants, Viridiana has the relaxed atmosphere of a bistro and black-and-white decor punctuated by prints from the classic Luis Buñuel anticlerical film after which this establishment is named. Iconoclast chef Abraham Garcia says "market-based" is too narrow a description for his creative menu, though the list does change every two weeks depending on what's locally available. Offerings include such varied fare as red onions stuffed with *morcilla* (black pudding); soft flour tortillas wrapped around marinated fresh tuna; and filet mignon in white truffle sauce. If it's available, be sure to try the superb duck pâté drizzled with sherry and served with Tokay wine. The tangy grapefruit sherbet is a marvel. *Juan de Mena 14, tel. 91/531–5222.*

Reservations required. Dress: stylish but casual. No credit cards. Closed. Sun., Easter week, and Aug.

★ **Zalacaín.** The deep apricot color scheme, set off by dark wood and gleaming silver, suggests the atmosphere of an exclusive villa. One of only two Spanish restaurants to be awarded three Michelin stars, Zalacaín introduced *nouvelle cuisine* to Spain and continues to set the pace after twenty years at the top. Splurge on prawn salad in avocado vinaigrette, scallops and leeks in Albariño wine, and roast pheasant with truffles. Service is correct but somewhat stuffy. A fixed-price tasting menu allows you to sample the best of Zalacaín for about 6,500 pesetas. *Alvarez de Baena 4, tel. 91/561–5935. Reservations required. Jacket and tie recommended. AE, DC, V. Closed Sat. lunch, Easter week, and Aug.*

$$$ **El Cenador del Prado.** A mecca for those with gourmet palates, Cenador features an innovative menu with French and Asian touches and some exotic Spanish dishes not often found in restaurants. Dine in the baroque salmon-and-gold salon or the less formal plant-filled conservatory. The house specialty is *patatas a la importancia*—sliced potatoes fried in a sauce of garlic, parsley, and clams. Equally rewarding are the shellfish consommé with ginger raviolis, veal and eggplant in béchamel, or wild boar with prunes. For dessert try *cañas fritas*, a cream-filled pastry treat once served only at Spanish weddings. *Calle del Prado 4, tel. 91/429–1561. Reservations advised. Jacket and tie recommended. AE, DC, MC, V. Closed Sat. lunch, Sun., Easter week, and 1st half of Aug.*

★ **Gure-Etxea.** Located in the heart of medieval Madrid on the trendy Plaza de Paja, this is the capital's most authentic Basque restaurant. The ground-floor dining room is airy, high-ceilinged, and elegant, while brick walls lining the downstairs eating area give it a rustic, farmhouse feel. As in the Basque country (but uncommon elsewhere in Europe), you are waited on by women. Classic dishes here include *bacalao pil-pil* (spicy cod fried in garlic and oil, making the "pil-pil" sound), *rape en salsa verde* (monkfish in green parsley sauce), and for dessert *leche frita* (fried custard). On weekdays a hearty and inexpensive plate of the day is added to the lunchtime menu. *Plaza de Paja 12, tel. 91/365–6149. Reservations advised. AE, DC, V. Closed Sun., Aug., and Easter week.*

Mentidero de la Villa. The decor of this intimate eatery is a bewitching blend of pastel colors, pale wood, and candlelight, with fanciful, rough-hewn rocking-horse sculptures. The menu is adventuresome—the chef's salad mixes fresh kelp and lettuce. Specialties include breast of squab in cherry vinegar, pheasant and chestnuts in wine, and halibut with a black-olive sauce. Apropos of the restaurant's moniker (the name means "gossip shop"), service is informal and chatty. *Santo Tomé 6, tel. 91/308–1285. Reservations advised. AE, MC, V. Closed Sat. lunch, Sun., and Aug.*

★ **El Pescador.** Spaniards swear that the seafood in Madrid is fresher than in the coastal towns where it was caught. That's probably an exaggeration, but it *seems* plausible, at least judging from El Pescador, one of Madrid's best-loved seafood restaurants. Stop for a drink at the bar before sitting down to dinner, and take in the delicious aromas wafting from the kitchen, where skilled chefs dressed in fishermen's smocks prepare shellfish just behind the counter. As tapas at the bar or as a first course of your meal, definitely try the incredible *salpicón de mariscos* (mussels, lobster, shrimp, and onions in vinaigrette). Named for the restaurant's owner, the *lenguado Evaristo* (grilled sole) is the best dish on the menu. The place is cheerful and noisy, and the decor is "dockside rustic," with lobster-pot lamps, red-and-white checked tablecloths, and rough-

74

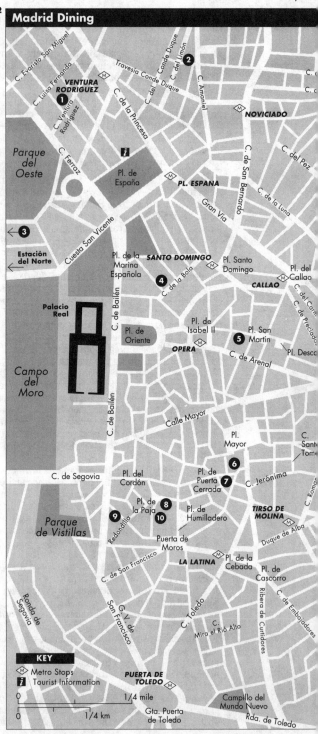

Madrid Dining

KEY

◇ Metro Stops
🛈 Tourist Information

0   1/4 mile

0   1/4 km

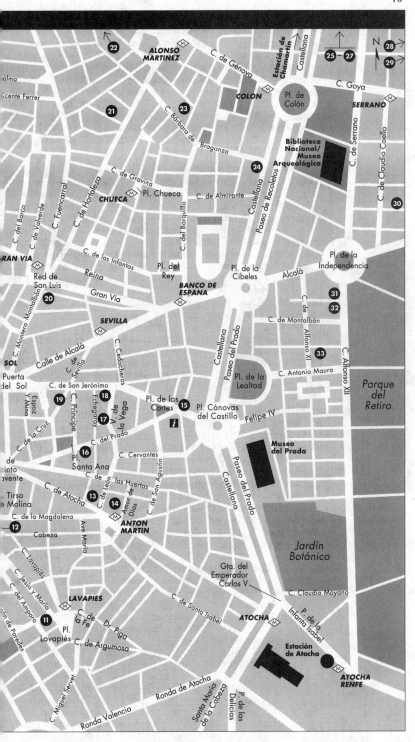

hewn posts and beams. *José Ortega y Gasset 75, tel. 91/402–1290. Reservations advised. MC, V. Closed Sun. and Aug.*

La Trainera. Fresh seafood—the best quality money can buy—is what La Trainera is all about. For decades this informal restaurant, with its nautical decor and maze of little dining rooms, has reigned as the queen of Madrid's seafood houses. Crab, lobster, shrimp, mussels, and a dozen other types of shellfish are served by weight in *raciones*. While most Spanish diners share several plates of these delicacies as their entire meal, the grilled hake, sole, or turbot make an unbeatable second course. Skip the listless house wine and go for a bottle from the cellar. *Lagasca 60, tel. 91/576–8035. Reservations advised. MC, V. Closed Sun. and Aug.*

$$ La Bola. First opened as a *botelleria* or wine shop in 1802, La Bola
★ developed slowly into a tapas bar and eventually a full-fledged restaurant. Tradition is what La Bola offers, from the blood-red paneling outside to the original bar and cozy dining nooks decorated with polished wood, Spanish tile, and lace curtains inside. It still belongs to the founding family, with the seventh generation currently in training to take over. Although it's open for dinner, La Bola's specialty is that quintessential Madrid meal, *cocido madrileño*, which is served only at lunch, and accompanied by crusty bread and a hearty red wine. *Bola 5, tel. 91/547–6930. Reservations advised for lunch. No credit cards. Closed Sun.*

Brasserie de Lista. For a gourmet meal in a comfortable, informal setting this bistro-style spot in a neighborhood of designer boutiques can't be beat. A long marble bar, lots of brass, and frosted glass create a turn-of-the-century ambience. Waiters in long white aprons serve Spanish specialties with nouvelle touches, grilled monkfish with toasted garlic or steak with *cabrales* blue cheese sauce, for example. The varied menu also includes international fare such as chicken and avocado salad with chutney and beef carpaccio. The weekday lunchtime special is a good value. *Ortega y Gasset 6, tel. 91/435–2818. Reservations advised for lunch and on weekends. AE, MC, V.*

La Cacharrería. The name of this restaurant in medieval Madrid means junkyard and it's reflected in the funky decor, a mix of dusty calico, old lace, and gilt mirrors. The cooking, however, is decidedly upscale, with a market-based menu that changes daily, and an excellent selection of wines. Venison stew and fresh tuna steaks with cava and leeks were among the specialties on a recent visit. Whatever else you order, save room for the homemade lemon tart. *Moreiria 9, tel. 91/365–3930. AE, DC, MC, V. Closed Sun.*

Café Balear. A sophisticated yet informal eatery that attracts a crowd of creative types from the fashion and advertising world, the Café Balear serves some of the best *paella* (rice dishes) in Madrid. Art prints and potted palms are the only nods to decoration in the stark white dining room. Specialties include *paella centolla* (rice with crab) and *arroz negro* (rice with squid in its ink). The perfectly prepared *paella mixta* combines seafood, pork, and vegetables. Also worth trying is the excellent and very affordable house cava. *Sagunto 18, tel. 91/447–9115. Reservations advised. AE, V. Closed Sun. and Mon. evenings.*

Cañas y Barro. Hidden away on an unspoiled plaza that was the 19th-century center of Madrid's university, this Valencian restaurant specializes in rice dishes with flair. The most popular is *arroz à la banda* (rice with peeled shrimp cooked in seafood broth). Another good choice is the *paella* Valenciana, made with chicken, rabbit, and vegetables. The service is friendly and unpretentious, and white plaster friezes lend the pink dining room a touch of elegance.

Amaniel 23, tel. 91/542–4798. Reservations advised on weekends. AE, DC, MC, V. Closed Sun. evening, Mon., and Aug.

★ **Casa Botín.** The *Guinness Book of World Records* calls this the world's oldest restaurant (1725) and Hemingway called it the best. The latter claim may contain a bit of hyperbole, but the restaurant *is* excellent and extremely charming, despite the hordes of tourists. There are four floors of tiled and wood-beamed dining rooms, and ovens dating back several centuries—which you'll pass if you're seated upstairs. There are also visits from traditionally garbed musical groups called *tunas.* Must-try specialties are *cochinillo asado* (roast suckling pig) and *cordero asado* (roast lamb). It is said Francesco Goya was a dishwasher here before he became successful as a painter. *Cuchilleros 17 (just off Plaza Mayor), tel. 91/366–4217. Reservations strongly advised (or you're in for a wait). AE, DC, MC, V.*

★ **Casa Paco.** This is a popular Castilian tavern that wouldn't have looked out of place two or three centuries ago. Squeeze your way past the old zinc-topped bar, always crowded with Madrileños downing shots of red wine, and into the tiled dining rooms. People come here to feast on thick slabs of red meat, served sizzling on plates so hot that it continues to cook at your table. The beef is superb and the Spanish consider overcooking a sin, so if you ask for your meat well done be prepared for nasty glares. You order the meat by weight, so remember that a *medio kilo* is more than a pound. For starters try the *pisto manchego* (the La Mancha version of ratatouille). *Puerta Cerrada 11, tel. 91/366–3166. Reservations advised. DC, V. Closed Sun. and Aug.*

Casa Vallejo. With its homey dining room, friendly staff, creative menu, and reasonable prices, this restaurant is the well-kept secret of Madrid's budget gourmets. Try the tomato, zucchini, and cheese tart or artichokes and clams for starters, then follow up with duck breast in prune sauce or meatballs made with lamb, almonds, and pine nuts. The fudge and raspberry pie alone makes it worth the trip. *San Lorenzo 9, tel. 91/308–6158. Reservations required. AE, MC, V. Closed Sat. lunch and Sun.*

Ciao Madrid. Always noisy and packed with happy diners, Ciao Madrid is the city's best Italian restaurant. Homemade pastas like tagliatelle with wild mushrooms or panzerotti stuffed with spinach and ricotta are popular as inexpensive main courses, but the kitchen also turns out credible versions of osso buco and veal scaloppine, accompanied by a good selection of Italian wines. The decor— mirrored walls and sleek black furniture—convincingly evokes fashionable Milan. A second location (Apodaca 20, tel. 91/447–0036), run by the owner's sons and daughter, also serves pizza. *Argensola 7, tel. 91/308–2519. Reservations essential. AE, MC, V. Closed Sat. lunch and Sun.*

Cornucopia en Descalzas. Run by former Boston caterer Deborah Hansen and her Madrid-born husband Julio de Haro, this young and friendly restaurant on the first floor of an old mansion just off the historic Plaza de las Descalzas Reales features a creative blend of nouvelle Spanish and American dishes. The menu changes with the seasons: In winter expect dishes like duck soup with duck meatballs, roast pork loin stuffed with apricots, or scallops in wine and cream; the lighter summer menu includes cold almond and garlic soup and grilled calamares with garlic mayonnaise. The mustard-and-burgundy-colored dining room is a tad ornate. *Flora 1, tel. 91/547–6465. Reservations advised for dinner. AE, MC, V. Closed Sat. and Sun. lunch, Mon., and Aug. 15–Sept. 15.*

★ **El Cosaco.** This romantic, candlelit Russian restaurant, tucked away on the ancient Plaza de Paja, is a favorite of young couples in love. While they may only have eyes for each other, the food here is definitely worth a look—savory blini stuffed with caviar, smoked trout, or salmon, and hearty beef dishes like woronof and stroganoff. The dining rooms are decorated with paisley wallpaper and dark red linens, and if the crackling fireplace's cheery glow in winter isn't enough to warm you there are eight types of vodka that ought to do the trick. *Plaza de Paja 2, tel. 91/365–3548. Reservations advised. AE, DC. Open for dinner only; lunch served on Sun.*

La Galette. Located just one block from Madrid's main shopping street, Calle Serrano, this is an intimate restaurant for a romantic lunch or supper by candlelight. The menu is primarily vegetarian, but includes some inventive meat dishes. Avoid the tasteless onion soup and go straight for the *Pimiento Persa* (green pepper stuffed with vegetables, rice, and cheese) or the *Cocotte Rusia* (beef stewed with laurel and plums, served over basmati rice). Luscious fruit tarts and brownies de Boston are irresistible dessert choices. *Conde de Aranda 11, tel. 91/576–0641. Reservations recommended. AE, V. Closed Sun.*

★ **La Gamella.** American-born chef Dick Stephens has created a new, reasonably priced menu at this hugely popular dining spot. The sophisticated rust-red dining room, batik tablecloths, oversize plates, and attentive service remain the same, but much of the nouvelle cuisine has been replaced by more traditional fare such as chicken in garlic, boeuf Bourguignon, or steak tartar à la Jack Daniels. A few of the old-favorite signature dishes like sausage and red pepper quiche and bittersweet chocolate pâté remain. The lunchtime *menú del día* is a great value at 1,700 pesetas. *Alfonso XII 4, tel. 91/532–4509. Reservations advised. AE, DC, MC, V. Closed Sun., Mon., and Aug. 15–Sept. 15.*

★ **La Pampa.** This excellent Argentine restaurant is secluded on a side street in the Lavapíes neighborhood. As you enter there's a small eating area to the left, but most patrons prefer to sit in the rustic dining room to the right. The massive and delicious *bife* La Pampa is the specialty of the house (enough steak, fried eggs, peas, and tomatoes for two light eaters), and contains sufficient protein for a week. Pasta dishes, such as cannelloni Rossini, are also good. The appearance of a second, more centrally located La Pampa (Bola 18, tel. 91/542–4412), testifies to its popular success. *Amparo 61, tel. 91/528–0449. AE, DC, MC, V. Closed Mon.*

Si Señor. One of Madrid's new crop of entertaining restaurants, Si Señor specializes in Mexican food and tequila slammers. There's a big bar in the entryway, which serves Mexican-style tapas (quesadillas or chips with guacamole). The huge, noisy dining hall is lined with oversized paintings, artfully executed in a unique Mexican pop-art style. While the drinks here are far better than the food, do try the beef enchiladas or *pollo pibil*, a spicy Yucatan-style chicken dish. *Paseo de la Castellana 128, tel. 91/564–0604. Reservations recommended. AE, DC, MC, V.*

$ ★ **Bodegon Logroñes.** This is a hidden treasure, a quiet, inexpensive restaurant masquerading as a gaudy cafeteria-style bar. At the back of the bar, walk downstairs and you'll emerge in the dining room in an old brick wine cellar with vaulted ceilings, decorated with hunting prints and lots of wrought iron. The sole waiter is friendly, even with those who speak no Spanish, and he'll help you pick a wine from the surprisingly fine list. The *pisto manchego* (vegetable stew) and the *paella* are good for starters. The *pimientos rellenos* (green peppers stuffed with meat) are excellent. *Plaza Tirso de Molina 5, tel. 91/369–1137. Reservations advised for Sun. lunch. No credit cards. Closed Mon.*

La Bodeguita del Caco. Salsa music and pink linoleum-topped tables give this place a tumble-down tropical feel that's just right for the Caribbean and Canary Island dishes served here. You won't go wrong ordering the avocado stuffed with shrimp or the *ropa vieja al estilo Canario*, which, although it literally means "old Canarian clothes," is in fact a tender brisket of beef stewed with potatoes, raisins, and olives. Be sure to ask for a plate of the *papas arrugadas* (wrinkled potatoes) that come with a garlicky sauce for dipping. *Echegaray 27, tel. 91/429–4023. No reservations. V. Closed Mon. and Aug.*

Cactus Charlie's. Homesick Americans aren't the only ones drawn to this spot just uphill from the Puerta del Sol. Young Spaniards are also attracted by the boisterous combination of rock and roll, hamburgers, and happy hour. The Mexican food is not as good as you can get back home, but the ribs are passable, and the cheeseburgers are terrific. Genuine Baskin Robbins 31 flavors of ice cream are available for dessert. *Caballero de Gracia 10, tel. 91/532–1976. Reservations advised on weekends. DC, MC, V.*

Café La Plaza. Strategically positioned between the Prado and Thyssen-Bornemisza art museums and open 10 AM to midnight, the Café La Plaza is an indispensable rest stop for tourists exploring Madrid. This is an upscale, self-service restaurant with a green-and-white, garden-party decor, situated among the exclusive boutiques of the Galería del Prado shopping center. Food is arranged on several circular tables. There's a do-it-yourself salad bar, a pasta bar, and an economical *menú del día*, which, depending on the day, might be Spanish-style chicken, breaded fish, or beef stew served with vegetables, bread, and wine. Breakfast, including bacon and eggs, is available until 12:30 PM, and the café is also a good place to remember for afternoon coffee and pastries. *Plaza de las Cortes 7, tel. 91/429–6537. AE, V.*

★ **Casa Mingo.** Resembling an Asturian cider tavern, Casa Mingo is built into a stone wall beneath the Estación del Norte train station, across the street from the hermitage of San Antonio de la Florida. It's a bustling place where you'll share long plank tables with other diners, and the only dishes offered are succulent roast chicken, salad, and sausages, all to be washed down with numerous bottles of *sidra* (hard cider). In summer small tables are set up on the sidewalk. *Paseo de la Florida 2, tel. 91/547–7918. No reservations. No credit cards.*

Inti de Oro. This Peruvian restaurant, located on one of Madrid's premier restaurant streets, is a big hit, thanks largely to the care the owners put into such traditional specialties of their native Peru as *cebiche de camarones* (shrimp in lime juice), *conejo con maní* (rabbit in peanut sauce), and *seco de cabrito* (goat meat stew). The dining room is light and the walls are adorned with handicrafts. *Ventura de la Vega 12, tel. 91/429–6703. No credit cards. Closed Sun. evening and Mon.*

El Molino de Siguero. One of the best bets for an inexpensive and tasty lunchtime *menú del día* in the Plaza España area, El Molino offers home-style Castilian food, such as lentil stew, roast meats, breaded fish, and excellent house wine. The busy dining room has dark wood wainscoting and is decorated with strings of sausages, hams, and antique farm implements. If you come here at night or order à la carte, prices rise from inexpensive to the moderate category. *Ventura Rodriguez 8, tel. 91/542–3524. AE, MC, V. Closed Sun.*

Puebla. Although the dining room decor lacks charm (the fake wood beams fool no one), you'd be hard pressed to find better-prepared food at such affordable prices anywhere in Madrid. Puebla opened in 1992 and is always crowded with bankers and congressmen from the nearby Cortes. There are two prices ranges for the *menú del día*, with more than a dozen choices in each. The selection changes frequently, but be sure to try the *berenjenas a la romana* (batter fried eggplant) if it's offered. The soups are always great, and other dishes include roast lamb, trout, calamari, and chicken. *Ventura de la Vega 12, tel. 91/429–6713. No credit cards. Closed Sun.*

Sanabresa. You can tell by the clientele what a find this place is. Working men and women who demand quality but don't want to spend much money come here daily, as does an international assortment of starving students from the nearby flamenco school. The menu is classic Spanish fare—hearty, wholesome meals like *pechuga villaroy* (chicken breast in béchamel, breaded and fried) and *paella* (Thursday and Sunday lunch only). The functional, green-tiled dining room is always crowded, so be sure to arrive by 1:30. *Amor de Dios 12, no phone. No reservations. No credit cards. Closed Sun. evening and Aug.*

Lodging

Hotel prices in Madrid have come down significantly since the glory days of the early '90s, especially in the upper price brackets. The Ritz and the Villamagna both once charged upward of $600 a night, but they each now offer a room rate comparable to that found in other world capitals—$250 to $300 a night. If that's still too steep, try bargaining. Surveys show that only 15% of hotel guests pay the posted room rate in Madrid. More savvy customers take advantage of a dizzying array of special offers. Be sure to ask for a business or professional discount, which can amount to up to 40% off. Since most hotels cater to business travelers, special weekend rates are widely available. You can generally save 50% on a Friday, Saturday, or Sunday night, and many hotels throw in extras, like meals or museum admissions.

There are booking services at the airport and the Chamartin and Atocha train stations. You can also contact the La Brujula agency (6th Floor, Torre de Madrid, Plaza de España, tel. 91/559–9705); the fee's a modest 150 pesetas. The staff speaks English and can book rooms and tours all over Spain.

If you're willing to embark on a serious hunt, you can also find *hostals* for 2,500 pesetas or even less. Most of these very cheap rooms are found in tiny hostals on the upper floors of apartment buildings. They are frequently full, however, and don't take reservations, so there is little use in listing them here; you simply have to go door to door and trust your luck. Many such places are concentrated in the old city between the Prado Museum and the Puerta del Sol. Start by looking around the Plaza Santa Ana.

All the rooms listed below come with complete baths. Highly recommended hotels are indicated by a star ★.

Category	Cost*
$$$$	over 20,000 ptas
$$$	12,000–20,000 ptas
$$	7,000–12,000 ptas
$	under 7,000 ptas

All prices are for a standard double room, excluding tax.

$$$$ **Fenix.** A magnificent marble lobby greets guests at this Madrid institution, overlooking Plaza de Colón on the Castellana, where a giant monument to the discoverers of the New World rises. The hotel is also just a few steps from the posh shopping street of Serrano. Its spacious rooms, decorated in beiges and golds, are carpeted and amply furnished. Flowers abound. *Hermosilla 2, 28001, tel. 91/431–6700, fax 91/576–0661. 204 rooms, 12 suites. Facilities: café, bar, catering, hairdressers, boutiques. AE, DC, MC, V.*

★ **Palace.** Built in 1912, this enormous Belle Epoque grand hotel is a creation of Alfonso XIII. At less than two thirds the price of the nearby Ritz, the Palace is a pleasure, though its attractions are concentrated in the opulent public areas, including a large cupola with a stained-glass ceiling. The rooms aren't impressive for a hotel of this caliber—they're plain and often small, with a pronounced 1960s American flavor. Bathrooms are spacious, however, with double sinks, tubs and separate shower stalls, and other welcome touches such as bathrobes and magnifying mirrors. The Palace looks and feels like a great aristocratic institution, and it is: President John F. Kennedy, the Aga Khan, and Mata Hari (just before she was captured and executed) stayed here. Long a symbol of bourgeois decadence, it was transformed during the civil war into a war orphanage. On the night of February 23, 1981, when a mad Civil Guard colonel held the nearby parliament at gunpoint in an attempt to return Spain to a Francoist dictatorship, the Palace became the de facto seat of Spanish government. *Plaza de las Cortes 7, 28014, tel. 91/429–7551, fax 91/429–8266. 480 rooms, 20 suites. Facilities: restaurant, bar, garage, shops, beauty salon. AE, DC, MC, V.*

★ **Ritz.** When Alfonso XIII was preparing for his marriage to the granddaughter of Queen Victoria of England, he realized, to his dismay, that Madrid had not a single hotel that could meet the exacting standards of his royal guests. Thus, the Ritz was born. Opened in 1910 by the king, who had personally overseen its construction, the Ritz is a monument to the Belle Epoque, furnished with rare antiques in every public room, hand embroidered linens from Robinson & Cleaver of London, and all manner of other luxurious details. The rooms are carpeted, hung with chandeliers, and decorated in pastel colors; many have good views of the Prado or the Castellana. A major renovation has made it, once again, Madrid's most exclusive hotel, just across the street from the Prado Museum. Visit the garden terrace even if you're not staying here. *Plaza de Lealtad 5, 28014, tel. 91/521–2857, fax 91/532–8776. 158 rooms. Facilities: restaurant, bar, beauty salon, garage. AE, DC, MC, V.*

Santo Mauro. A turn-of-the-century mansion that once housed the Canadian embassy was opened in 1992 as an intimate luxury hotel. The neoclassical architecture is complemented by contemporary furnishings such as suede armchairs, and sofas in such colors as mustard, teal, and eggplant. Twelve of the rooms are in the main building, which also houses a popular gourmet restaurant. Other rooms are in a new annex, are all split-level, and have stereo systems and VCRs. *Zurbano 36, 28010, tel. 91/319–6900, fax 91/308–5477. 37 rooms. Facilities: restaurant, bar, garden, garage, satellite TV. AE, DC, MC, V.*

Villamagna. Favored by visiting financiers and reclusive rock stars, the modern Villamagna ranks among Madrid's most exclusive hotels and boasts a staff dedicated to personal attention. Its green-and-white lobby exudes elegance, and a pianist provides soothing music in the lounge at lunchtime and during the cocktail hour. Rooms all have desks and working space, as well as luxury details such as hidden TVs, VCRs, and green plants in the bathrooms. The restaurant, Berceo, has cozy walnut paneling and the feel of an English library;

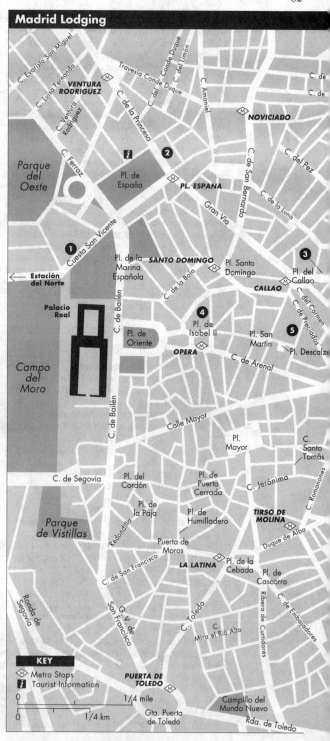

Madrid Lodging

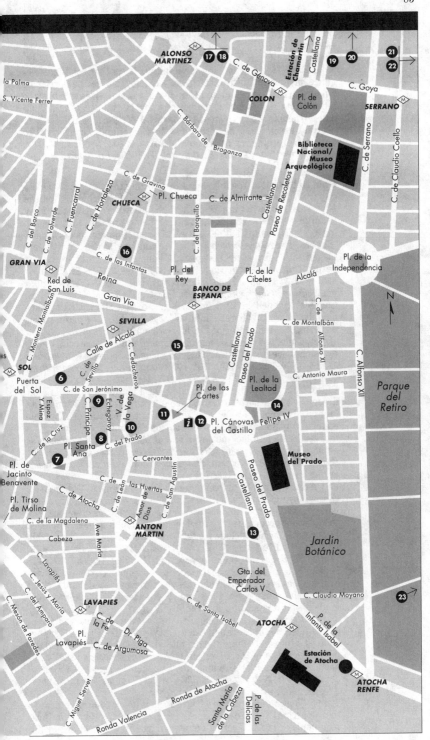

its garden terrace is open for dinner in warm weather. *Paseo de la Castellana 22, 28046, tel. 91/576–7500, fax 91/575–9504. 164 rooms, 18 suites. Facilities: restaurant, bar, sauna, beauty salon, garage, shops. AE, DC, MC, V.*

Villa Real. If you're looking for a luxury hotel that combines elegance, modern amenities, and great location, this may be the ticket. Opened in 1989, its simulated 19th-century facade gives way to large lobbies dotted with potted palms and a tiny bar that seats about half a dozen people. Each room has a character of its own, albeit with an overall French feel. The hotel faces the Cortes and is convenient to almost everything. *Plaza de las Cortes 10, 28014, tel. 91/420–3767, fax 91/420–2547. 94 rooms, 20 suites. Facilities: bar, garage, boutiques. AE, DC, MC, V.*

\$\$\$ **Gran Hotel Colón.** You'll have some traveling to do to get to the old city from this sprawling hotel on the far side of Retiro Park, but the prices are somewhat less than they'd be elsewhere, given the many amenities it offers. It's a massive, functional structure that went up in the 1960s, and its lobbies have the airport-lounge look typical of that era. The rooms, which are sizable and well lit, are brightly furnished with kelly-green bedspreads, aqua curtains, and brown carpeting. *Calle Dr. Esquerdo 117–119, 28007, tel. 91/573–5900, fax 91/573–0809. 390 rooms. Facilities: 3 restaurants, 2 cafeterias, outdoor pool, sauna, 3 bars, shops, beauty salon. AE, DC, MC, V.*

Lagasca. Opened in 1993 in the heart of the elegant Salamanca neighborhood, this hotel combines large brightly decorated rooms with an unbeatable location two blocks from Madrid's main shopping street, Calle Serrano. The marble lobbies border on the coldly functional, but are fine to use as a meeting place. *Lagasca 64, 28001, tel. 91/575–4606, fax 91/575–1694. 100 rooms. Facilities: restaurant, bar, garage, satellite TV. AE, DC, MC, V.*

Plaza. This aging hotel, overlooking the Plaza de España, is a bit dreary, with leatherette overstuffed furniture setting the tone in its lobby. The rooms are a step up, fairly bright and comfortable enough. A major attraction is the rooftop swimming pool and bar—a marvelous spot to look out over one of Madrid's major squares at night. *Gran Vía 84, 28013, tel. 91/547–1200, fax 91/548–2389. 306 rooms. Facilities: cafeteria, restaurant, bar, child care, hairdresser, barbershop. AE, DC, MC, V.*

El Prado. Wedged in between the classic buildings of Old Madrid, this skinny new hotel is within stumbling distance of the city's best bars and nightclubs. Rooms are surprisingly spacious, and are virtually soundproofed from street noise by double-paned windows. Decorative touches include pastel floral prints and gleaming marble baths. *Calle Prado 11, 28014, tel. 91/369–0234, fax 91/429–2829. 50 rooms. Facilities: cafeteria, garage, satellite TV. AE, DC, MC, V.*

★ Reina Victoria. The Tryp chain recently bought and extensively renovated what is one of Madrid's most historic and loved hotels. Now, besides the remarkable glass and steel exterior that faces two of Madrid's most charming squares, the Victoria boasts a ritzy lobby and far more upscale clientele than in the era when it served down-at-the-heels bullfighters and American writers like Ernest Hemingway. The rooms are huge and bright, with new furnishings, and the best have views of the Plaza Santa Ana. Reservations usually are needed because it's becoming very popular. *Plaza del Angel 7, 28014, tel. 91/531–4500, fax 91/522–0307. 110 rooms. Facilities: bar. AE, DC, MC, V.*

Suecia. The chief attraction of the Suecia is its location right next to the superchic Círculo de Bellas Artes (arts society/café/movie/theater complex). It's on a very quiet street, a definite advantage in Madrid. Though recently remodeled, its lobby is still somewhat soulless. The rooms are trendy, with modern art on the walls and futuristic light fixtures. *Marqués de Riera 4, 28014, tel. 91/531-6900, fax 91/521-7141. 119 rooms, 9 suites. Facilities: 2 restaurants and bar. AE, DC, MC, V.*

★ **Tryp Ambassador.** Ideally located on an old street between Gran Vía and the Royal Palace, this hotel opened in 1991 in the renovated 19th-century palace of the Dukes of Granada. A magnificent front door and a graceful three-story staircase are reminders of the building's aristocratic past; the rest has been transformed into an elegant hotel favored by business executives. The lobby, in the palace's former patio, is decorated in French Provincial style, with a glass roof that gives the space a bright and airy feel. Bedrooms are large, with separate sitting areas, and have mahogany furnishings and floral drapes and bedspreads. A greenhouse bar filled with plants and songbirds is especially pleasant on cold days. *Cuesta Santo Domingo 5 and 7, 28013, tel. 91/541-6700, fax 91/559-1040. 182 rooms. Facilities: restaurant, bar, garage. AE, DC, MC, V.*

Zurbano. Just a few steps from the Castellana, in the northern part of the city, the Zurbano is a hotel of gleaming modern lobbies and equally gleaming rooms. The decor, in a word, is minimalist; the rooms, like the lobby, have tile floors, and the linens, walls, and rugs are generally monochromatic—muted blues, greens, or other colors. *Zurbano 79-81, 28003, tel. 91/441-4500, fax 91/441-3224. 269 rooms. Facilities: restaurant, cafeteria, bar. AE, DC, MC, V.*

$$ **Atlántico.** Don't be put off by the location on a noisy stretch of Gran Vía, or by the rather shabby third-floor lobby. Bright, clean accommodations at good prices is what the Atlántico is all about. Rooms are small but comfortable, with fabric wall-coverings and new furniture. All have tile baths. A member of the Best Western chain, this hotel is a favorite with British travelers and is almost always full, so it's a good idea to book well in advance. *Gran Vía 38, 28013, tel. 91/522-6480, fax 91/531-0210. 60 rooms. Facilities: snack bar. AE, MC, V.*

Carlos V. For those who like to be right in the center of things, this classic hotel in a quiet pedestrian zone may be one of the best options for value and convenience. It's just a few steps away from the Puerta del Sol and Plaza Mayor. A suit of armor decorates the tiny lobby, while crystal chandeliers add elegance to a second-floor guest lounge. All rooms are bright and carpeted. *Maestro Victoria 5, 28013, tel. 91/531-4100, fax 91/531-3761. 67 rooms. AE, MC, V.*

★ **Inglés.** This little gem is smack in the center of the old city's bar and restaurant district. Virginia Woolf was one of its first discoverers, but since then it's attracted more than its share of less famous artists and writers. The interior is a bit faded, but its offbeat rooms and lobby—which has a glass-cased model ship—are still appealing. Many of the rooms are gigantic—suites for the price of normal doubles. The balconies overlooking Calle Echegaray give you an unusual view of the medieval look of the old city from the air, all red Mediterranean tiles and ramshackle gables. *Echegaray 8, 28014, tel. 91/429-6551, fax 91/420-2423. 58 rooms. Facilities: cafeteria, bar, parking lot (essential in this neighborhood), gym. AE, DC, MC, V.*

★ **Paris.** For a remarkably fair price, the Paris offers delightful Old-World charm, right at the corner of the busy Puerta del Sol and Calle de Alcalá; you can't get more central than this. The odd-shaped rooms are clean, spacious, and decorated with orange bedspreads and curtains. The lobby is dark, woody, and somehow redolent of times long past. There's no bar, but three meals are served in a bright second-floor restaurant. All in all, the Paris is an unusual deal. *Alcalá 2, 28014, tel. 91/521–6496. 114 rooms. Facilities: restaurant. MC, V.*

Príncipe Pío. This hotel appears to have seen better days, but despite the fading velveteen and linoleum look of the lobby, it's convenient to much of Madrid's west side: the Royal Palace and its gardens, Plaza de España, and the Norte railway station. The rooms are surprisingly pleasant once you're past the lobby; they're bright, with fine views of the Royal Palace, and furnished with white bedside tables and orange carpeting. Also offered are "apartosuites," complete with kitchen and up to two bedrooms. *Cuesta de San Vicente 14–16, 28008, tel. 91/547–0800, fax 91/541–1117; for apartosuites, tel. 91/542–5900. Facilities: restaurant, bar, garage. AE, DC, MC, V.*

$ **Lisboa.** Clean, small, and central, the Lisboa has for years been a well-kept secret just off the Plaza Santa Ana. It offers no frills, but is in a marvelous location on a busy bar and restaurant street and is easy on most budgets. Past a tiny lobby, the rooms tend to vary greatly in size and quality. Most of them are sparsely furnished, with tile floors and papered walls, and the linen doesn't always match; but they are clean and functional. *Ventura de la Vega 17, 28014, tel. 91/429–9894. 22 rooms. AE, DC, MC, V.*

Monaco. Just a few steps from the tiny Plaza de Chueca, the Monaco is an eccentrically opulent delight. The lobby's resplendent with red carpeted stairs, potted plants, brass rails, and mirrors—and the rooms are similar, with Louis XIV–style furniture and mirrored walls. The owner is Portuguese and very gracious. *Barbieri 5, 28004, tel. 91/522–4630, fax 91/521–1601. 33 rooms. Facilities: cafeteria, bar. AE, MC, V.*

★ **Mora.** Directly across the Paseo del Prado from the Botanical Gardens, the Mora underwent a complete renovation in 1994 and now offers a sparkling faux-marble lobby and bright, carpeted hallways. The guest rooms are modestly decorated but large and comfortable; those on the street side have great views of the gardens and Prado Museum (they're also fairly quiet, thanks to double-paned windows). *Paseo del Prado 32, 28014, tel. 91/420–1569, fax 91/420–0564. 61 rooms. AE, DC, MC, V.*

Ramón de la Cruz. If you don't mind a longish metro ride from the center, this medium-size hotel is a find. The rooms are large, with modern bathrooms, and the lobby's spacious and stone-floored. Given Madrid prices, it's a bargain. *Don Ramón de la Cruz 94, 28006, tel. 91/401–7200, fax 91/402–2126. 103 rooms. Facilities: cafeteria. MC, V.*

The Arts and Nightlife

The Arts

Madrid's cultural scene is so lively that it's hard to keep pace with the constantly changing offerings and venues. As its reputation has skyrocketed in recent years, artists and performers of all kinds are coming here. The best way to stay abreast of events is through the weekly *Guía de Ocio* (published Mondays) or daily listings in the leading newspaper, *El País*. Both sources are relatively easy to figure out, even if you don't read Spanish. Tickets to performances usually are best purchased at the venues themselves; in the case of major popular concerts, the larger Corte Inglés and Galerías Preciados department stores have **Discoplay** outlets that sell advance tickets.

The city puts on major arts festivals in each of the four seasons. While you'll have to look up ever-changing details, events include world-class jazz, salsa, African music, and rock; arts exhibitions of all kinds; movie festivals; and more—all at more than reasonable prices. The venues are more often than not outdoors in city parks and amphitheaters.

Theater English-speaking performances are a rarity, and when they do come to town, they may play on any of a dozen Madrid stages; you'll have to check local newspapers. One you won't need the language for is the **Teatro de la Zarzuela** (Jovellanos 4, tel. 91/429–8225), which puts on the traditional Spanish operettas known as *zarzuela*, a kind of bawdy comedy. The **Teatro Español** (Príncipe 25, tel. 91/429–6297) specializes in Spanish Golden Age classics.

Concerts Opened in 1988, the **Auditorio Nacional de Música** (Príncipe de Vergara 136, tel. 91/337–0100) is Madrid's principal concert hall for classical music, and regularly hosts major orchestras from around the world.

Movies Almost a dozen theaters regularly show undubbed foreign films, the majority of them English-language. These are listed in newspapers and in the *Guía de Ocio* under "V.O."—meaning original version. Leading V.O. theaters include the **Alphaville** and **Renoir,** both on Martín de los Heros, just off Plaza de España, and each with four theaters. The city offers excellent classic V.O. films that change daily at the **Filmoteca Cine Dore** (Santa Isabel 3).

Nightlife

It's a commonplace in Spain that Madrileños hardly sleep, and that's largely because of the amount of time they spend in bars—not drunk, but socializing in the easy, sophisticated way that is unique to the capital. This is true of old as well as young, though the streets that are famous for their bars tend to be patronized by a younger clientele (these include Huertas, Moratín, Segovia, Victoria, and the areas around Plaza Santa Ana, Plaza de Anton Martin). Adventuresome travelers may want to explore the scruffier bar scene around the Plaza Dos de Mayo in the Malasaña neighborhood, where trendy, smoke-filled places line both sides of Calle San Vicente Ferrer.

Tapas Bars Spending the early evening hours going from bar to bar and eating tapas is so popular that the Spanish have a verb to describe it: *tapear*. The selection is endless and the best-known tapas bars are the *cuevas* that cluster around Cava de San Miguel (*see* Tour 4, *above*). Here are a few more suggestions:

Aloque (Torrecilla del Leal 20) is one of Madrid's few wine bars, with more than 200 offerings by the bottle and half a dozen Spanish varieties sold by the glass. Plates of hearty stews and tapas are also served as classical music plays in the background.

Bocaíto (Libertad 6) is said by some to serve the best tapas in all Madrid—a heady claim. In any case, you can have a full meal here or just partake of a few tapas before heading on to the many other fine places in the immediate vicinity.

Las Bravas (Alvarez Gato 3), hidden away in an alley off the Plaza Santa Ana, isn't much to look at, but it's here that *patatas bravas* (potatoes in a spicy tomato sauce) were invented. They're now a classic Spanish tapa.

Casa Alberto (Huertas 18) is an atmospheric place with a pewter and marble bar, beautifully carved wooden ceilings, and some great tapas. Like many Madrid bars, there's no seating—you're meant to stand while you imbibe.

La Chuleta (Echegaray 20) is a cheery corner bar hung with bull-fight memorabilia and offering a colorful selection of tapas on the bar. You *can* sit down here.

La Dolores (Plaza de Jesús 4) is a crowded, noisy, and wonderful place that's rightly reputed to serve the best draft beer in Madrid. Located just behind the Palace Hotel, it offers a very few tables in the back.

Mesón Gallego (León 4) is a hole in the wall that serves a wonderfully hearty Galician potato soup (a famous cure for those who've drunk too much) called *caldo gallego*. Not for everyone is the *ribeira* (the somewhat acidic white wine made with grapes from Galician river-banks).

The Reporter (Fúcar 6), true to its English name, is hung with great Spanish and world news photos. Its other great attraction is a garden terrace shaded by a grapevine trellis. The raciones are very good, and the pâté plate is terrific.

El Rey de Pimiento (Plaza Puerta Cerrada) serves some 40 different kinds of tapas including *pimientos* (peppers)—the roasted red variety, as well as the intermittently hot *pimientos de padrón*.

Taverna del Alabardero (Felipe V 6) is an upscale and cheerful bar with a twin in Washington, DC. Their specialty is garlicky *patatas a la pobre*.

La Trucha (Manuel Fernández y Gonzalez 3) is hung with hams and garlic and has the feel of an inn of the Middle Ages. It's also a restaurant, but the wonderful tapas that line its aging bar are a far better bet.

El Ventorrillo (Bailén 14) is a place to go between May and October, when tables are set up in the shady park of Las Vistillas overlooking the city's western edge. Specialties include croquettes and mushrooms. This is Madrid's premier spot from which to watch the sun go down.

Other Bars There are countless bars in Madrid, and while almost all offer something to eat, some are known more for their atmosphere than their food. Some recommendations:

Cafe Gijon (Paseo de Recoletos 24) may be Madrid's most famous café-bar. For more than a century, it's been the venue of the city's most highfalutin *tertulias* (discussion groups that meet regularly to muse on all manner of topics).

Casa Pueblo (corner of calles del Prado and León) stays open later than most (4 AM on weekends) and has a wonderful Jazz Age feel to it.

Cervantes (León 8) is a bright, tiled bar where you can also get a pizza or pasta in a small dining room at the back. It caters to a young neighborhood crowd.

La Champañeria Gala (Moratín 24) is one of the city's better-known champagne bars, offering especially good Catalan *cavas* (as Spanish champagnes are known).

Chicote (Gran Vía 12) was immortalized in several Hemingway short stories of the Spanish civil war and still makes an interesting stop.

Los Gabrieles (Echegaray 17) is featured in most of the tourist literature on Madrid for its remarkable tile walls, but the place's clientele is mostly hip Spaniards, not foreigners.

Hermanos Muñiz (Huertas 29) is the quintessential Spanish neighborhood bar, neither trendy nor touristy. The tapas here are uniformly excellent, and the men who serve them both friendly and superbly professional.

Palacio de Gaviria (Arenal 9) is an impeccably restored 19th-century baroque palace hidden away on the upper floors of a tawdry commercial street between Puerta del Sol and the Royal Palace. Allegedly built to house one of the queen's lovers, the palace now serves drinks in an elegant setting with live jazz late at night.

Taberna de Antonio Sanchez (Meson de Paredes 13) is reputedly the oldest bar in Madrid (the proprietors claim it's been in business since 1830). Order wine and tapas at the old zinc bar in front; head to the back to order a full meal.

La Venecia (Echegaray 7) is a trendy but engaging sherry bar in a rustic 19th-century setting. Examples of the best sherries, both sweet and dry, are available.

Viva Madrid (Manuel Fernández y Gonzalez 7) is an extremely popular and atmospheric bar with a Brassai motif. Packed with Spaniards and foreigners, it has become something of a hip singles scene recently. There are tables—and food served—in the rear.

Nightclubs Jazz, rock, flamenco, and classical music are all popular in the many small clubs that dot the city. Here are a few of the more interesting:

Café Central (Plaza de Ángel 10), the city's best-known jazz venue, is chic and well run. The musicians are often very good, with performances generally beginning at 10 PM.

Cafe del Foro (San Andrés 38) is a funky, friendly club on the edge of the Malasaña neighborhood with live music every night starting at 11:30.

Café Jazz Populart (Huertas 22) is a club featuring jazz, Brazilian music, reggae, and salsa.

Café Maravilla (San Vicente Ferrer 33) is physically reminiscent of the futuristic milk bar in Stanley Kubrick's film *A Clockwork Orange*, but the music—often a kind of flamenco-jazz fusion—is more trendsetting still. Prices can be outrageous.

Clamores (Albuquerque 14), another famous jazz club, offers a wide selection of French and Spanish champagnes.

La Fídula (Huertas 57) features nightly chamber music (starting around 11:30 PM) in a subdued and pleasant setting.

Teatriz (Hermosilla 15) is a restaurant that converts to a sophisticated nightspot after hours. Its theatrical decor is entertaining in and of itself, plus the place includes a tiny discotheque.

Torero (Cruz 26), a thoroughly modern club despite the name, is one of Madrid's chicest spots. You'll have to come looking good, though—a doorman ensures that only those judged *gente guapa* (beautiful people) may enter.

Flamenco Madrid is not a great city for flamenco, but for those who aren't traveling south, here are a few possibilities:

Café de Chinitas (Torija 7, tel. 91/547–1502) is the city's best-known show, and the tourists it draws have included such diplomatic guests as former Nicaraguan president Daniel Ortega. It's expensive, but the food and dancing are good. Plan to reserve in advance; it often sells out.

Corral de la Moreria (Moreria 17, tel. 91/365–8446) serves dinners à la carte, and features well-known flamenco stars who perform along with the resident group.

Corral de la Pacheca (Juan Ramon Jiménez 26, tel. 91/359–2660) offers good performances, if a little touristy, and the prices are more reasonable than those of Chinitas.

Cabaret If you're looking for Las Vegas–style topless revues, head for **La Scala Melía**, a cabaret in the gigantic Melía Castilla Hotel (Rosario Pino 7, tel. 91/571–4411).

Casino **Casino Gran Madrid,** 29 km (18 mi) northwest of the capital on N VI, is said to handle more money per year than any of its counterparts at

Monte Carlo, Deauville, and Baden Baden. The casino, with a night-club, three restaurants, and four bars, is open daily from 5 PM to 4 AM. Men are required to wear jackets and ties, October to April. Free buses to the casino depart from in front of Plaza de España 6 at 5, 7, and 9 every evening, with return trips at 7, 8, and 10. Bring your passport. (Admission: 500 pesetas. Tel. 91/856–1100.)

Discos Madrid's hottest new discotheque is in a converted public bathhouse predictably called **Baños** (Escalinata 10). Owned by the same people behind Viva Madrid and Archy's, the locale doubles as a café during the day, but a pounding disco beat takes over from midnight to 4. **Joy Eslava** (Arenal 11), a downtown disco in a converted theater, remains popular, as does **Pacha** (Barceló 11), while the well-heeled crowd likes to be seen at **Archy's** (Marqués de Riscal 11). Salsa music has become a permanent fixture of the Spanish capital and the best place to dance to these Latin-American rhythms is the **Café del Mercado** (Ronda de Toledo 1).

4 Around Madrid

By Michael
Jacobs

Updated by
Deborah
Luhrman

Traveling around Madrid will take you to an enormous variety of
landscapes and places. The impressive Sierras of Guadarrama and
Gredos to the north and west of Madrid attract skiers. Farther
north runs the fertile valley of the Duero, with extensive vineyards
producing excellent wines. Bare hills alternating with densely
wooded valleys make up much of the landscape northeast of Madrid,
while south of here, the river courses turn into harsh and dramatic
gorges. South of Cuenca and Toledo begin the vast, featureless
plains of La Mancha. In the course of your travels, you will find, furthermore, that each of the main towns that you visit has a very distinctive character in terms of architecture, gastronomy, popular
traditions, and the inhabitants themselves.

Yet for all the many facets that make up the surroundings of Madrid,
there is an underlying unity. The region covered in this section is
Castile—more accurately Old and New Castile, the former north of
Madrid, the latter south (and known as "New" because it was captured from the Moors at a slightly later date). Castile is essentially a
vast, windswept plateau, famed for its clear skies and endless vistas. Over the centuries poets and others have characterized it as an
austere and melancholy region, most notably Antonio Machado,
whose experiences early this century at Soria inspired his memorable and haunting *Campos de Castilla (Fields of Castile)*.

Stone is one of the dominant elements of the Castilian countryside
and it has, to a large extent, molded the character of the region.
Gaunt mountain ranges frame the horizons, gorges and rocky out-
crops break up many a flat expanse, and the fields around Ávila and
Segovia are littered with giant boulders. The villages are predominantly of granite, and their solid, formidable look contrasts marked-
ly with the whitewashed walls of most of southern Spain. The
presence of so much stone perhaps helps to explain the rich sculptural tradition of this region—few parts of Europe have such a wealth of
outstanding sculptural treasures as does Castile, a wealth testified
to by the unrivaled National Museum of Sculpture at Valladolid.

Whereas southern Spaniards are traditionally passive and peace loving, Castilians have been a race of soldiers. The very name of the region refers to the great line of castles and fortified towns built in the
12th century between Salamanca in the west and Soria in the east.
The Alcázar at Segovia, the intact surrounding walls of Ávila, and
countless other military monuments are among the greatest tourist
attractions of Castile, and some of them—for instance, the castles at
Sigüenza and Ciudad Rodrigo—are also splendid hotels.

Faced with the austerity of the Castilian environment, many here
have taken refuge in the worlds of the spirit and the imagination.
Ávila is closely associated with two of the most renowned of
Europe's mystics, St. Teresa and her disciple St. John of the Cross;
Toledo, meanwhile, was the main home of one of the most spiritual of
all western painters, El Greco. As for the escape into fantasy, this is
famously illustrated by Cervantes's hero Don Quixote, in whose formidable imagination even the dreary expanse of La Mancha—one of
the bleakest parts of Spain—could be transformed into something
magical. A similarly fanciful mind has characterized many of the region's architects. Castile in the 15th and 16th centuries was the main
center of the Plateresque, a style of ornamentation of extraordinary
intricacy and boundless fantasy, suggestive of silverwork. Developed in Toledo and Valladolid, it reached its exuberant climax in the
university town of Salamanca.

Essential Information

Arriving and Departing by Plane

The only international airport in both Old and New Castile is Madrid Barajas. Valladolid Airport has flights to Barcelona.

Getting Around

By Train All the main towns covered in this section are accessible by train from Madrid, and it is quite possible to visit each in separate day trips. There are commuter trains from Madrid to Segovia (3 hours), Alcalá de Henares (30 minutes), Guadalajara (50 minutes), and Toledo (1½ hours). Train travel, however, is generally slow, and it is always quicker, if not as interesting, to get to your destination by bus. The one important town that can be reached only by train is Sigüenza, which, like most places surrounding Madrid (including Segovia, Ávila, and Salamanca), is served by Madrid's Chamartín Station. Atocha is the station for trains to Toledo, Cuenca, and other destinations south of Madrid.

By Bus The bus connections between Madrid and the two Castiles are excellent. Two of the most popular services with tourists and day-trippers are to Toledo (1 hour) and Segovia (1½ hours); buses to the former leave every half hour from the Estación del Sur (Canaria s/n, tel. 91/468–4200) and to the latter every hour from La Sepulvedana (Paseo de la Florida 11, tel. 91/527–9537). Buses to Soria (3 hours) and Burgo de Osma (2½ hours) leave from Continental Auto (Calle Alenza 20, tel. 91/533–0400), while Auto Res (Plaza Conde de Casal 6, tel. 91/551–7200) runs services to Ávila (2 hours), Cuenca (2 hours, 50 minutes), Valladolid (2½ hours), and Salamanca (3 hours). Services between the provincial towns are not as good as those to and from Madrid: If you are traveling between, say, Cuenca and Toledo, you will find it quicker to return to Madrid and make your way from there. Reservations are rarely necessary; in cases of extra demand, additional buses are usually put into service.

By Car A series of major roads with extensive stretches of divided highway—the N I, II, III, IV, and V—radiate from Madrid in every direction and make communications with the outlying towns only too easy; if possible, however, you should avoid returning to Madrid on these roads at the end of a weekend or public holiday. The side roads are variable in quality and rarely of the high standard that you find, say, in provincial France. Nonetheless, these roads constitute one of the great pleasures of traveling around the Castilian countryside by car—you are constantly coming across unexpected architectural delights and wild and spectacular vistas; above all, you can enjoy the feeling that you have all these beautiful places to yourself because you will rarely come across other tourists.

Important Addresses and Numbers

Tourist Offices The main provincial tourist office in Madrid is on the Plaza de España (Princesa 1, tel. 91/541–2325). Useful information and excellent town plans can be obtained from the following local offices:

Alcalá de Henares (Callejón de Santa María, tel. 91/889–2694), **Aranjuez** (Plaza Santiago Rusiñol, tel. 91/889–2694), **Ávila** (Plaza de la Catedral 4, tel. 918/21–13–87), **Ciudad Real** (Av. Alarcos 21, tel. 926/21–29–25), **Ciudad Rodrigo** (Puerta de Amayuelas 5, tel. 923/

46–05–61), **Cuenca** (Calle Dalmacio García Izcara 8, tel. 966/22–22–31), **Guadalajara** (Plaza Mayor 6, tel. 911/22–06–98), **Salamanca** (Gran Vía 41, tel. 923/26–85–71), **Segovia** (Plaza Mayor 10, tel. 911/43–03–28), **Soria** (Plaza Ramón y Cajal s/n, tel. 975/21–20–52), **Toledo** (Puerta de Bisagra s/n, tel. 925/22–08–43), **Valladolid** (Plaza de Zorrilla 3, tel. 983/35–18–01), and **Zamora** (Calle Santa Clara 20, tel. 988/53–18–45).

Car Rental It is often cheaper to rent cars in advance, while still in the United States, through international firms such as Hertz and Avis (*see* Before You Go in Chapter 1). Spain's leading car rental agency is **Atesa** (Infanta Mercedes 90, Madrid, tel. 91/571–2145).

Guided Tours

City Tours Current information on city tours can be obtained from the local tourist offices, where you can also find out about hiring guides. You should be especially wary of the local guides at Ávila and Toledo; they can be quite ruthless in trying to impose their services on you. Do not buy goods in the shops that they take you to because you will probably end up paying more than the normal prices.

Special-Interest Tours For a special art tour of Castile, including Salamanca, contact **Prospect Music & Art Tours Ltd.**, a London-based company (10 Barley Mow Passage, Chiswick, London W4 4PH, tel. 081/995–2163). At the same address is by far the best of Great Britain's cultural tour specialists, **Martin Randall Travel** (tel. 081/994–6477), which offers an excellent five-day trip that includes Madrid and Toledo.

Exploring Around Madrid

Orientation

Aranjuez, Ávila, Segovia, and Toledo tend to be visited by tourists on day trips from Madrid. Salamanca and all the other major places discussed in this section can also be seen on a day's outing from the capital, but in these cases you will find yourself spending more time traveling than actually being there. Ideally, especially if you have a car, you should undertake at least a four-day trip around the area, staying at Toledo, Segovia, and Salamanca and passing through Ávila. Both Toledo and Segovia have an extra charm at night, not only because their monuments are so beautifully illuminated, but also because they are free of the great crowds of tourists that congest them by day. To visit all the main sights around Madrid would require at least another three to six days and feature overnight stays as well in Zamora, Soria, Sigüenza, and Cuenca.

Highlights for First-time Visitors

The walls of Ávila (*see* Tour 2)
The Casas Colgadas, Cuenca (*see* Tour 7)
The fountains of La Granja (*see* Tour 1)
The National Museum of Religious Sculpture, Valladolid (*see* Tour 5)
Salamanca (*see* Tour 3)
Segovia (*see* Tour 1)
Toledo (*see* Tour 8)

Tour 1: Segovia and Its Province

Numbers in the margin correspond to points of interest on the Around Madrid and Segovia maps.

❶ Outstanding Roman and medieval monuments, embroideries and textiles, and excellent cuisine make beautifully situated **Segovia** one of the most popular destinations for excursions from Madrid. An important military town in Roman times, Segovia was later established by the Arabs as a major textile center. Captured by the Christians in 1085, the town was enriched by a royal residence, and indeed, in 1474 the half-sister of Henry IV, Isabella the Catholic (Isabel la Católica, of Castile, wife of Ferdinand of Aragón), was proclaimed queen of Castile here. By that time Segovia was a bustling city of about 60,000 inhabitants (there are 54,000 today), but its importance was soon to diminish as a result of its taking the side of the Comuneros in the popular revolt against the Emperor Charles V. Though the construction in the 18th century of a royal palace at nearby La Granja helped somewhat to revive its fortunes, it was never to recover its former vitality. At the turn of the century, its sleepy charm came to be appreciated by numerous artists and writers—for instance, the painter Ignacio Zuloaga and the poet Antonio Machado. Today, it swarms with tourists and day-trippers from Madrid and you may want to avoid it in the summer months, especially on weekends or public holidays. On weekdays in the winter you can appreciate fully the haunting peace of the town.

When you approach Segovia driving west from Madrid along N603, the first building that you see is the cathedral, which seems from here to rise directly above the fields. Between you and Segovia lies, in fact, a steep and narrow valley, which shields the old town from view. Only when you descend into this valley does the spectacular position of the old town begin to become apparent, rising as it does on top of a narrow rock ledge shaped like a ship. As soon as you reach the modern outskirts of Segovia, turn left onto the Paseo E. Gonzalez and follow the road marked **"Ruta Panorámica."** Soon you will find yourself descending on the narrow and winding Cuesta de los Hoyos, a road that takes you to the bottom of the wooded valley that dips to the south of the old town. Above, in the old town, you can see the Romanesque church of San Martín to the right; the cathedral in the middle; and on the far left, at the point where the rock ledge tapers out, the turrets, spires, and battlements of the castle, known as the Alcázar.

The Cuesta de los Hoyos comes to an end at a bridge crossing the River Eresma, which runs below the northern side of the town; turn right on the other side of the bridge and then, after 100 m (328 ft), make a short detour to the left, up several hundred yards to the ❷ church of **Vera Cruz.** This isolated Romanesque structure, in the warm orange stone of the area, was built in 1208 for the Knights Templar; like other buildings associated with this order, it is round, inspired by the Holy Sepulcher in Jerusalem. A visit here is rewarded by the climb up the bell tower for a view of the whole town profiled against the Sierra de Guadarrama, which in the winter is capped with snow. *Admission: 150 pesetas. Open May–Sept., Tues.–Sun. 10:30–1:30 and 3:30–7; Oct.–Apr., Tues.–Sun. 10:30–1:30 and 3–6.*

Return to the road, turn left (east), and you will soon cross the river again. Continue to drive below the walls, and you will pass on your left a 15th-century building that functioned from 1455 until 1730 as the **mint** where all Spanish coinage was struck. Farther on is the

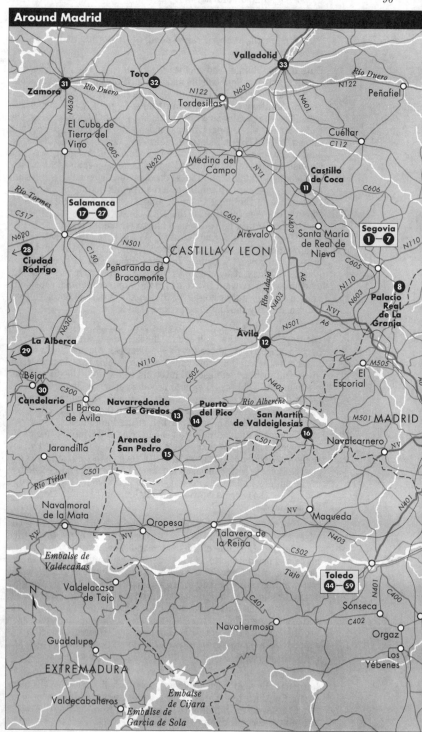

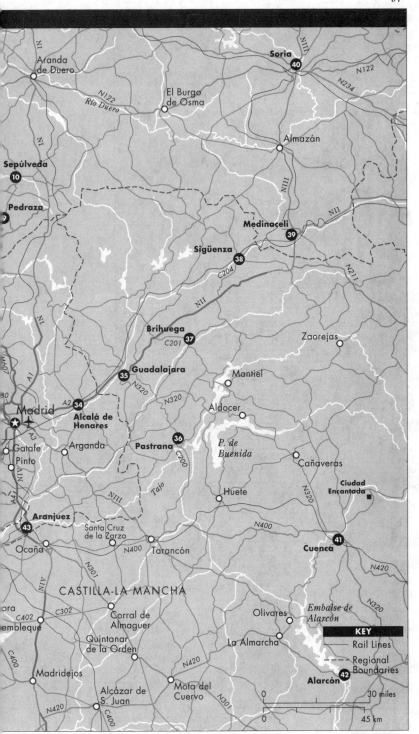

N1

Aranda
de Duero

N122

Río Duero

El Burgo
de Osma

Soria
40

N122

NIII

N234

Almazán

Sepúlveda
10

NI

Pedraza
9

NIII

Medinaceli
39

NII

Sigüenza
38

C204

N211

Zaorejas

Brihuega
37

C201

Guadalajara
35

NII

AM607

A1

Mantiel

30

A2

34

N320

N320

Aldocer

Madrid

Alcalá de
Henares

A3

Pastrana
36

C200

P. de
Buenida

Cañaveras

Getafe
Pinto

Arganda

NIII

Tajo

Huete

Ciudad
Encantada

A42

N320

Aranjuez
43

Santa Cruz
de la Zarza

N400

Ocaña

N400

Tarancón

Cuenca
41

N420

NIV

N301

CASTILLA-LA MANCHA

Embalse de
Alarcón

N320

ora

C402

C302

Corral de
Almaguer

Olivares

embleque

Quintanar
de la Orden

La Almarcha

C400

N420

Madridejos

Alcázar de
S. Juan

C400

Mota del
Cuervo

N301

Alarcón
42

0   30 miles

0   45 km

N420

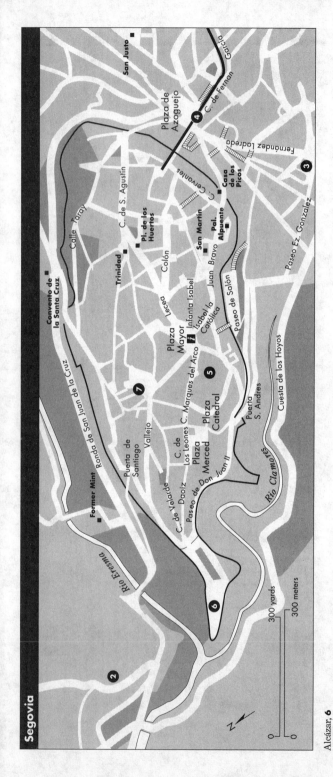

Segovia

Alcázar, **6**
Catedral, **5**
Roman aqueduct, **4**
San Esteban, **7**
San Millán, **3**
Vera Cruz, **2**

Convento de la Santa Cruz, founded in the 13th century near a cave inhabited by Santo Domingo de Guzmán, founder of the Dominican order; the church was rebuilt in the 15th century by Ferdinand and Isabella. At the church the road forks; a left turn takes you up to the modern parador, from which there is another extensive panorama of Segovia and the Guadarrama. If you take the right-hand turn, you will come to Segovia's Roman aqueduct, on the other side of which is the Avenida Fernández Ladreda, the main street through the lower, modern half of town. Near its end is the Paseo E. Gonzalez. Continue your visit on foot.

❸ The 12th-century church of **San Millán,** nearby on Fernández Ladreda, is a perfect example of the Segovian Romanesque and perhaps the finest church in town, apart from the cathedral. The exterior is notable for its arcaded porch, where church meetings were once held. The virtually untouched Romanesque interior is dominated by massive columns supporting capitals beautifully carved with such scenes as the Flight into Egypt and the Adoration of the Magi; the vaulting of the crossing shows the Moorish influence on Spanish medieval architecture. *Admission free. Open for mass only, daily 10:30 AM and 7 PM.*

From San Millán, walk down the Avenida Fernández Ladreda until ❹ you come to the **Roman aqueduct,** which ranks with the Pont du Gard in France as one of the greatest surviving examples of Roman engineering. Spanning the dip that stretches from the walls of the old town to the lower slopes of the Sierra de Guadarrama, it is about 900 m (2,952 ft) long, and—above the square to which Avenida Fernández Ladreda leads—rises in two tiers to a height of 35 m (115 ft). The raised section of stonework in the center originally carried an inscription, of which only the holes for the bronze letters remain. The massive granite blocks that make up the vast structure are held up by neither mortar nor clamps. Nonetheless, the aqueduct has managed to remain standing from the time of the emperor Augustus (3rd century BC), and the only damage it has suffered is the demolition of 35 of its arches by the Moors (these were later replaced on the orders of Ferdinand and Isabella).

Steps at the side of the aqueduct lead up to the walls of the old town, offering at the top a breathtaking side view of the structure. Turn left along a narrow alley that follows the walls, and you will eventually emerge beside the late-15th-century **Casa de los Picos,** so called because its walls are studded with diamond shapes. The Calle de Juan Bravo, a pedestrian shopping street, leads from here toward the center of the old town. Just off to the left, a few meters from the Casa de los Picos, is the Late Gothic **Palacio de los Condes de Alpuente** (Palace of the Counts of Alpuente), covered with plasterwork incised with regular patterns; this type of plasterwork, known as *esgrafiado*, is characteristic of the buildings of Segovia and was probably introduced by the Moors. Head once more toward the center and you will soon cross the small, delightful Plaza Martín, on which rises another porticoed Romanesque church, San Martín.

A turning from the south side of the square will lead you down to the Paseo de Salón, a small promenade at the foot of the town's southern walls that was very popular with Spain's 19th-century queen, Isabel II; it offers good views over the wooded valley to the south and toward the Guadarrama range. Back on the Calle de Juan Bravo, turn right at the Calle Isabel la Católica and into the arcaded main square, on which stand the 17th-century **Ayuntamiento** (Town Hall), the tourist office, and the cathedral.

Time Out The Plaza Mayor, lined with bars and terraces, makes an ideal place for a lunch break or early evening drink. The most elegant of the bars, and the one with the most renowned *tapas* (savory tidbits), is **La Concepción** (Plaza Mayor 15), adjacent to the cathedral; excellent homemade pâtés are served here.

⑤ The **catedral** (cathedral) was begun in 1525 to replace an earlier one near the Alcázar that was destroyed during the revolt of the Comuneros. Completed only 65 years later, it is one of the most harmonious in Spain, and one of the last great examples of the Gothic style in the country. The designs were drawn up by the leading Late Gothicist Juan Gil de Hontañon, but executed by his son Rodrigo, in whose work can be seen a transition between the Gothic and Renaissance styles. The tall proportions and buttressing are pure Gothic, but much of the detailing—for instance, on the crossing tower—is classical. The golden interior, illuminated by 16th-century Flemish windows, is remarkably light and uncluttered, the one major distracting detail being the wooden neoclassical choir. You enter the building through the north transept, and the first chapel you come to on the right has a lamentation group in polychromed wood by the Baroque sculptor Gregorio Fernández.

On the southern transept is a door opening into the Late Gothic cloister; this and the delightfully elaborate door leading into it were transported from the old cathedral and are the work of Juan Guas, the architect of the church of San Juan de Los Reyes, in Toledo. Under the pavement immediately inside the cloisters are the tombs of Juan and Rodrigo Gil de Hontañon: That these two men should lie in a space designed by Guas is appropriate, for these three men together dominated the last phase of the Gothic style in Spain. Off the cloister a small museum of religious art, installed partly in the first-floor chapter house, is worth a visit for the white-and-gold paneled ceiling of the 17th century, a late and splendid example of Mudéjar *artesonado* work. *Admission to museum: 200 pesetas. Open June–Sept., daily 10–7; Oct.–May, 10–1 and 3–6, Sun. and holidays 9:30–6.*

The Calle de Los Leones, lined with tourist shops, slopes gently down from the cathedral toward the western extremity of the old town's ridge. Finally, you'll come to the partially shaded Plaza del Alcázar, where there are excellent views to the north and south. At ⑥ the western end of the square is the famous **Alcázar,** which dates possibly to Roman times, but was considerably expanded in the 14th century, remodeled in the 15th, altered again toward the end of the following century, and completely redone after being gutted by a fire in 1862, when the building was used as an artillery school. The exterior, especially when seen from the Ruta Panorámica, is certainly imposing, but it is little more than a medieval sham, with the exception of the keep through which you enter, the last remnant of the original structure. Crowned by crenellated towers that seem to have been carved out of icing sugar, the keep can be climbed and offers superb views. The rest of the garishly colored interior of the Alcázar is disappointing. *Tel. 911/43–01–76. Admission: 350 pesetas. Open May–Sept., daily 10–7; Oct.–Apr., daily 10–6.*

You can return to the Roman aqueduct through the northern half of town, leaving the Plaza del Alcázar on the Calle de Velarde, and ⑦ passing shortly afterward the porticoed church of **San Esteban,** the third of the town's major Romanesque monuments. Though the interior has a Baroque facing, the exterior has kept some splendid capitals, as well as an exceptionally tall and elegant tower. Due east of the attractive square on which the church stands is the Capilla de San Juan de Dios, next to which is the former pension where the poet Antonio Machado spent his last years in Spain. The family who looked after him still own the building and will show you on request the poet's room, with its paraffin stove, iron bed, and round table.

Numbers in the margin correspond to points of interest on the Around Madrid map.

The major attraction within the immediate vicinity of Segovia is ⑧ without question the **Palacio Real** (Royal Palace) **de La Granja,** which is built in the town of La Granja de San Ildefonso on the northern slopes of the Guadarrama range, 11 km (7 mi) southeast of Segovia on the N601 (the route is well-marked with road signs). It stands on a site previously occupied by a hunting lodge and a shrine to San Ildefonso administered by Hieronymite monks from the Segovian monastery of El Parral. Commissioned by the Bourbon king Philip V in 1719, the palace has sometimes been described as the first great building of the Spanish Bourbon dynasty; the English 19th-century writer Richard Ford likened it to "a theatrical French chateau, the antithesis of the proud, gloomy Escorial, on which it turns its back." The architects who brought the building to completion in 1739 and gave it its distinction were, in fact, not French but Italian—Juvarra and Sachetti. They were responsible for the imposing garden facade, a Late Baroque masterpiece articulated throughout its whole length by a giant order of columns. The interior has been badly gutted by fire, and the few rooms that were undamaged are heavy and monotonous; the main interest is the collection of 15th- to 18th-century tapestries, which have been gathered together in a special museum. It is the gardens of La Granja that you should come to see. Terraces, ornamental ponds, lakes, classical statuary, woods, and elaborate Late Baroque fountains dot the slopes of the Guadarrama, permitting hours of wandering. On Wednesday, Saturday, and Sunday evenings in the summer (from 6 to 7, May 1–Sept. 30), the fountains are turned on, one by one, creating one of the most exciting spectacles to be seen in Europe (*see* What to See and Do with Children, *below*). *Tel. 911/47-00-20. Admission: 500 pesetas. Open Oct.–May, Tues.–Sat. 10–1:30 and 3–5, Sun. 10–2; June–Sept., Tues.–Sun. 10–6. Admission to gardens: free. Open daily 10–sunset.*

Another delightful excursion from Segovia is to the villages of Pedraza and Sepúlveda. Head northeast from Segovia on N110, following the northern slopes of the Guadarrama range; after 24 km (15 mi), turn left (north) onto the road marked "Pedraza" and continue for another 10.5 km (6½ mi). Though it has been commercialized and ⑨ overprettified in recent years, **Pedraza** is still a striking 16th-century village. Crowning a rocky outcrop and completely encircled by its walls, it is perfectly preserved, with wonderful views of the Guadarrama Mountains. Farther up, at the very top of the tiny village, is a Renaissance castle, which was bought in this century as a private residence by the painter Ignacio Zuloaga. Two sons of the French king Francis I were kept hostage here after the Battle of Pavia, together with their majordomo, the father of the Renaissance poet Pierre de Ronsard. In the center of the village is the attractive main square, irregularly shaped, lined with rustic wooden porticoes, and dominated by a Romanesque bell tower.

⑩ **Sepúlveda,** another walled village with a commanding position, lies 24 km (15 mi) to the north of Pedraza. It, too, has a charming main square, but its principal attraction is the 11th-century Church of El Salvador, the highest monument within the walled perimeter. Older than any of Segovia's Romanesque churches, it has a crude but amusing example of the porches that are to be found in later Segovia buildings: The carvings of its oversize capitals, probably the work of a Moorish convert, are purely fantastical and have little to do with Christianity.

Perhaps the most famous medieval sight in the Segovia area is the **⑪ Castillo de Coca** (Castle of Coca), situated near recently planted forests, 52 km (32 mi) northwest of Segovia; it merits a detour between Segovia or Ávila and Valladolid. The shortest approach from Segovia is to take C605 northwest to Santa María la Real de Nieva and then, just beyond the town, turn right and head north for 20½ km (13 mi) on the tiny and poorly surfaced SG341. Built in the 15th century for Archbishop Alonso de Fonseca I, the castle is a turreted structure in plaster and red brick, surrounded by a deep moat. It looks like a stage set for a fairy tale and, indeed, was intended not for any defensive function, but as a place for the notoriously pleasure-loving Archbishop Fonseca to hold riotous parties. The interior, now taken over by a forestry school, can be visited only with special permission (tel. 911/58–60–62). The once-lavish rooms have been modernized, with only fragments of the original decoration preserved.

Tour 2: Ávila and the Sierra de Gredos

⑫ Ávila looks wild and slightly sinister in the middle of a windswept plateau littered with giant primeval-looking boulders. Ugly modern development on the outskirts of the town only partially obscures Ávila's intact surrounding **walls**. Though restored in parts, these walls look exactly as they would have in the Middle Ages. Begun in 1090, shortly after the town had been reclaimed from the Moors, they were completed in only nine years—a feat accomplished by the daily employment of an estimated 1,900 men. Featuring nine gates and 88 cylindrical towers bunched closely together, these walls are unique to Spain in form and very unlike the Moorish defense system that the Christians adapted elsewhere. For the most extensive view, cross the Adaja River and walk to a large cross off the Salamanca road.

The walls of Ávila are a telling reflection of the town's importance in the Middle Ages. Populated by Alfonso VI mainly with Christians from Asturias, the town soon came to be known as "Ávila of the Knights," on account of the high proportion of nobles among the inhabitants. Decline set in at the beginning of the 15th century, with the gradual departure of the nobility to the court of Charles V at Toledo. Ávila's fame in later years was due largely to St. Teresa, patroness of Spain (St. James, the apostle, is Spain's male patron saint). Born here in 1515, she spent much of her life in Ávila, leaving a legacy of various convents and the ubiquitous *yemas* (egg-yolk sweets), originally distributed free to the poor, but now sold for high prices to tourists. Ávila today is well preserved, but with a sad, austere, and slightly desolate atmosphere.

Any tour of the town should begin with the **catedral** (cathedral), whose battlemented apse forms the most impressive part of the town's walls. The apse was built mainly in the late 12th century, but the construction of the rest of the cathedral continued until the 18th century. Entering the town gate to the right of the apse, you'll reach the sculpted north portal (originally the west portal until it was moved in 1455 by the architect Juan Guas) by turning left and walking a few steps. The present west portal, flanked by 18th-century towers, is notable for the crude carvings of hairy male figures on each side. These figures, known as "wild men," are often found in Castilian palaces of this period, but are of disputed significance.

The Transitional Gothic interior, with its granite nave, is heavy and austere. The Lisbon earthquake of 1755 deprived the building of its Flemish stained glass, so the main note of color appears in the curious mottled stone in the apse, tinted yellow and red. Exceptionally elaborate Plateresque choir stalls built in 1547 complement the powerful high altar of c. 1504 by the painters Juan de Borgoña and Pedro Berruguete. On the wall of the ambulatory, look for the extraordinary early 16th-century marble sepulcher of Bishop Alonso de Madrigal, a remarkably lifelike representation of the bishop seated at his writing table. Known as "El Tostado" for his swarthy complexion, the bishop was a tiny man of enormous intellect, the author of 54 books. When on one occasion Pope Eugenius IV ordered him to stand—mistakenly thinking him to be still on his knees—the bishop indicated the space between his eyebrows and hairline, retorting, "A man's stature is to be measured from here to here!" *Tel. 918/21-16-41. Admission: 200 pesetas. Open May–Sept., daily 10–1 and 3:30–7; Oct.–Apr., daily 10–2.*

Outside the walls, a few minutes' walk to the east of the cathedral apse, is the 15th-century **Casa de Deanes** (Dean's House), now a cheerful provincial museum of local archaeology and folklore. *Tel. 918/21-10-03. Admission: 200 pesetas. Open Tues.–Fri. 10–2 and 4:30–7:30.*

Just north of the museum is the Romanesque **Basilica de San Vicente** (Basilica of St. Vincent), a much-venerated church founded on the supposed site where St. Vincent was martyred in 303, together with his sisters Saints Sabina and Cristeta. The west front, shielded by a narthex, has damaged but expressive Romanesque carvings featuring the death of Lazarus and the parable of the rich man's table. The sarcophagus of St. Vincent, surrounded with delicate carvings of this period, forms the centerpiece of the basilica's Romanesque interior; the extraordinary, Oriental-looking canopy that rises over the sarcophagus is a 15th-century addition, paid for by the Knights of Ávila. *Admission: 50 pesetas. Open May–Sept., Tues.–Sun. 10–2 and 4–7; Oct.–Apr., Tues.–Sun. 10–2 and 4–6.*

Reenter the walled town through the splendid gate directly in front of San Vicente and follow the quiet Calle de Lopez Nuñez until you reach the **Capilla de Mosen Rubi.** Try to persuade the nuns in the adjoining convent to let you inside this particularly elegant chapel (c. 1516), illuminated by Renaissance stained glass by Nicolás de Holanda.

Continue parallel to the town's north walls and you will soon come to the parador, housed in one of the austere granite palaces characteristic of old Ávila. One of the ancient stone bulls that the Iberians mysteriously deposited on the Castile landscape occupies the middle of its courtyard. From the gardens of the parador, you can climb up to the town's battlements and walk for 100 m (328 ft) or so along them.

At the bottom of the walls, just above the river, is the small but memorable **Ermita de San Secundo** (Hermitage of St. Secundus). This Romanesque structure, partly hidden by poplars in an enchanting farmyard setting, was founded on the site where the remains of St. Secundus, a follower of St. Peter, were reputedly found. Inside is a realistic and expressive marble monument to the saint, carved by Juan de Juni. *Admission: tip to caretaker in adjoining house. Open any reasonable hour if caretaker is in.*

Return to the old town through **La Puerta del Puente** (the bridge gate) and walk uphill to the Palace of the Counts of Polentinos (now a police station), one of the grandest palaces of 15th-century Ávila. Turn right here and you will come to the **Convento de Santa Teresa,** which was founded in the 17th century on the site of the saint's birthplace. Her famous written account of an ecstatic vision she had, involving an angel piercing her heart, was to influence many Baroque artists, including the Italian Bernini. There are three small museums dedicated to the saint in Ávila alone, one of which is in this convent; you can also see the small and rather gloomy garden where Teresa —the daughter of a noble family of Jewish origin—played as a child. *Admission free. Open daily 9:30–1 and 3:30–7.*

The other two museums are on the outskirts of the city, in the Convento de La Encarnación (due north of the parador) and the Convento de San José, or de Las Madres (due east of the cathedral). The **Convento de la Encarnación** is where the saint first took orders, and where she was to remain based for more than 30 years; its museum has an interesting drawing of the crucifixion by her disciple, St. John of the Cross, and a reconstruction of the cell used by the saint when she was a prioress here. *Admission: 50 pesetas. Open May–Sept., daily 9:30–1 and 4–7; Oct.–Apr., daily 9:30–1:30 and 3:30–6.*

The museum in the **Convento de San José** displays the musical instruments used by the saint and her nuns at Christmas; she herself specialized in percussion. *Admission: 50 pesetas. Open May–Sept., daily 10–1:30 and 4–7; Oct.–Apr., daily 10–1:30 and 4–6.*

On the town's outskirts the chief monument of architectural interest is the **Monasterio de Santo Tomás.** Leave the old town through the Puerta de Santa Teresa (next to the convent of that name), walk east along the walls to the neighboring Puerta de Rastro, and then take the street that descends from here in a southeasterly direction. The monastery's location, a good 10-minute walk from the walls among blackened housing projects, is certainly not where you would expect to find one of the most important religious institutions in Castile. The founders were Ferdinand and Isabella, assisted financially by the notorious Inquisitor-General Tomás de Torquemada, who is buried in the sacristy here; further funds were provided by the confiscated property of converted Jews who fell foul of the Inquisition. Three extensively decorated cloisters, each progressively larger, lead you to the church. Inside, a masterly high altar (c. 1506) by Pedro Berruguete overlooks a delicate and serene marble tomb by the Italian artist Domenico Fancelli. This influential work was one of the earliest examples of the Italian Renaissance style in Spain; it was made for Prince Juan, the only son of Ferdinand and Isabella, who died when only 19 while at Salamanca University. After his burial here, his heartbroken parents found themselves unable to return to the institution that they had founded. In happier times, they had frequently attended Mass in the church, seated in the upper choir behind a balustrade exquisitely carved with their coats of arms; the choir can be reached from the upper part of the Kings' Cloister. *Admission to cloister: 50 pesetas. Admission to Museum of Eastern Art, containing works collected in Dominican missions in Vietnam: 50 pesetas. Open daily 10–1 and 4–7.*

Return to the Puerta de Rastro and walk due north (past the imposing Palacio de Abrantes) to end your tour in the pleasant but distinctly unlively main square (the Plaza de la Victoria). Due east from here is the cathedral, in front of which is the grand 15th-century palace housing the Palacio de Valderrábanos hotel (*see* Dining and Lodging, *below*).

The gaunt Sierra de Gredos, the most dramatic mountain range in Castile, lies just to the south of Ávila and provides in the winter months a majestic snowy backdrop to the town. To approach it, take N110 southwest toward Piedrahita, then turn left at the fork about 5 km (3 mi) onto the small C502. Head south and about 26 km (16 mi), past the village of Mengamuñoz, the road begins to ascend steeply, and its surface rapidly degenerates. You enter a rocky, treeless landscape. After another 15 km (9 mi), there is a turning to the right (west on the C500, which will be marked "Parador"), which will take you 12½ km (7¾ mi) to the modern parador at **Navarredonda de Gredos** (*see* Dining and Lodging, *below*), an excellent base for skiing in the winter and hiking excursions in the summer. Back on C502, you continue to ascend in a southerly direction to the **Puerto del Pico** (1,352 m/4,435 ft), from which there are extensive views. The route you have taken from Ávila has followed a road dating to Roman times, when it was used for the transport of oil and flour from Ávila in exchange for potatoes and wood. Soon after you descend from the Puerto del Pico, you will see below you a perfectly preserved stretch of the Roman road, zigzagging its way down into the valley and crossing the modern road every now and then. Today it is used by hikers, as well as by shepherds transporting their flocks to lower pastures in early December.

The medieval town of **Arenas de San Pedro,** farther down the mountain (turn right, or west, of the C501 when you cross it), is surrounded by pretty villages, such as Mombeltrán, Guisando, and Candeleda, with wooden balconies decorated with flowers. A common and colorful sight in Candeleda is wicker baskets with pimiento for sale. Guisando, incidentally, has nothing to do with the famous stone bulls of that name, which are situated 60 km (37 mi) to the east.

If you decide to see the bulls, head back east from Arenas on the C501 to **San Martín de Valdeiglesias.** This is a pleasant drive through green and fertile countryside bordered to the north by the southern side of the Gredos range. Just 6 km (3¾ mi) before San Martín, on the right-hand side of the road, is a stone inscription placed in front of a hedge; this records the site where in 1468 Isabella the Catholic was acknowledged as rightful successor to Henry IV by the assembled Castilian nobility. On the other side of the hedge stand the forlorn stone bulls of Guisando, now a symbol of the Spanish Tourist Board. These are just three of many such bulls that once were scattered around the Castilian countryside; probably they marked the frontier of a Celto-Iberian tribe. The three here, in their evocative rustic setting, have an undoubted pathos and power. Return to Ávila by turning left and heading north on N403 from San Martín de Valdeiglesias, a 58-km (36-mi) drive along a winding but well-surfaced road, past a beautifully situated reservoir.

Tour 3: Salamanca and Its Province

Numbers in the margin correspond to points of interest on the Around Madrid and Salamanca maps.

Approached from Ávila and Madrid, **Salamanca** is first seen rising up on the northern banks of the wide and murky River Tormes. In the foreground is its sturdy 15-arch Roman bridge, while, above this, dominating the view, soars the bulk of the old and new cathedrals. Piercing the skyline to the right is the Renaissance monastery and church of San Esteban, the second most prominent ecclesiastical structure in Salamanca. Behind both San Esteban and the cathedrals, and largely out of sight from the river, extends a stunning

Salamanca

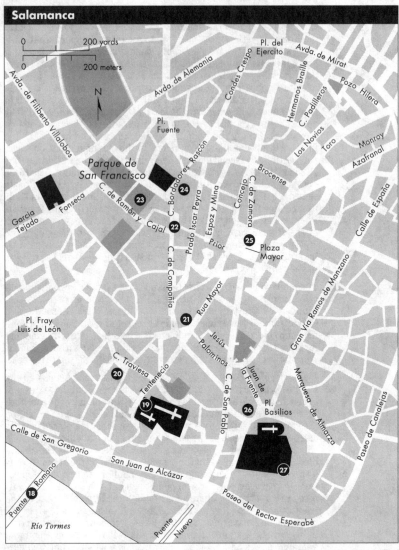

Casa de Las
Conchas, **21**

Casa de Las
Muertes, **24**

Catedral, **19**

Convento de las
Dueñas, **26**

Convento de Las
Ursulas, **23**

Palacio de
Monterrey, **22**

Plaza Mayor, **25**

Puente Romano, **18**

San Esteban, **27**

Universidad, **20**

series of palaces, convents, and university buildings, culminating in the Plaza Mayor, one of the most elegant squares in Spain. Despite considerable damage over the centuries, Salamanca remains one of Spain's greatest cities architecturally and certainly one of the showpieces of the Spanish Renaissance. The beauty of its buildings is enhanced by the color of the local stone, a soft sandstone that has worn over the centuries to a golden reddish brown.

Already an important settlement in Iberian times, Salamanca was captured by Hannibal in 217 BC and later flourished as a major Roman station on the road between Mérida and Astorga. Converted to Christianity by at least the end of the 6th century, it later passed back and forth between Christians and Moors and began to experience a long period of stability only after the Reconquest of Toledo in 1085. The later importance of the town was due largely to its university, which grew out of a college founded around 1220 by Alfonso IV of León.

Salamanca thrived in the 15th and early 16th centuries, and the number of students in attendance at its university rose to almost 10,000. Its greatest royal benefactor was Isabella the Catholic, who generously financed both the magnificent New Cathedral and the rebuilding of the university. A dual portrait of her and her husband, incorporated into the facade of the main university building, commemorates her patronage.

The other outstanding buildings of Renaissance Salamanca nearly all bear the five-star crest of the all-powerful and everostentatious Fonseca family. Alonso de Fonseca I, the most famous of the Fonsecas, was archbishop first of Santiago and then of Seville; Alonso was also a notorious womanizer and one of the major patrons of the Spanish Renaissance.

Salamanca and its university began to decline in the early 17th century, corrupted by ultraclericalism and devastated by a flood in 1626. Something of the town's former glory was recovered in the 18th century with the construction of the Plaza Mayor by the Churrigueras; natives of Salamanca, they were among the most influential architects of the Spanish Baroque. The town suffered in the Peninsular War of the early 19th century and was damaged by ugly modern development initiated by Franco after the civil war. In compensation, the university has revived in recent years and is again one of the most prestigious in Europe.

18 Both chronologically and in terms of available parking space, the well-preserved **Puente Romano** (Roman Bridge) makes a good starting point for a tour of Salamanca. This is a quiet and evocatively decayed part of town, with a strong rural character. Next to the bridge is an Iberian stone bull, and, opposite the bull, a recent statue commemorating Lazarillo de Tormes, the eponymous young hero of an anonymous 16th-century work that is one of the masterpieces of Spanish literature.

19 In front of the bridge the narrow Tentenecio climbs up steeply toward the **catedral** (cathedral) complex. For a complete tour of the buildings' exterior (an arduous 10-minute walk), take the first street to the right and circle the complex in a counterclockwise direction. Nearest the river stands the **Catedral Vieja** (Old Cathedral), which was built in the late 12th century. It is one of the most interesting examples of the Spanish Romanesque. Because the dome of the crossing tower features strange plumelike ribbing, it is known as the Torre del Gallo (the rooster's tower). The much larger **Catedral Nueva** (New Cathedral) dates mainly from the 16th century, though some parts, including the dome over the crossing and the bell tower attached to the west facade, had to be rebuilt after the Lisbon earthquake of 1755. Work was begun in 1513 under the direction of the distinguished Late Gothic architect Juan Gil de Hontañon. As at Segovia cathedral, Juan's son Rodrigo took over the work after his father's death in 1526. Of the many outstanding architects active in 16th-century Salamanca, Rodrigo Gil de Hontañon left the greatest mark, becoming one of the leading exponents of the Classical Plateresque. The New Cathedral's north facade (where the main entrance is situated) is ornamental enough, but the west facade is dazzling in its sculptural complexity. Try to come here in the late afternoon, when the sun shines directly on it.

The interior of the New Cathedral is as light and harmonious as that of Segovia cathedral, but larger. Furthermore, you are treated to a triumphant Baroque conception designed by the Churrigueras. From a door in the south aisle, steps descend into the Old Cathedral, where boldly carved capitals supporting the vaulting feature a delightful range of foliage, strange animals, and touches of pure fantasy. Then comes the extraordinary crossing of the dome, which seems to owe much to Byzantine architecture: It is a remarkably light structure raised on two tiers of arcaded openings. Not the least of the Old Cathedral's attractions are its furnishings, including many sepulchers of the 12th and 13th centuries and a curved high altar, comprising 53 colorful and delicate scenes by the mid-15th-century artist Nicolás Florentino. In the apse above, Florentino painted an astonishingly fresh Last Judgment fresco.

From the south transept of the Old Cathedral, a door leads into the cloister, which was begun in 1177. From about 1230 until the construction of the main university building in the early 15th century, the chapels around the cloister served as classrooms for the university students. In the chapel of St. Barbara, on the eastern side, theology students answered the grueling questions put to them by their doctoral examiners. The chair in which they sat is still there, directly in front of a recumbent effigy of Bishop Juan Lucero, on whose head the students would place their feet for inspiration. Also attached to the cloister is a small cathedral museum that contains a 15th-century triptych of St. Catherine by Salamanca's greatest native artist, Fernando Gallego. *Admission to New Cathedral free. Admission to Old Cathedral: 200 pesetas. Open daily 10–2 and 4–7.*

㉟ After seeing the two cathedrals, your next stop should be the main building of the **universidad** (university), the plain back of which faces the New Cathedral's west facade. Its walls, like those of the cathedral and of numerous other structures in Salamanca, are covered with large ocher lettering recording the names of famous university graduates—it is this golden coloring, which seems to glow throughout the city, that you will remember above all things after leaving Salamanca. The earliest names are said to have been written in the blood of the bulls killed celebrating the successful completion of a doctorate. To reach the main facade, walk along the Calle Calderón and then turn right into the enchanting quadrangle known as the **Patio de Las Escuelas** (Schools' Square). The main university building (Escuelas Mayores) is to your right, while adjacent to it, on the southern side of the square, is the Escuelas Menores, which was built in the early 16th century as a secondary school preparing candidates for the university proper. In the middle of the square is a modern statue of the 16th-century poet and philosopher Fray Luis de León, one of the greatest teachers in the history of the university.

The **Escuelas Mayores** dates to 1415, but it was not until more than 100 years later that an unknown architect provided the building with its gloriously elaborate frontispiece, generally acknowledged as one of the finest works of the Classical Plateresque. Immediately above the main door is the famous double portrait of Isabella and Ferdinand, surrounded by ornamentation that makes much play on the yoke-and-arrow heraldic motifs of the two monarchs. The double-eagle crest of Charles V flanked by portraits of the emperor and empress in classical guise dominates the middle layer of the frontispiece. On the highest layer is a panel recently identified as representing Pope Martin V (one of the greatest benefactors of Salamanca University), accompanied by cardinals and university rectors. The whole is crowned by a characteristically elaborate Plateresque balustrade.

The interior of the Escuelas Mayores, which has been drastically restored in parts, comes as a slight disappointment after the splendor of the facade. The fancifully shaped arches of the courtyard (a form peculiar to Salamanca, known as Salamantine) lost some of their charm in a recent glazing. The large classrooms that lie off the courtyard, though medieval in date, have a similarly modern, institutional character. The *aula* (lecture hall) of Fray Luis de León, the place where Cervantes, Calderón de la Barca, and numerous other luminaries of Spain's Golden Age sat, is of particular interest. Here Fray Luis, returning after five years' imprisonment for having translated the Song of Solomon into Spanish, began his lecture, "As I was saying yesterday. . . ."

Your ticket to visit the Escuelas Mayores also permits entrance to the Escuelas Menores nearby. Passing through a gate crowned with the double-eagle crest of Charles V, you'll come to a large green, on the other side of which is a modern building housing a strange and fascinating ceiling fresco of the zodiac, originally in the library of the main university building. This painting, a fragment of a much larger whole, is generally attributed to Fernando Gallego. *Tel. 923/29–44–00, ext. 1150. Admission: 200 pesetas. Open Mon.–Sat. 10–2 and 4–8; Sun. 10–1.*

You might like to pay a quick visit to the **Museo de Salamanca,** on the west side of the Patio de Las Escuelas. Consisting mainly of minor 17th- and 18th-century paintings, it is interesting largely for the 15th-century building, which belonged to the physician to Isabella the Catholic, Alvárez Abarca. *Tel. 923/21–22–35. Admission: 200 pesetas. Open Tues.–Sat. 10–2 and 4–8; Sun. 10–2.*

As you head now toward the Plaza Mayor, numerous distractions may slow your progress, beginning with the **Casa de Las Conchas** (House of Shells), which looms in front of you as you walk north from the Patio de Las Escuelas on the Calles Libreros and San Isidro. It was built around 1500 for Dr. Rodrigo Maldonado de Talavera, professor of medicine at the university and a doctor at the court of Isabella. The scallop shell motif was a reference to his recently having been made chancellor of the Order of Santiago, whose symbol is the shell. Among the playful Plateresque details, note the two lions over the main entrance in a fearful tug-of-war with the Talavera crest. The interior has been converted into a public library. You can also visit the elaborate courtyard, which has an upper balustrade carved with virtuoso intricacy in imitation of basketwork. *Tel. 923/26–93–17. Admission free. Open Mon.–Fri. 9–9, Sat. 9–2.*

Turn left at the Casa de Las Conchas and head north along the Calle de Compañía. The next palace that draws attention is at the inter-

㉒ section of Calle Agustinas. This building, the **Palacio de Monterrey** (Palace of Monterrey), was built after 1538 by Rodrigo Gil de Hontañón for an illegitimate son of Alonso de Fonseca I. Only one of its four wings was completed, but this alone makes the palace one of the most imposing in Salamanca. As in Rodrigo's other palaces in this town, the building is flanked on each side by towers and has an open arcaded gallery running the whole length of the upper level. Such galleries—which, in Italy, you would expect to see on the ground floor of a building—are common features in Spanish Renaissance palaces and were intended as areas where the women of the house could exercise unseen and undisturbed; they also had the advantage of cooling the floor below during the summer months.

You can make an interesting detour from here to the **Colegio de Los Irlandeses** by turning left up the Calle de Ramón y Cajal and then left again past the Monastery of San Francisco (which faces the park of that name). This university college was founded in 1521 by Alonso de Fonseca II and is referred to as the Irish College because it served at one time as an institution for the training of young Irish priests. Today, it is a residence hall for guest lecturers at the university. The surroundings are not attractive; this part of town was the most severely damaged during the Peninsular War and still has a slightly derelict character. The interior of the building, however, is a treat. Immediately inside to the right is an elegant and spacious Late Gothic chapel, while beyond is one of the most classical and genuinely Italianate of Salamanca's many beautiful courtyards; the architect was possibly Diego de Siloe, Spain's answer to Michelangelo. *Tel. 923/21–45–02. Admission: 100 pesetas. Open Tues.–Sun. 10–2 and 4–6.*

㉓ Return to the Calle de Compañía along the northern side of the Parque de San Francisco, passing the **Convento de Las Ursulas** (Convent of the Ursulines). Archbishop Alonso de Fonseca I lies buried here, in a splendid marble tomb by Diego de Siloe. *Tel. 923/21–98–77. Admission: 100 pesetas. Open daily 10–1 and 4:30–7.*

㉔ Facing the apse of the convent church, on the other side of a small square, is the bizarre **Casa de Las Muertes** (House of the Dead). Built in about 1513 for the majordomo of Alonso de Fonseca II, it received its sinister name on account of four small skulls that decorate the facade. Alonso de Fonseca II had them put there to commemorate his recently deceased uncle, the licentious archbishop who lies in the church opposite. For this reason, too, the facade bears a portrait of the archbishop.

The square on which the House of the Dead stands was a favorite haunt of the poet, philosopher, and university rector Miguel de Unamuno, whose statue stands here. At the outbreak of the civil war of 1936–39, Unamuno supported the Nationalists under Franco, but then turned decisively against them. Placed under virtual house arrest, he died in the house adjacent to the House of the Dead in 1938 (plaque). During the Franco period, his statue was frequently daubed red by students, as a symbol that his heart still bled for Spain.

Head down the Calle de Compañía, and you come back to the Monterrey. From here, it is a five-minute walk along Calle Prior to the ㉕ **Plaza Mayor.** One of the largest squares in Spain, the Plaza Mayor was built in the 1730s by Alberto and Nicolás Churriguera; it is dominated on its northern side by the grandly elegant, pinkish **Ayuntamiento** (Town Hall). Along the square's arcades and in its traffic-free center gather most of Salamantine society.

So, you're getting away from it all.

Just make sure you can get back.

AT&T Access Numbers
Dial the number of the country you're in to reach AT&T.

*AUSTRIA†††	022-903-011	*GREECE	00-800-1311	NORWAY	800-190-11
*BELGIUM	078-11-0010	*HUNGARY	00◊-800-01111	POLAND†♦²	0◊010-480-0111
BULGARIA	00-1800-0010	*ICELAND	999-001	PORTUGAL†	05017-1-288
CANADA	1-800-575-2222	IRELAND	1-800-550-000	ROMANIA	01-800-4288
CROATIA†♦	99-38-0011	ISRAEL	177-100-2727	*RUSSIA† (MOSCOW)	155-5042
*CYPRUS	080-90010	*ITALY	172-1011	SLOVAKIA	00-420-00101
CZECH REPUBLIC	00-420-00101	KENYA†	0800-10	S. AFRICA	0-800-99-0123
*DENMARK	8001-0010	*LIECHTENSTEIN	155-00-11	SPAIN •	900-99-00-11
*EGYPT¹ (CAIRO)	510-0200	LITHUANIA♦	8◊196	*SWEDEN	020-795-611
*FINLAND	9800-100-10	LUXEMBOURG	0-800-0111	*SWITZERLAND	155-00-11
FRANCE	19◊-0011	F.Y.R. MACEDONIA	99-800-4288	*TURKEY	00-800-12277
*GAMBIA	00111	*MALTA	0800-890-110	UKRAINE†	8◊100-11
GERMANY	0130-0010	*NETHERLANDS	06-022-9111	UK	0500-89-0011

Countries in bold face permit country-to-country calling in addition to calls to the U.S. **World Connect**℠ prices consist of **USADirect**® rates plus an additional charge based on the country you are calling. Collect calling available to the U.S. only. *Public phones require deposit of coin or phone card. ◊Await second dial tone. †May not be available from every phone. †††Public phones require local coin payment through the call duration. ♦Not available from public phones. • Calling available to most European countries. ¹Dial "02" first, outside Cairo. ²Dial 010-480-0111 from major Warsaw hotels. ©1994 AT&T.

Here's a travel tip that will make it easy to call back to the States. Dial the access number for the country you're visiting and connect right to AT&T. It's the quick way to get English-speaking AT&T operators and can minimize hotel telephone surcharges.

If all the countries you're visiting aren't listed above, call **1 800 241-5555** for a free wallet card with all AT&T access numbers. Easy international calling from AT&T. **TrueWorld Connections.**

AT&T

American Express offers Travelers Cheques built for two.

Cheques *for Two*^{SM} from American Express are the Travelers Cheques that allow either of you to use them because both of you have signed them. And only one of you needs to be present to purchase them.

Cheques *for Two* are accepted anywhere regular American Express Travelers Cheques are, which is just about everywhere. So stop by your bank, AAA* or any American Express Travel Service Office and ask for Cheques *for Two*.

Time Out The Plaza Mayor and its surroundings offer innumerable possibilities for a leisurely drink, a snack, or a full meal. One of the most popular cafés is on the north side, the **Cafetería Las Torres** (at No. 26), a very large establishment with an enormous array of snacks and pastries.

Leave the Plaza Mayor and walk down the Calle de San Pablo. Halfway down, on your left, you will pass a verdant square, bordered on the northern side by a late-15th-century tower topped by fantastic battlements (the **Torre del Clavero,** built for the *clavero,* or key warden, of the order of Alcántara). To your right is the **Palacio de La Salina,** another Fonseca palace designed by Rodrigo Gil de Hontañón. Try to pop inside to have a glimpse of the courtyard, where you will find a projecting gallery supported by wooden consoles carved with expressive nudes and other dynamic forms.

㉖ Toward the end of the street, on the left-hand side, is the Dominican **Convento de las Dueñas** (Convent of Las Dueñas). Founded in 1419, it has a 16th-century cloister that is the most fantastically decorated in Salamanca, if not in the whole of Spain. The capitals of its two superimposed Salamantine arcades are crowded with a baffling profusion of grotesques that could absorb you for hours. There is another good reason for visiting this convent: The nuns here make excellent sweets and pastries. *Tel. 923/21–54–42. Admission: 100 pesetas. Open daily 10:30–1 and 4:15–5:30 (until 7 in summer).*

㉗ Facing Las Dueñas, atop a monumental flight of steps, is the church and monastery of **San Esteban.** The vast size of this building is a measure of its importance in the history of the town: Its monks were among the most enlightened teachers at the university, among the first to take Columbus's ideas seriously (hence his statue in the square below), and helpful in gaining his introduction to Isabella the Catholic. The architecture of San Esteban was the work of one of its monks, Juan de Alava. The door to the right of the west facade leads you into a gloomy cloister with Gothic arcading, interrupted by tall, spindly columns adorned with classical motifs. From the cloister, you enter the church at its eastern end. The interior is unified and uncluttered, but also dark and severe. The one note of color is provided by the sumptuously ornate and gilded high altar of 1692, a Baroque masterpiece by José Churriguera. The most exciting feature of San Esteban, though, is the massive west facade, a thrilling Plateresque work in which sculpted figures and ornamentation are piled up to a height of over 30 m (98 ft). *Tel. 923/21–50–00. Admission: 150 pesetas. Open May–Sept., daily 9–1 and 5–8; Oct.–Apr., daily 9–1 and 4–7.*

From San Esteban, it is a short walk to the river and back to the Roman bridge.

Numbers in the margin correspond to points of interest on the Around Madrid map.

㉘ The most interesting town in Salamanca province outside the capital is **Ciudad Rodrigo,** which lies 88 km (54 mi) to the west, along N620. Surveying the fertile valley of the River Agueda, Ciudad Rodrigo is entirely surrounded by its medieval walls, within which little has changed over the centuries. This small and surprisingly little-visited town (which makes an excellent overnight stop on the way between Spain and Portugal) has numerous well-preserved palaces and churches.

The **cathedral** is a combination of Romanesque and Transitional Gothic styles, with much fine sculpture. Among its furnishings, the early 16th-century choir stalls by Rodrigo Alemán, elaborately carved with entertaining grotesques, deserve attention. The cloister has carved capitals, and the four cypresses in its center contribute to its tranquillity. Note that the cathedral's outer walls are still scarred by cannonballs fired during the Peninsular War. *Admission: 50 pesetas. Open daily 8–1 and 4–8.*

The town's other chief monument is its sturdy medieval **castillo** (fortress), part of which has been turned into a parador. From here, you can climb the town's battlements.

A half-hour's drive due east of Ciudad Rodrigo on the C515 will take you into wild, mountainous scenery bordering on the once-savage and notoriously poor Extremaduran region of Las Hurdes. Follow C515 for 49 km (30 mi) until you reach the village of El Cabaco, and then head south into the wooded range known as the Sierra de La Peña de Francia (there's only one right turn possible in the village).
㉙ After 10 km (6 mi), you will come to **La Alberca,** a pretty village full of narrow alleys overhung with wooden balconies supporting a riot of flowers. The place has been overexploited in recent years, and its balcony-lined main square is now almost cloyingly quaint. At La Alberca head east, following signs for **Miranda del Castañar,** a hilltop village of equally excessive prettiness. Farther east still, you hit the C512; turn left, and after a short drive you rejoin C515. Once across the River Alagón, this road climbs in an easterly direction into the wilder Sierra de Béjar, a continuation of the Gredos range. The small medieval town of **Béjar,** 30 km (18 mi) from Miranda del Castañar, makes a good base for skiing and hiking. Southward 4 km
㉚ (2½ mi) is the village of **Candelario,** singularly attractive if also slightly spoiled, with balconied houses overlooking steep alleys and rushing streams. It is known for its folklore, and some of the older women still wear their hair in a style that could only be described as baroque. The local sausages are excellent; one of the more famous 18th-century tapestries at El Escorial is even entitled *The Sausage-Seller from Candelario.* From Béjar, Salamanca is 70 km (43 mi) north along N630.

Tour 4: Zamora and Toro

The province of Zamora is densely fertile country, divided by the River Duero into two distinct zones, the "land of bread," to the north, and the "land of wine," to the south. The province is of interest, above all, for its Romanesque churches, the finest of which are concentrated in the towns of Zamora and Toro.

㉛ **Zamora,** rising on a bluff above the Duero, is not a conventionally beautiful place, as its many interesting monuments are isolated from one another by ramshackle 19th- and 20th-century development. It does have a lively, old-fashioned character, making it a pleasant stop for a night or two. Calle Santa Clara leads from Avenida Alfonso IX, near the old bus station, to the medieval center of town. On the south side of the Plaza Mayor is the Romanesque **Church of San Juan,** remarkable for its elaborate rose window. *Admission free. Open for Mass only.*

The rest of the square seems to have changed little since the 19th century. North of the Plaza Mayor, at the end of Calle Reina, is one of the surviving medieval gates of the town, and if you turn left here along the Avenida Santa María, you will reach the Romanesque church of that name.

Zamora is famous for its Holy Week celebrations, and next to the Church of Santa María is a hideous modern building housing the **Museo de Pasos,** a museum of the processional sculptures that are paraded around the streets during that week. These works, of relatively recent date, have an appealing provincial quality. You will find, for instance, a Crucifixion group filled with apparently all the real contents of a hardware shop, including bales of rope, a saw, a spade, and numerous nails. *Admission: 300 pesetas adults, 150 pesetas children. Open Mon.–Sat. 11–2 and 4–6 (until 8 in summer).*

From the Church of Santa María, the Calle Carniceros leads west to a large square. Continue west along the Calle Ramos Carrión to the hauntingly attractive cathedral square, situated at the highest and westernmost point of old Zamora. The bulk of the **cathedral** is Romanesque, and the most remarkable feature of the exterior is its dome, which is flanked by turrets, articulated by spiny ribs, and covered in overlapping stones like scales. The dark interior is notable for its early 16th-century choir stalls. The austere late-16th-century cloister has a small museum upstairs, with an intricate *custodia* (monstrance, or receptacle for the Host) by Juan de Arce and some badly displayed but intriguing Flemish tapestries of the 15th and 16th centuries. *Admission: 200 pesetas adults, 100 pesetas children. Open daily 11–2 and 4–6 (until 8 in summer).*

Surrounding the cathedral to the north is an attractive park incorporating the town's much-restored **castle.** The Calle Trascastillo, which descends south from the cathedral to the river, affords views of the fertile countryside to the south and of the town's old Roman bridge. Follow the river east until you reach the bridge and then turn onto Calle del Puente. Shortly, on your left, you will see an amusing 15th-century house with a sculpted rope decorating its facade. Turning north from here, you now climb up to the **parador,** which is located in a Renaissance palace, with excellent views and a patio adorned with classical medallions of mythological and historical personages (*see* Dining and Lodging, *below*). The main entrance to this building overlooks the principal street through old Zamora. Turn east and you will pass to your right the Calle Herreros, a small street lined with 14 bars, most serving good tapas. One street farther on and you will be back at the Plaza Mayor.

㉜ **Toro,** 33 km (20 mi) east of Zamora along N122, stands above a loop of the River Duero and commands particularly extensive views over the vast plain to the south. It, too, was a provincial capital, but was absorbed into Zamora province in 1833, a loss of status that, in some ways, was to its advantage. Zamora developed into a thriving modern town, but Toro slumbered and thus was able to preserve its old appearance. The latter is crowded with Romanesque churches, of which the most important is the **Colegiata,** begun in 1160. The protected west portal (the Portico de La Gloria) has colorfully painted early 13th-century statuary that is perfectly preserved. Famous, too, is its Serbian-Byzantine dome. In the sacristy is an anonymous 15th-century painting of the Virgin: This touching work, in a so-called Hispano-Flemish style, is called *The Virgin of the Fly* because of the fly painted on the Virgin's robe, a most unusual detail. *Admission free, but you'll have to arrange a visit by asking at the tourist office or calling a local association of English-speaking personal guides (tel. 988/52–69–53).*

Tour 5: Valladolid

③ **Valladolid** is a large, dirty, and singularly ugly modern-looking town in the middle of one of the flattest and dreariest parts of the Castilian countryside. It has one outstanding attraction, however—the **Museo Nacional de Escultura Religiosa** (National Museum of Religious Sculpture)—as well as many other interesting sights. It is also historically one of the most important Spanish towns. Ferdinand and Isabella were married here, Philip II was born and baptized here, and Philip III turned the town, for six years, into the capital of Spain.

To cope with this chaotic city, take a taxi—from the bus station, the railway station, or wherever you have parked your car—and head for the National Museum of Religious Sculpture, in the northernmost part of the old town. The late-15th-century Colegio de San Gregorio in which this museum is housed would alone make a trip to Valladolid worthwhile. It's a masterpiece of the so-called Isabelline or Gothic Plateresque, an ornamental style of exceptional intricacy featuring a plethora of playful, naturalistic detail. The retable facade is especially fantastic, with ribs in the form of pollarded trees, branches sprouting everywhere, and—to accentuate this forest imagery—a row of wild men bearing mighty clubs.

The museum is beautifully arranged in rooms off an elaborate arcaded courtyard. Its collections do for Spanish sculpture what those in the Prado do for Spanish painting. The only difference between the museums is that while most people have heard of Velázquez, El Greco, Goya, and Murillo, few know anything about Alonso de Berruguete, Juan de Juni, and Gregorio Fernández, the three great names represented here.

Arrows and attendants encourage you to tour the museum in a chronological order, beginning on the ground floor with Alonso de Berruguete's remarkable sculptures from the dismantled high altar in the Valladolid church of San Benito (1532). Berruguete, who trained in Italy under Michelangelo, is the most widely appreciated of Spain's postmedieval sculptors. He strove for pathos rather than realism, and his works have an extraordinarily expressive quality. The San Benito altar was the most important commission of his life, and fragments in this museum at least allow one to study, at close hand, his powerful and emotional art. In the museum's elegant chapel (which you normally see at the end of the tour) is a retable by him, dated 1526, his first known work. On either side of Berruguete's retable kneel gilt bronze figures by the Italian-born Pompeo Leoni, whose polished and very decorative art is diametrically opposed to that of Berruguete.

To many critics of Spanish sculpture, decline set in with the late-16th-century artist Juan de Juni, who used glass for eyes, and pearls for tears. But to his many admirers, the sculptor's works are intensely exciting; they comprise the highlights of the museum's upper floor. Many of the 16th-, 17th-, and 18th-century sculptures on this floor were originally paraded around the streets during Valladolid's celebrated Easter processions; should you ever attend one of these thrilling pageants, the power of Spanish Baroque sculpture will become evident to you.

Dominating Castilian sculpture of the 17th century was the Galician-born Gregorio Fernández, in whose works the dividing line between sculpture and theater becomes a tenuous one. Respect for Fernández has been diminished by the large number of vulgar imitators that his work has spawned, right up to the present day. At Valladolid you see his art at its very best, and the enormous, dramatic, and very moving sculptural groups that have been assembled in the museum's last series of rooms (on the ground floor near the entrance) form a suitably spectacular climax to this impressive collection. *Calle Cadenas San Gregorio 1, tel. 983/25–03–75. Admission: 200 pesetas. Open Tues.–Sat. 10–2 and 4–6; Sun. 10–2.*

Turn right from the museum and walk toward the Plaza de San Pablo. **Felipe II's birthplace** is the brick mansion on the Plaza at the corner of Calle Angustias. The late-15th-century **Church of San Pablo** has another overwhelmingly elaborate retable facade. The city's **cathedral,** which can be reached by walking the length of the Calle Angustias, is disappointing. Though its foundations were laid in Late Gothic times, the building owes much of its appearance to designs executed in the late 16th century by Juan de Herrera, the architect of the Escorial; further work was carried out by Alberto de Churriguera in the early 18th century, but even so, the building remains only a fraction of its intended size. The altarpiece by Juni is the one bit of color and life in an otherwise cold and intimidatingly severe place. *Tel. 983/30–43–62. Admission: 200 pesetas. Open Tues.–Fri. 10–1:30 and 4:30–7; weekends 10–2.*

Far more appealing is the main **university** building, which stands on the southern side of the verdant space south of the cathedral. The exuberant and dynamic Late Baroque frontispiece is by Narciso Tomé, the creator of the remarkable *Transparente* in the Toledo cathedral (*see* Tour 8, *below*). The Calle Librería will lead you south from this building to the magnificent **Colegio de Santa Cruz,** a large university college begun in 1487 in the Gothic style and completed in 1491 by Lorenzo Vázquez in a tentative and pioneering Renaissance mode; inside is a harmonious courtyard.

Turning west onto Calle del Cardenal Mendoza, you will come to Calle Colón, where you can see the extensively rebuilt house where Columbus died in 1506; within is the excellent **Museo de Colón,** featuring a well-arranged collection of objects, models, and information panels relating to the life and times of the explorer. *Tel. 983/29–13–53. Admission free. Open Tues.–Sat. 10–2 and 4–6; Sun. 10–2.*

A more interesting survival from Spain's Golden Age is the tiny house where the writer Miguel de Cervantes lived from 1603 to 1606, **Casa de Cervantes.** A haven of peace set back from a noisy commercial thoroughfare, this house is far from the other main monuments in town and is best reached by taxi. Furnished in the early 20th century in a pseudo-Renaissance style by the Marquis of Valle-Inclan—the creator of the El Greco Museum in Toledo—it has a cozy, appealing atmosphere. *Calle Rastro s/n, tel. 983/30–88–10. Admission: 200 pesetas. Open Tues.–Sat. 10–3:30, Sun. 10–3.*

Tour 6: East of Madrid: Alcalá de Henares, Guadalajara, Sigüenza, Medinaceli, and Soria

Though off the main tourist routes, the provinces of Guadalajara and Soria have much to offer and, what is more, are—for a change—easily accessible by train. The line from Madrid to Zaragoza passes through all the towns mentioned above, making possible a manageable and interesting excursion of about two to three days. If you travel by car, you can extend this trip by detouring into beautiful, unspoiled countryside.

34 Alcalá de Henares is on the eastern edge of Madrid province, 30 minutes from the capital off the A2/N II (entrances to the town are well-marked on both roads). Its fame in the past was due largely to its university, founded in 1498 by Cardinal Cisneros. In 1836 the university was moved to Madrid, and Alcalá's decline was hastened. The civil war destroyed much of the town's artistic and architectural heritage, and in recent years Alcalá has emerged as a dormitory town of Madrid, with extensive high-rise development. Nevertheless, enough survives of old Alcalá to give a good impression of what it must have been like during its Golden Age heyday.

The town's main monument of interest is its enormous **Universidad Complutense** (university) building, constructed between 1537 and 1553 by the great Rodrigo Gil de Hontañón. Though it is one of the earliest and most important examples in Spain of a building in an Italian Renaissance style, most Italian architects of the time would probably have had a fit had they seen its principal facade. The use of the classical order is all wrong, the main block is out of line with the two that flank it, and the whole is crowned by a heavy and elaborate gallery. All this is typically Spanish, as is the prominence given to the massive crest of Cardinal Cisneros and to the ironwork, both of which form an integral part of the powerful overall design. Inside are three patios, of which the most impressive is the first, comprising three superimposed arcades. A guided tour of the interior will take you to a delightfully decorated room where exams were once held and to the chapel of San Ildefonso, with its richly sculpted Renaissance mausoleum of Cardinal Cisneros. *Plaza San Diego s/n. Admission: 150 pesetas (free to citizens of EC countries). Open May–Sept., Tues.–Sun. 11–2 and 5–8; Oct.–Apr., Tues.–Sun. 11–2 and 4–7.*

On one side of the university square is the **Convento de San Diego,** where Clarissan nuns make and sell the *almendras garrapiñadas* (caramelized almonds) that are a specialty of the town. The other side adjoins the large and arcaded **Plaza de Cervantes,** the animated center of Alcalá. Off this runs the arcaded Calle Mayor, which still has much of the appearance that it had in the 16th and 17th centuries.

Miguel de Cervantes y Saavedra was born in a house on this street in 1547; a charming replica, **Casa de Cervantes,** built in 1955, contains a small Cervantes museum. *Mayor 48. Admission free. Open Tues.–Fri. 10–2 and 4–7; weekends 10–2.*

35 Guadalajara, 17 km (10 mi) east of Alcalá on N II, is a provincial capital that was severely damaged in the civil war of 1936–39. The **Palacio del Infantado,** built between 1461 and 1492 by Juan Guas, is one of the most important palaces of its period in Spain, a bizarre and potent mix of Gothic, classical, and Mudéjar influences. The main facade is rich, the lower floors studded throughout with diamond shapes, and the whole crowned by a complex Gothic gallery supported on a frieze pitted with intricate Moorish cellular work (honeycomb motif). Inside is a fanciful and exciting courtyard, though little else, the magnificent Renaissance frescoes that once covered all the palace's rooms having largely been obliterated in the civil war. On the ground floor is a modest provincial art gallery. *Admission: 100 pesetas. Open Tues.–Sat. 10–2 and 4–7; Sun. 10–2.*

East of Guadalajara extends the Alcarria, an area of high plateau intercut with rivers forming verdant valleys. It was made famous in the 1950s by one of the great classics of Spanish travel literature, Camilo José Cela's *Journey to the Alcarria*. Cela evoked the backwardness and remoteness of an area barely an hour away from Madrid. Even today, despite growing numbers of day-trippers, you can feel far removed from the modern world here. **Pastrana,** 42 km (26 mi) southeast of Guadalajara on C200 (south from N320), is high on a hill, its narrow, secretive lanes merging into the landscape. It is a pretty village of Roman origin, once the capital of a small duchy. The tiny museum (admission: 125 pesetas; open weekends only 1–3 and 4–6) attached to its Collegiate Church displays a glorious series of Gothic tapestries. The village of **Brihuega** has kept its medieval fortifications and a castle dating to Moorish times. From Guadalajara, continue northeast on N II and turn right at Torija (22 km/13 mi); Brihuega lies 15 km (9 mi) to the east.

The next major stop on the journey east from Madrid is **Sigüenza,** one of the most beautiful of all the Castilian towns. From the Brihuega turning, continue east along N II for another 30 km (18 mi), and then head due north along C204 for 26 km (16 mi). The journey by train between Guadalajara and Sigüenza is beautiful, following as it does the narrow, poplarlined valley of the River Henares. An attractive shaded promenade leads from the station up the hill on which this small town lies. Halfway up the hill, turn left onto the Calle del Cardenal Mendoza, and you will come soon to Sigüenza's remarkable **cathedral.** Begun around 1150 and not completed until the early 16th century, the building presents an anthology of Spanish architecture from the Romanesque period to the Renaissance. The sturdy west front has a forbidding, fortresslike appearance, and your first impression of the interior might well be one of austere Romanesque gloom. It contains, however, a wealth of ornamental and artistic masterpieces. Go directly to the sacristan (the Sacristy is at the north end of the ambulatory) for an informative guided tour of the building; he will turn on lights and unlock doors for you. The Sacristy is an outstanding Renaissance structure, covered in a barrel vault designed by the great Alonso de Covarrubias; its coffering is studded with hundreds of portrait heads, which stare at you disarmingly. The tour will take you, among other places, into the Late Gothic cloister, off which is situated a room lined with Flemish 17th-century tapestries. You will also have illuminated for you the ornate late-15th-century sepulcher of Dom Fadrique of Portugal (in the north transept), an early example of the Classical Plateresque. The cathedral's high point is the Chapel of the Doncel (to the right of the sanctuary), in which is to be found the most celebrated of Spain's funerary monuments, the tomb of Don Martín Vázquez de Arca. It was commissioned by Isabella the Catholic, to whom Don Martín served as *doncel* (page) before dying young at the gates of Granada in 1486. The reclining Don Martín is portrayed in a most lifelike way, an open book in his hands and a wistful melancholy in his eyes. More than a memorial to an individual, this tomb, with its surrounding Late Gothic foliage and tiny mourners, is like an epitaph of the Age of Chivalry, a final flowering of the Gothic spirit. *Admission: 150 pesetas. Open daily 11:30–2:30 and 4–6.*

Adjacent to the cathedral's west facade, in a refurbished early 19th-century house, is the **Museo Diocesano de Arte Sacro** (Diocesan Art Museum), with a prehistoric section and much religious art from the 12th to the 18th century, including an outstanding painting by Zurbarán. *Admission: 50 pesetas. Open Tues.–Sun. 11:30–2 and 3–7:30 (4–8:30 in summer).*

The south side of the cathedral overlooks the arcaded Plaza Mayor, a harmonious Renaissance square commissioned by Cardinal Mendoza. By now you will have entered a virtually intact Old Quarter, full of small palaces and cobbled alleys. Walk the length of the square and continue uphill along the Calle Mayor, past the palace that belonged to the doncel's family. At the top is the **castle,** founded by the Romans but rebuilt at various later periods; most of the present structure was put up in the 14th century, when it was transformed into a residence for the queen of Castile, Doña Blanca de Borbón, who was banished here by her husband, Peter the Cruel. This enchanting castle, above Sigüenza and overlooking wild, hilly countryside, is now a parador (*see* Dining and Lodging, *below*).

Continuing toward Soria, take C114 east to Alcolea del Pinar (20 km/ 12 mi), where you will rejoin N II. Your first stop within Soria province should be **Medinaceli,** 19 km (12 mi) farther on. The original village of Medinaceli commands an exhilarating position on top of a long, steep ridge and can be reached from the train station by a sharply winding 2-km (1-mi) side road or by a more direct but arduous footpath (an exhausting 20minute walk). Dominating the skyline is a Roman triumphal arch of the 2nd or 3rd century AD, the only triple archway of this period to survive in Spain. (The arch's silhouette is now featured on signposts to national monuments throughout the country.) The surrounding village, once the seat of one of Spain's most powerful dukes, had virtually been abandoned by its inhabitants by the end of the 19th century, and if you come here during the week, you will find yourself in almost a ghost town. Numerous Madrileños have weekend houses here, and there are also various Americans in part-time residence. It is undeniably beautiful, with extensive views, picturesquely overgrown houses, and unpaved lanes leading directly into wild countryside. The former palace of the dukes of Medinaceli is currently undergoing restoration, and Roman excavations are also being carried out in one of the squares.

The town of **Soria** lies 74 km (46 mi) north of Medinaceli on N III. This provincial capital, which has prospered for centuries as a center of sheep farming, has been spoiled by modern development and is frequently beset by biting cold winds. Yet its situation in the wooded valley of the Duero is splendid, and it has a number of fascinating Romanesque buildings. The main roads to Soria converge onto the wide modern promenade called El Espolón, where you will find the **Museo Numantino,** a collection of local archaeological finds that was founded in 1919. A large postmodern structure has recently been built for it, which opened in September 1989. Few other museums in Spain are laid out quite as well or as spaciously as this; the collections are rich in prehistoric and Iberian finds, and there is one section—on the top floor—dedicated to the important Iberian/Roman settlement at nearby Numantia (*see below*). *Tel. 975/22–13–97. Admission: 200 pesetas. Open May–Sept., Tues.–Sat. 10–2 and 5–9, Sun. 10–2; Oct.–Apr., Tues.–Sat. 9:30–6:30, Sun. 10–2.*

Soria has strong connections with Antonio Machado, Spain's most popular 20th-century poet after García Lorca. From the eastern end of the Espolón, follow the pedestrian Calle Marqués de Vadillo to the Plaza San Esteban; to the right is the fine Romanesque church of **San Juan de Ribanera,** but turn left instead, to reach (at the junction of Calles La Aduana Vieja and Instituto) the **school** where Machado taught from 1909 to 1911. A large bronze head of the poet is set outside the building, and, in the room where he taught (now called the Aula Machado), there's a tiny collection of memorabilia relating to him. The Seville-born poet lived a bohemian life in Paris for many years, but returned to Spain and became a French teacher at Soria. Here he fell in love with and married the 16-year-old daughter of his landlady. When she died only two years later, the heartbroken poet felt he could no longer stay in this town so full of her memories. He moved on to Baeza in his native Andalucía, and then went to Segovia, where he spent his last years in Spain (he died early in the civil war, shortly after escaping to France). His most successful work, the *Campos de Castilla,* was greatly inspired by Soria and by his dead wife, Leonor; the town and this woman both haunted him until his death.

At the top of the Calle Aduana Vieja is the late-12th-century church of **San Domingo,** with its richly carved Romanesque west facade. Turn right down the Calle Estudios, on the left of which is the imposing 16th-century palace of the counts of Gomara (now a law court). Calle Estudios will take you to Calle Collado, which ends in the uninspiring Plaza Mayor. Walking down the ugly Calle Real toward the River Duero, you pass between two hills, the one to the south dominated by the parador Antonio Machado (*see* Dining and Lodging, *below*), which stands in a park that also contains the ruins of the town's castle. Machado loved the views of the town and valley from this hill. Calle de Santiago, which leads to the parador, passes on its way the church and cemetery of El Espino, where Leonor is buried. Just before the river stands the **catedral** (cathedral)—a Late Gothic hall church attached to a large Romanesque cloister.

On the other side of the river, you are virtually in open countryside. To the left of the bridge, in a wooded setting overlooking the river, is the deconsecrated church of **San Juan de Duero,** once the property of the Knights Hospitalers. Outside the church are the curious ruins of a Romanesque cloister, featuring a rare Spanish example of interlaced arching; the church itself, now looked after by the Museo Numantino, is a small, didactic museum of Romanesque art and architecture. *Admission: 200 pesetas. Open Apr.–Oct., Tues.–Sat. 10–2 and 4–6, Sun. 10–2; Nov.–Mar., Tues.–Sat. 10:30–2 and 3:30–6, Sun. 10:30–2.*

It is an evocative half-hour walk along the Duero to the **Ermita de San Saturio.** Return to the bridge and follow the Zaragoza road until it turns away from the river. From here, a riverside path (accessible by car) lined by poplars leads to the hermitage, which was built above a cave where the Anchorite San Saturius fasted and prayed. Entering the cave, you can climb up to the 18th-century hermitage. *Admission free. Open daily 10–2 and 4–sundown.*

Seven km (4 mi) north of Soria, off the Logroño road and accessible only by car, are the bleak hilltop ruins of **Numantia,** an important Iberian settlement, which was viciously besieged by the Romans in 135–134 BC; the inhabitants chose death rather than surrender. Most of the foundations that have been unearthed are from the time of the Roman occupation. *Admission: 200 pesetas. Open Apr.–Oct., Tues.–Sat. 10–2 and 4–7, Sun. 10–2; Nov.–Mar., Tues.–Sat. 10:30–1:30 and 3:30–6, Sun. 10:30–2.*

The N122 back to Madrid passes through **El Burgo de Osma,** 56 km (35 mi) west of Soria. This village is a virtually intact medieval and Renaissance town, dominated by a Gothic cathedral and a Baroque bell tower. Thirteen km (8 mi) farther west, turn south onto N110, and join N I after 71 km (44 mi); from this point, it is 98 km (61 mi) to Madrid.

Tour 7: Cuenca

Situated in wild and rocky countryside intercut with dramatic
gorges, **Cuenca** offers a haunting atmosphere and outstanding cuisine. Arriving either by bus or by train, you reach the old town by
heading due north along the Calle Ramón y Cajal until you come to a
small bridge crossing the narrow River Huécar. On the other side of
the river, the old town rises steeply, hugging a spine of rock thrust
up between the gorges of the Huécar and the Júcar and bordered on
two sides by sheer precipices, over which plunges the odd hawk or
eagle. The lower half of the old town is a maze of tiny streets, any of
which will take you up to the Plaza del Carmen. From here the town
narrows, and just a single street, the Calle Alfonso VIII, continues
the ascent up to the Plaza Mayor, which you reach after passing under the arch of the Town Hall.

You have still some way to climb before reaching the very top of the
town, but from this point onward, all is sheer enchantment. Walk up
the central Calle San Pedro and take the first alley to your left,
which will lead you to the tiny **Plaza San Nicolás,** a picturesquely dilapidated square clinging to the western edge of the town. Continue
from here along the unpaved Ronda del Júcar, which hovers over the
Júcar gorge and commands remarkable views over the mountainous
landscape. The best views of all are from the square in front of the
castle, at the very top of Cuenca, where the town tapers out to the
narrowest of ledges. Gorges are on each side of you, while directly in
front, old houses sweep down toward a distant plateau. The castle
itself, which for many years served as the town prison, is expected to
open as a parador by 1994. Inquire at the tourist office for more information.

Return to the Plaza Mayor by following the Calle de Julian Romero,
a street hung over the town's eastern precipice. Back at the Plaza
Mayor, take the Calle Obispo Valero, which skirts the southern side
of the undistinguished cathedral, and follow signs pointing toward
the Casas Colgadas. Halfway down on the left, in what were formerly the cellars of the Bishop's Palace, a **Museo Diocesano de Arte Sacro**
(Diocesan Museum of Sacred Art) has recently been installed; in its
beautifully clear display you will find a jewel-encrusted Byzantine
diptych of the 13th century, a Crucifixion by the 15th-century Flemish artist Gerard David, and two small El Grecos. *Tel. 966/21–20–
11. Admission: 150 pesetas. Open Tues.–Sat. 11–2 and 4–6, Sun.
11–2.*

At the bottom of the street is one of the finest and most curious of
Spain's museums, housed in the most famous of Cuenca's buildings,
the **Casas Colgadas** (Hanging Houses). This group of joined houses,
literally projecting over the town's eastern precipice, originally
formed a 15th-century palace; later they served as a town hall, before falling into disuse and decay in the 19th century. During the
restoration campaign of 1927, the cantilevered balconies that had
once hung over the gorge were rebuilt. Finally, in 1966, the painter
Fernando Zóbel decided to create inside them the first museum in
the world devoted exclusively to abstract art. The works he gathered are almost all by the remarkable generation of Spanish abstract
artists who grew up in the 1950s and were forced to live abroad. The
major names include Carlos Saura, Eduardo Chillida, Muñoz,
Millares, Antoni Tàpies, and Zóbel. Even if you have had no previous
interest in abstract art, this museum is likely to win you over, with
its honeycomb of dazzlingly white rooms and vistas of sky and gorge.

Admission: 200 pesetas. Open Tues.–Fri. 11–2 and 4–6, Sat. 11–2 and 4–8, Sun. 11–2:30.

From the museum, you can walk down to the Puente de San Pablo, an iron footbridge built over the Huécar gorge in 1903 for the convenience of the Dominican monks of San Pablo, who live on the other side. If you have a head for heights, cross the narrow bridge, with its vertiginous view down to the river below and equally thrilling panorama of the Casas Colgadas. A path from the bridge descends to the bottom of the gorge, landing you by the bridge that you crossed to enter the old town.

The most popular car excursion from Cuenca is to the **Ciudad Encantada** (Enchanted City). (Drive north for 30 km/18 mi along CU991, then turn right, following signs, and continue 5 km/3 mi.) The so-called city comprises a series of large and fantastic rock formations erupting in a landscape of pines.

42 South of Cuenca (69 km on N320, then right onto N111) is the village of **Alarcón,** also situated on the River Júcar. This fortified village on the edge of the great plains of La Mancha stands impressively on a high spur of land encircled almost entirely by a bend of the river. The principal monument is its **castle,** which dates to Visigothic times; in the 14th century it came into the hands of the infante Don Juan Manuel, who wrote a collection of moral tales that rank among the great treasures of Spanish medieval literature. The castle is today one of the finest of Spain's paradors (*see* Dining and Lodging, below).

Tour 8: South of Madrid: Aranjuez and Toledo

Toledo can be reached by bus or car from Madrid on N401 in just under an hour. With a slightly longer drive by way of N IV/A4, you can **43** break your journey at **Aranjuez,** an oasis in the middle of the parched Castilian plateau. Once the site of a Habsburg hunting lodge on the banks of the Tajo, Aranjuez became in the 18th century a favorite summer residence of the Bourbons, who constructed a large palace and other buildings, created extensive gardens, and planted woods; in the following century, it developed into a popular retreat for the people of Madrid. Today, the spaciously and regularly laid-out small town that grew up in the vicinity of the palace retains a faded elegance. The **Palacio Real** (Royal Palace) itself reflects French grandeur. The high point of the sumptuous interior is a room covered entirely with porcelain; there are also numerous elaborate clocks and a good museum of costume. Shaded riverside gardens, full of statuary and fountains, afford pleasant relaxation after the palace tour. *Tel. 91/891–0740. Admission: 500 pesetas. Open May–Sept., Tues.–Sun. 10–6:30; Oct.–Apr., Tues.–Sun. 10–5:30. Admission to gardens free. Open May–Sept., daily 8–6:30; Oct.–Apr., daily 8–8:30.*

The charming **Casa del Labrador** (Farmer's Cottage), a small and intimate palace at the eastern end of Aranjuez, built by Carlos IV in 1804, has a jewellike interior bursting with color and crowded with delicate objects. Between the Royal Palace and the Casa del Labrador is the **Casa de Marinos:** (Sailors' House), where you will see a gondola that belonged to Felipe V and other plushly decorated pleasure boats that once plied the river. *Admission to Casa del Labrador and Casa de Marinos: 500 pesetas. Open May–Sept., Tues.–Sun. 10–6:30; Oct.– Apr., Tues.–Sun. 10–5:30; closed Mon.*

④④ The contrast between Aranjuez and nearby **Toledo** could hardly be more marked. From the sensuous surroundings and French-style elegance of the former, you move to a place of drama and austerity, tinged with mysticism, that was long the spiritual and intellectual capital of Spain. No matter which route you take from Madrid, your first glimpse of Toledo will be of its northern gates and battlements rising up on a massive granite escarpment. The flat countryside comes to an end, and a steep range of ocher-colored hills rises on each side of the city.

Numbers in the margin correspond to points of interest on the Toledo map.

④⑤ At the main northern gate of Toledo—the sturdy, freestanding **Puerta de Bisagra**—turn right to the large traffic circle called the Plaza de Alfonso VI. Follow the walls around to the west, cross a modern bridge, and then turn left onto the Carretera de Circunvalación. It slowly climbs up the brush-covered southern slopes of the gorge, passing the occasional villa. Almost immediate-
④⑥ ly to your left is the **Puente de San Martín,** a pedestrian bridge dating to 1203 and featuring splendid horseshoe arches. High above this, and the most prominent monument in western Toledo, is the late-15th-century church of **San Juan de los Reyes.** A much better and more extensive view of Toledo is to be had from the eastern end of the gorge. Continue driving along the Circunvalación, passing below the modern parador (*see* Dining and Lodging, *below*), and you will eventually come to a belvedere where you can park your car (except in the middle of the day, when buses line up) and look down over almost all the main monuments of Toledo.

The rock on which Toledo stands was inhabited as far back as prehistoric times, and there was already an important Iberian settlement here when the Romans came in 192 BC. On the highest point of the rock—on which now stands the Alcázar, the dominant building on the Toledo skyline—the Romans built a large fort, and this was later remodeled by the Visigoths, who had, by the middle of the 6th century AD, transformed the town into their capital. In the early 8th century, the Moors arrived.

During their occupation of Toledo, the Moors furthered its reputation as a great center of learning and religion. Enormous tolerance was shown toward those who continued to practice Christianity (the so-called Mozarabs), as well as to the town's exceptionally large Jewish population. Today, the Moorish legacy is evident in the strong crafts tradition here, in the mazelike arrangement of the streets, and in the predominance of brick rather than stone. To the Moors, beauty was a quality to be found within and not to be shown on the surface, and it is significant that even the cathedral of Toledo—one of the most richly endowed in the whole of Spain—is difficult to see from the outside, being largely obscured by the warren of houses that surrounds it. Long after the departure of the Moors, Toledo remained secretive, its life and treasures hidden behind closed doors and austere facades.

Alfonso VI, aided by El Cid, captured Toledo in 1085 and styled himself "Emperor of Toledo." Under the Christians, the strong intellectual life of the town was maintained, and Toledo became famous for its school of translators, who spread to the West a knowledge of Arab medicine, law, culture, and philosophy. Religious tolerance continued, and during the rule of Peter the Cruel (so named because he allegedly had members of his own family murdered to advance himself), a Jewish banker, Samuel Levi, became royal treasurer and

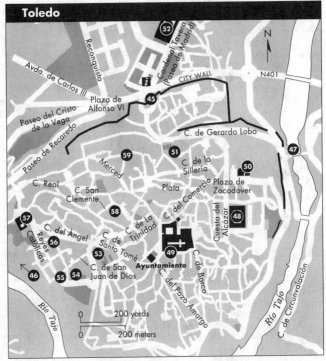

one of the wealthiest and most important men in town. By the early 15th century, however, hostility toward both Jews and Arabs grew as Toledo developed more and more into a bastion of the Catholic Church.

As Florence had the Medici and Rome the papacy, so Toledo had its long and distinguished line of cardinals, most notably Mendoza, Tavera, and Cisneros. Under these great patrons of the arts, Renaissance Toledo emerged as a center of humanism. Economically and politically, however, Toledo had already begun to decline in the 16th century. The expulsion of the Jews from Spain in 1492 had particularly serious economic consequences for Toledo, the decision in 1561 to make Madrid the permanent center of the Spanish court led to the town's loss of political importance, and the expulsion from Spain of the converted Arabs (Moriscos) in 1601 resulted in the departure of most of Toledo's celebrated artisan community. The years the painter El Greco spent in Toledo—from 1572 to his death in 1614—were those of the town's decline. Its transformation into a major tourist center started in the late 19th century, when the works of El Greco came to be widely appreciated after years of neglect. Today, Toledo is prosperous and conservative, high priced, silent at night, and closed in atmosphere. Yet Spain has no other town of this size with such a concentration of major monuments and works of art.

Leaving the belvedere and continuing around the gorge in a counterclockwise direction, you pass on your left the **Puente de Alcántara,** the oldest of the town's bridges, of Roman origin. On your right is a heavily restored castle built after the Christian capture of 1085, and above this stands a vast and depressingly austere military academy, a typical example of Fascist architecture under

Franco. The Circunvalación will deposit you back at the Puerta de Bisagra. Toledo's maze of narrow streets was not made for cars; park either at your hotel or outside the walls.

48 The **Alcázar** is the monument with the earliest opening time. The entrance is on the north side, but to get there from the Cuesta del Alcázar (the street that leads up to the Alcázar from Toledo's main square), you have to do almost a full circle of the building. The south facade, the most severe, is the work of Juan de Herrera, of Escorial fame; the east facade, meanwhile, gives a good idea of the building's medieval appearance, incorporating a large section of battlements. The finest of the facades is undoubtedly the northern, one of many works executed in Toledo by Alonso de Covarrubias, who did more than any other architect to introduce the Renaissance style to this town.

Within the building is both a military headquarters and a large military museum—one of Spain's few remaining homages to Francoism, hung with tributes from various right-wing military groups and figures from around the world. Architecturally, its highlight is Covarrubias's harmonious Italianate courtyard, which, like most other parts of the building, was largely rebuilt after the civil war of 1936–39, when the Alcázar was besieged by the Republicans. Though the Nationalists' ranks were depleted, they managed to hold on to the building. Franco later turned the Alcázar into a monument to Nationalist bravery; the office of the Nationalist general who defended the building, General Moscardó, has been left in exactly the same state as it was after the war, complete with peeling ceiling paper and mortar holes. The gloomy tour can continue with a visit to the dark cellars, where living conditions at the time of the siege are evoked.

More cheerful is a ground-floor room full of beautifully crafted swords, a Toledan specialty introduced by the Moorish silver workers. At the top of the grand staircase, which apparently made even Carlos V "feel like an emperor," are rooms displaying a vast collection of toy soldiers. *Tel. 925/22–30–38. Admission: 125 pesetas. May–Sept., Tues.–Sun. 9:30–1:30 and 4–6:30; Oct.–Apr., Tues.–Sun. 9:30–1:30 and 4–5:30.*

49 From opposite the southwestern corner of the Alcázar, a series of alleys descends to the east end of the **catedral** (cathedral), affording good views of the cathedral tower. Make your way around the southern side of the building, passing the mid-15th-century **Puerta de los Leones,** with magnificently detailed and realistic carvings by artists of northern descent. Emerging into the small square in front of the cathedral's west facade, you will see to your right the elegant **Ayuntamiento,** begun by the young Herrera and completed by El Greco's son, Jorge Manuel Theotokópoulos. Jorge Manuel was also responsible for the cathedral's Mozarabic chapel, the elongated dome of which crowns the right-hand side of the west facade; the rest of this facade is mainly of the early 15th century and features as its centerpiece a representation of the Virgin presenting her robe to Toledo's patron saint, the Visigothic Ildefonsus.

Enter the cathedral from the 14th-century cloisters to the left of the west facade. The primarily 13th-century architecture is inspired by the great Gothic cathedrals of France, such as Chartres; the squat proportions, however, give it a Spanish feel, as do the wealth and heaviness of the furnishings and the location of the elaborate choir in the center of the nave. Immediately to your right as you enter the building is a beautifully carved Plateresque doorway by Covarrubias, marking the entrance to the Treasury. The latter houses a small Crucifixion by the Italian painter Cimabue and an extraordinarily intricate late-15th-century monstrance by Juan del Arfe, a silversmith of German descent; the ceiling is an excellent example of Mudéjar workmanship.

From here, walk around to the ambulatory, off the right-hand side of which is a chapter house featuring a strange and quintessentially Spanish mixture of Italianate frescoes by Juan de Borgoña. In the middle of the ambulatory is a dazzling and famous example of Baroque illusionism by Narciso Tomé, known as the *Transparente*, a blend of painting, stucco, and sculpture.

Finally, off the northern end of the ambulatory, you will come to the sacristy, where a number of El Grecos are to be found, most notably the work known as *El Espolio* (Christ being stripped of his raiment). One of El Greco's earliest works in Toledo, it fell foul of the pedantic Inquisition, which accused the artist of putting Christ on a lower level than some of the onlookers. El Greco was thrown into prison, and there his career might have ended had he not by this stage formed friendships with some of the more enlightened clergy of the town. Before leaving the sacristy, look up at the colorful and spirited Late Baroque ceiling painting by the Italian Luca Giordano. *Admission: 350 pesetas. Open Tues.–Sat. 10:30–1 and 3:30–6 (until 7 in summer), Sun. 10:30–1:30 and 4–6.*

On leaving the cathedral, turn right outside the cloister's entrance and then turn right again. You will find yourself on the Calle del Comercio, the town's narrow and lively pedestrian thoroughfare, lined with bars and shops and shaded in the summer months by awnings suspended from the roofs of tall houses. The street ends in the Plaza Zocodover, the town's main square, built in the early 17th century as part of an unsuccessful attempt to impose a rigid geometry on the town's chaotic Moorish ground plan.

Time Out On the south side of the square, and on the narrow street leading off the middle of it, are numerous bars, cafés, and modest restaurants. Those on the square—one of which features in Luis Buñuel's movie *Tristana*—have chairs and tables outside.

50 Next, you can visit the **Museo de la Santa Cruz,** which can be reached from Plaza de Zocodover by going through the Moorish arch on the square's eastern side and descending a few steps. One of the joys of this museum is that it is housed in a beautiful Renaissance hospital with a stunning classical Plateresque facade. Unlike the other monuments in town, the museum is open all day without a break and in the early hours of the afternoon is delightfully quiet. The light and elegant interior has changed little since the 16th century, the main difference being that works of art have replaced the hospital beds. Look for the paintings by El Greco on the upper floor—in particular, the *Assumption* of 1613, the artist's last known work. A small **Museo de Arqueología** has been arranged in and around the hospital's delightful cloister, off which a beautifully decorated staircase by Alonso de Covarrubias can also be found. *Tel. 925/22–10–36. Admission: 200 pesetas. Open Tues.–Sat. 10–6:30, Sun. 10–2, Mon. 10–2 and 4:30–6:30.*

Back on the Plaza de Zocodover, cross to the western side of the square and enter the Calle de la Sillería. The third main turn to your right, the Cuesta del Cristo de la Luz, will take you to the **Capilla del Cristo de la Luz** (Chapel of Christ of the Light), which lies behind railings in a small park above the town's northern ramparts. The gardener will open the gate for you and show you around, but in case he is not there, inquire at the house opposite. The exposed chapel was originally a tiny Visigothic church, transformed into a mosque during the Moorish occupation; the arches and vaulting of the mosque survive, making this the most important relic of Moorish Toledo. The story behind the chapel's name is that the horse of Alfonso VI, who was riding in triumph into Toledo in 1085, knelt in front of the building; it was then discovered that behind the masonry was a candle that had burned continuously throughout the time that the Infidels had been in power. The first Mass of the Reconquest was said here, and later a Mudéjar apse was added (now shielded by glass). After you have looked at the chapel, the gardener will take you across the ramparts to climb to the top of the Puerta del Sol, a 12th-century Mudéjar gatehouse. *Admission: tip to gardener. Open any reasonable hour.*

Walking outside the walls and passing through Covarrubias's imposing Puerta de Bisagra, you will come to a long and slightly decayed square, the Paseo de Merchán, dominated at its northern end ⑤② by the **Hospital de Tavera,** Covarrubias's last work. Unlike the Hospital of Santa Cruz, this complex is unfinished and slightly dilapidated. It is nonetheless full of character and has an evocatively ramshackle museum in its southern wing, looked after by two exceptionally friendly and eccentric women. The most important work in the museum's miscellaneous collection is a painting by the 17th-century artist José Ribera. In the hospital's monumental chapel is the *Baptism of Christ* by El Greco and the exquisitely carved marble tomb of Cardinal Tavera, the last work of Alonso de Berruguete. Descend into the crypt to experience some bizarre acoustical effects. *Tel. 925/22–04–51. Admission to hospital: 300 pesetas; admission to adjoining church: 500 pesetas. Open daily 10:30–1:30 and 3:30–6.*

⑤③ El Greco's most famous painting can be found in the church of **Santo Tomé;** ideally, you should get here as soon as it opens in the morning, for later on in the day, especially in the summer months, you may well have to wait in line to get inside. To walk to the chapel from the cathedral, head west along the Calle de la Trinidad and join the Calle de Santo Tomé. The church is on the left-hand side, adorned by an elegant Mudéjar tower. The entrance to the specially built chapel housing El Greco's *Burial of Count Orgaz* is on the other side of the building and can be reached by turning left down the Travesía de Santo José, and then left again. The painting—the only one by the artist to have been consistently admired over the centuries— portrays the benefactor of the church being buried with the post-humous assistance of St. Augustine and St. Stephen, who miraculously appeared at the funeral to thank him for all the money he had given to religious institutions named after them. Though the count's burial took place in the 14th century, El Greco painted the onlookers in contemporary costumes and included people he knew; the boy in the foreground is one of El Greco's sons, while the sixth figure on the left is said to be the artist himself. *Admission: 100 pesetas. Open Oct.–Apr., daily 10–1:45 and 3:30–5:45; May–Sept., daily 10–1:45 and 3:30–6:45.*

You are now in the tourist heart of Toledo, and from Santo Tomé all the way to San Juan de los Reyes stretches a succession of souvenir ⑤④ shops. **Casa de El Greco** (El Greco's House), another tourist magnet, is farther down the hill from Santo Tomé, off the Calle de San Juan de Dios. The property belonged to Peter the Cruel's Jewish treasurer, Samuel Levi, and it is known that the artist once lived in a house owned by this man; whether he lived in this one, however, is pure conjecture. The interior, done up in the late 19th century to resemble a "typical" house of El Greco's time, is a pure fake, albeit quite a pleasant one. The once-drab museum attached to it is currently being restored and remodeled; one of the few works to be seen at present is a large panorama of Toledo by El Greco, featuring in the foreground the Hospital of Tavera. *Tel. 925/22–40–46. Admission: 200 pesetas. Open Tues.–Sat. 10–2 and 4–6, Sun. 10–2.*

55 The **Sinagoga del Tránsito** (Tránsito Synagogue), at the bottom of the street, is a 14th-century structure financed by Samuel Levi. Plain on the outside, the walls of this simple rectangular structure are sumptuously covered inside with intricate Mudéjar decoration, as well as Hebraic inscriptions glorifying God, Peter the Cruel, and Levi himself. The upper, women's gallery has recently been opened to the public for the first time following loving restoration; the rooms adjoining the main hall reopened in 1991 as a small museum of Jewish culture in Spain. *Admission: 200 pesetas. Open Tues.–Sat. 10–2 and 4–6, Sun. 10–2.*

Turn right onto the wide Calle de Los Reyes Católicos and you will **56** come shortly to the town's other synagogue, **Santa María la Blanca.** Nearly two centuries older than the Tránsito Synagogue, it has a white interior featuring a forest of columns supporting capitals of the most enchanting filigree workmanship. Stormed in the early 15th century by a Christian mob led by St. Vincent Ferrer, the synagogue was later put to a variety of uses—as a carpenter's workshop, a store, a barracks, and a refuge for reformed prostitutes. *Admission: 100 pesetas. Open Oct.–Apr., daily 10–2 and 3:30–6; May–Sept., daily 10–2 and 3:30–7.*

A few steps from Santa María la Blanca, at the western end of town, **57** is the convent church of **San Juan de los Reyes,** erected by Ferdinand and Isabella to commemorate their victory at the battle of Toro in 1476 and intended originally to be their burial place. The building is largely the work of Juan Guas, who considered it his masterpiece and asked to be buried here himself. Guas, one of the greatest exponents of the Gothic, or Isabelline, was an architect of prolific imagination and great decorative exuberance. The white interior, in true Plateresque fashion, is covered with inscriptions and heraldic motifs. *Admission: 100 pesetas. Open Oct.–Apr., daily 10–1:30 and 3:30–5:45; May–Sept., daily 10–1:45 and 3:30–6:45.*

Walk uphill from San Juan de Los Reyes on the Calle del Ángel and you will rejoin the Calle de Santo Tomé; from there, it is a short walk back to the cathedral. For a diversion into a virtually unspoiled part of town, turn left by the church of Santo Tomé onto the Plaza Valdecaleros. At the top of this square, turn left again and then immediately right onto the Calle San Clemente; the **Convento de San Clemente** (on the left-hand side) has a richly sculpted portal by Covarrubias.

58 **San Román,** at the top of the street, is an early 13th-century Mudéjar church, with extensive remains of frescoes inside; it has been deconsecrated and now serves as a **Museo de los Concilios y de la Cultura Visigoda** (Museum of Visigothic Art), featuring statuary, manuscript illustrations, and delicate jewelry. *Admission: 100 pesetas. Open Tues.–Sat. 10–2 and 4–6:30, Sun. 10–2.*

Almost every wall in this exceptionally quiet part of town belongs to a convent, and the empty streets here make for contemplative walks. This was a district much loved by the Romantic poet Gustavo Adolfo Bécquer, author of *Rime,* the most popular book of Spanish

verse before García Lorca's *Romancero Gitano*. His favorite corner
was the tiny square in front of the 16th-century convent church of
Santo Domingo, a few minutes' walk to the north of San Román, below the Plazuela de Padilla. You will find here not only the earliest of
El Greco's Toledo paintings, but also the artist's coffin. The friendly
nuns at the convent will show you around an eccentric little museum,
which includes documents bearing El Greco's signature. *Admission: 150 pesetas. Open Mon.–Sat. 11–2 and 4–7, Sun. 4–7.*

What to See and Do with Children

Unquestionably, the greatest treat that you could give your children, and probably yourself, is to take them to see the **fountains at
La Granja,** 6 km (4 mi) south of Segovia (*see* Tour 1, *above*). Installed
in the late 18th century, they were immediately hailed as among the
great artistic and technological marvels of the age. Of exceptional
intricacy and ingenuity, they benefit from the very strong water
pressure provided by their location on the slopes of the Sierra de
Guadarrama. Every Wednesday, Saturday, and Sunday evening at
6, from May 1 to September 30, crowds of noisy Spanish children
gather at the gates of La Granja as a man turns on the water with a
large key. The jets shoot up from unpredictable places and angles,
so be prepared for a good soaking.

Shopping

Salamanca Salamanca has a reputation for **leatherwork;** the most traditional
shop in town where you can buy it is **Salón Campero** (Plaza Corrillo
5).

Segovia After Toledo, **Segovia province** ranks next in importance for its
crafts. **Glass** and **crystal** are a specialty of **La Granja,** while **ironwork, lace,** and **embroidery** are famous in Segovia itself. In search of
the old, authentic article, go to **San Martín 4** (Plaza San Martín 4,
Segovia), an excellent **antiques** shop. You can buy good **lace** from the
Gypsies in Segovia's **Plaza del Alcázar,** but be prepared for a lot of
strenuous bargaining and never offer more than half the opening
price.

Toledo The most renowned center for crafts in Castile, if not in the whole of
Spain, is **Toledo province.** Here, the Moors established **silverwork,
damascene** (metalwork inlaid with gold or silver), **embroidery,** and
pottery traditions that are still very much alive. Next to the church
of San Juan de los Reyes in Toledo is a turn-of-the-century art school
that teaches these various crafts and helps to maintain standards.
For much cheaper pottery, you would be better off stopping at the
large roadside emporia on the outskirts of the town, on the main
road to Madrid. Better still, go to **Talavera la Reina,** 76 km (47 mi)
west of Toledo, where most of this pottery is made. The finest embroidery in the province is from **Oropesa** and **Lagartera.**

Sports

Golf There are golf courses at Alcalá de Henares, Salamanca, and numerous smaller places in the immediate surroundings of Madrid. For
further information, contact the **Real Federación Española de Golf**
(Capitán Haya 9, 28020 Madrid, tel. 91/555–2682).

Hiking and The best area for both hiking and mountaineering is the Sierra de
Mountaineering Gredos, and you could base yourself here at the Gredos Parador (*see*

Dining and Lodging, *below*). The range has six mountain huts with limited accommodations and facilities; for information on these and on mountaineering in general, contact the **Federación Española de Montañismo** (Alberto Aguilera 3, 28015 Madrid, tel. 91/445–1382).

Hunting and Fishing These are the most traditional Castilian leisure activities. Most of the private game reserves are in the provinces of Toledo and Guadalajara, where the red-legged partridge is one of the most sought-after species. The Spanish ibex can be hunted in the Sierra de Gredos. Information can be obtained from **ICONA** (Gran Vía de San Francisco 4, tel. 91/347–6000) and **Federación Española de Caza** (Av. Reina Victoria 72, 28006 Madrid, tel. 91/553–9017). Hunting and fishing permits must be obtained locally (not in Madrid); inquire at local tourist offices.

The most common fish in Castile's rivers are trout, pike, black bass, and blue carp; among the main trout rivers are the Eresma, Alto Duero, Júcar, Jarama, Manzanares, Tajo, and Tormes. Obtain permits and information from ICONA (*see above*) and from the **Federación Española de Pesca** (Navas de Tolosa 3, 28013 Madrid, tel. 91/532–8353).

Skiing Skiing is popular in the Sierra de Gredos and in the Guadarrama resorts of La Pinilla (Segovia), Navacerrada (Madrid), Valdesquí (Madrid), and Valcotos (Madrid). Current information on skiing conditions can be obtained from **ATUDEM** (tel. 91/458–1557), although you'll do better to call the slope you're planning on visiting; general information is available from **Federación Española de Deportes de Invierno** (Claudio Coello 32, 28001 Madrid, tel. 91/575–0576).

Dining and Lodging

Dining

The classic dishes of Castile are *cordero* (lamb) and *cochinillo* (suckling pig) roasted in a wood oven. These are the particular specialties of Segovia, which is widely thought of as the gastronomic capital of Castile, thanks largely to the international reputation of such long-established restaurants as the Mesón de Cándido and the Mesón Duque. In the Segovian village of Pedraza, superb roast lamb is served with hearty red wine.

The mountainous districts of Salamanca are renowned for their hams and sausage products—in particular, the villages of Guijuelo and Candelario. Bean dishes are a specialty of El Barco (Ávila) and La Granja (Segovia), while *trucha* (trout) and *cangrejos de río* (river crab) are common to Guadalajara province. Game is abundant throughout Castile, two famous dishes being *perdiz en escabeche* (the marinated partridges of Soria) and *perdiz estofada a la Toledana* (the stewed partridges of Toledo). The most exotic and complex cuisine in Castile is perhaps that of Cuenca, where you will find two outstanding restaurants, Figon de Pedro and Los Claveles. A strong Moorish influence prevails here—for instance, in *gazpacho pastor* (a hot terrine made with a variety of game, topped with grapes).

Among the region's sweets are the *yemas* (sugared egg yolks) of Ávila, *almendras garrapiñadas* (candied almonds) of Alcalá de Henares, *mazapan* (marzipans) of Toledo, and *ponche Segovia* (egg toddy of Segovia). La Mancha is the main area for cheeses, while Aranjuez is famous for its strawberries and asparagus.

Much of the cheap wine in Spain comes from La Mancha, south of Toledo. Far better in quality, and indeed among the most superior Spanish wines, are those from the Duero Valley, around Valladolid. Look, in particular, for the Marqués de Riscal whites from Rueda and the Vega Sicilia reds from Valbuena; Peñafiel is the most common of the Duero wines. An excellent, if extremely sweet, Castilian liqueur is the *resolí* from Cuenca made from aquavit, coffee, vanilla, orange peel, and sugar and often sold in bottles in the shape of Cuenca's Casas Colgadas.

Dress in restaurants of this region is usually casual, unless otherwise indicated. Reservations are not necessary unless so specified.

Highly recommended restaurants are indicated by a star ★.

Category	Cost*
$$$$	over 6,500 ptas
$$$	4,000–6,500 ptas
$$	2,500–4,000 ptas
$	under 2,500 ptas

* *per person for a three-course meal, including wine, excluding tax*

Lodging

The most stylish of Spain's hotels are usually the paradors. Though this holds true in the region around Madrid, the oldest and most beautiful of the paradors here are generally to be found in the lesser towns, such as Ciudad Real and Sigüenza, rather than in the major tourist centers. The paradors at Salamanca, Toledo, Segovia, and Soria are all in ugly or nondescript modern buildings, albeit with magnificent views. Fortunately, the region has many other memorable alternatives to paradors, such as the beautifully and centrally situated Los Linajes in Segovia, the Palacio de Valderrábanos in Ávila (a 15th-century palace next to the cathedral), and Cuenca's Posada San José, a 16th-century convent in a spectacular situation.

Highly recommended hotels are indicated by a star ★.

Category	Cost*
$$$$	over 13,000 ptas
$$$	8,000–13,000 ptas
$$	4,000–8,000 ptas
$	under 4,000 ptas

* *All prices are for a standard double room, excluding tax.*

Alarcón
Lodging

Parador Nacional Marqués de Villena. For indulging in medieval fantasies, this parador is virtually unrivaled. Set in a 14th-century castle with a spectacular position above a gorge, the hotel has only 13 small rooms, some of which are in the corner towers and have as windows the narrow slots once used to shoot arrows out of; other rooms have window niches where the women of the household would sit to do needlework. Dinners are served in a high-arched baronial hall adorned with shields, armor, and a gigantic fireplace recalling medieval banquets. *Av. Amigos de los Castillos 3, 16213, tel. 966/33–13–50, fax 966/33–11–07. 13 rooms. Facilities: restaurant, garden. AE, DC, MC, V. $$$$*

Alcalá de Henares
Dining

Hostería del Estudiante. One of the original buildings acquired by Spain's parador chain, this restaurant is magnificently set around a 15th-century cloister and features wood-beam ceilings, a large and splendid fireplace, and glass-and-tin lanterns. Appropriate to such a traditional setting is the good and simple Castilian food, a particular specialty being roast lamb. *Los Colegios 3, tel. 91/888–0330. AE, DC, MC, V. No dinner July and Aug. Closed Mon. $$*

Ávila
Dining
★

El Molino de la Losa. Few restaurants could have a better or more exciting situation than this one. Standing in the middle of the River Adaja, with one of the best views of the town's walls, it occupies a 15th-century mill, the working mechanism of which has been well preserved and provides much distraction for those seated in the animated bar. Lamb here is roasted in a medieval wood oven, and there is fish freshly caught from the river; this is also a good place to try the beans from nearby El Barco (*judías de El Barco*). In the beautiful garden outside is a small playground for children. *Bajada de la Losa 12, tel. 918/21–11–01 or 918/21–11–02. AE, MC, V. Closed Mon. in winter. $$*

Mesón del Rastro. The best alternative after El Molino de la Losa, this restaurant occupies a wing of the medieval Abrantes Palace and has an attractive old-style interior. Once again, try the lamb and the El Barco beans; also good is the *caldereta de cabrito* (goat stew). The place suffers somewhat from its popularity with tour buses, and service is slow and impersonal. *Plaza Rastro 1, tel. 918/21–12–18. AE, DC, MC, V. $$*

Lodging
★

Palacio de Valderrábanos. The hotel stands right in front of the cathedral and occupies a 15th-century palace that originally belonged to the first bishop of Ávila. The medieval splendor of the sculpted granite exterior shields a luxury hotel of distinctly old-fashioned character. The spacious rooms retain a 1920s-style decor. *Plaza de la Catedral 9, 05001, tel. 918/21–10–23, fax 918/25–16–91. 73 rooms with bath. Facilities: restaurant, conference room. AE, DC, MC, V. $$$*

Parador Nacional Raimundo de Borgoña. This largely rebuilt medieval castle attached to the town walls has none of the character or architectural interest of the Palacio de Valderrábanos, but it does have slightly more sophisticated furnishings. It also has the advantage of a beautiful garden, from which you can climb up onto the town's ramparts. *Marqués de Canales y Chozas 16, 05001, tel. 918/ 21–13–40, fax 918/22–61–66. 62 rooms with bath. Facilities: restaurant, parking, garage, garden, conference room. AE, DC, MC, V. $$$*

Ciudad Rodrigo
Dining

Mayton. This restaurant has a most engaging wood-beamed interior, bursting with a wonderful and eccentric collection of antiques, ranging from pestles and mortars to Portuguese yokes and old typewriters. In contrast to the decor, the emphasis of the cooking is on simple preparation; the specialties are fish, seafood, goat, and lamb. *La Colada 9, tel. 923/46–07–20. AE, DC, MC, V. $$*

Lodging

Parador Nacional Enrique II. Occupying part of the magnificent castle built by Enrique II of Trastamara to guard over the Agueda Valley, this parador is a series of small white rooms along the sturdy and gently sloping outer walls of the building; ask for room No. 10 if you want one that has kept its original vaulting. A special feature throughout the hotel is the under-floor heating in the bathrooms.

Some of the rooms, as well as the restaurant, overlook a beautiful garden that runs down to the River Agueda; beyond the river the view surveys fertile plains. *Plaza Castillo 1, 37500, tel. 923/46–01–50, fax 923/46–04–04. 27 rooms. Facilities: parking, garden, conference room. AE, DC, MC, V. $$$*

Conde Rodrigo. A good and cheaper alternative to the parador, this hotel is situated in a dignified old building on the town's cathedral square. The clean and simply furnished rooms are modern and lack character, but those on the front have balconies with excellent views of the cathedral. *Plaza del Salvador 7, 37500, tel. 923/46–14–04, fax 923/46–14–08. 35 rooms. Facilities: restaurant, parking, conference hall. AE, MC, V. $$*

Cuenca
Dining
★

Figón de Pedro. The owner of this restaurant, Pedro Torres Pacheco, is one of the famed restaurateurs of Spain and has done much to promote the excellence of Cuenca cuisine. In this pleasantly low-key and modest-looking establishment in the lively heart of the modern town, you can try such unusual local specialties as *gazpacho pastor* (a hot terrine made here with partridge, hare, and rabbit), *ajo arriero* (a paste made with pounded salt cod), and *alaju* (a sweet of obvious Moorish origin and consisting of honey, bread crumbs, almonds, and orange water). You can finish off your meal with resolí, the Cuenca liqueur. *Cervantes 13, tel. 966/22–45–11. Weekend reservations advised. AE, DC, MC, V. Closed Sun. evening and Mon. $$$*

Mesón Casas Colgadas. Run by the management of the Figón de Pedro, it offers much the same fare, but more pretentiously, in an ultramodern white dining room in the spectacularly sited Casas Colgadas, next to the Museum of Abstract Art. *Canónigos s/n, tel. 966/22–35–09. Weekend and holiday reservations required. AE, DC, MC, V. Closed Tues. evening. $$$*

★ **Los Claveles.** In a quiet and attractive part of the new town, with a colorful, homey interior filled with curiosities and posters (even on the ceiling), this is, in many ways, one of the most agreeable restaurants in Castile. The present owner's father bought the establishment in 1950, following a drunken spree after a bullfight; he realized what he had done only the next day, but fortunately persevered with the place and soon helped win for it a great local popularity. His widow still does the cooking, which is every bit as good as that of El Figón, with perhaps a more authentic character: You feel that she is perpetuating family traditions that go back centuries. All the Cuenca specialties can be found here, including *morteruelo* (an even richer and more elaborate version of gazpacho pastor, containing liver and ham). The gazpacho pastor here is served with the traditional grapes, a truly Moorish touch. *Torres 34, tel. 966/21–38–24. Closed Thurs. and Sept. MC, V. $$*

Lodging **Cueva del Fraile.** This luxurious hotel, 7 km (4½ mi) out of town on the Buenache road, occupies a 16th-century building in dramatic surroundings. The white rooms have reproduction traditional furniture, stone floors, and some wood ceilings. *Ctra. Cuenca-Buenache, 16001, tel. 966/21–15–71, fax 966/21–15–73. 54 rooms with bath. Facilities: garden, pool, parking, garage, tennis courts, conference room. Closed Jan. 10–Mar. 2. $$$*

Parador de Cuenca. Spain's newest parador (opened in 1993) is in an exquisitely restored 16th-century monastery situated in the gorge below Cuenca's famous hanging houses. The guest rooms are furnished in a lighter and more luxurious style than one usually finds in Castilian houses of the same vintage. *Paseo Hoz de Huecar s/n, 16001, tel. 969/23–23–20, fax 969/23–25–34. 124 rooms with bath. Facilities: restaurant, bar, indoor pool, tennis. AE, DC, MC, V. $$$*

★ **Posada San José.** This is still the only hotel in the Old Town, and it's just as good, if somewhat more modest, than the nearby parador. Tastefully installed in a 16th-century convent, it clings to the top of the Huécar gorge, which most of its rooms overlook. The furnishings are traditional and in the spirit of the building. The atmosphere is friendly and intimate. Reservations are essential, preferably well ahead. *Julián Romero 4, 16001, tel. 966/21–13–00. 16 rooms with bath, 9 without. MC, V. $$*

El Burgo de Osma
Dining

Virrey Palafox. One of Castile's famed restaurants, this is a family-run establishment set in a modern building. Inside, decor is traditional Castilian style, complete with white walls and a timber-beamed ceiling. The long dining room, adorned with old furnishings, is divided into smoking and nonsmoking sections. The emphasis is on fresh, seasonal produce. Vegetables are home-grown, and there is excellent local game throughout the year. The specialty of the house is fish, in particular *merluza Virrey* (hake stuffed with eels and salmon). On February and March weekends, a pig is slaughtered and a marvelous and very popular banquet is held (about 4,500 pesetas). *Universidad 7, tel. 975/34–02–22. AE, DC, MC, V. Closed Sun. evening in winter and Dec. 15–Jan. 15. $$–$$$*

Lodging

Virrey II. Twenty clean, modest, and inexpensive rooms are to be found above the famous restaurant of this name. For more stylish accommodation, try this new hotel, opened by the same management in 1990 a few hundred yards away. Situated on the village's beautiful main square, it adjoins the 16th-century Convent of San Agustín and appears to form part of it. Though of recent construction, the hotel is built with traditional materials and has an Old World look. The rooms, most of which overlook the square, have marble floors, stone walls, and tastefully simple decoration. *Calle Mayor 2, 42300, tel. 975/34–13–11, fax 975/34–08–55. 52 rooms. Facilities: conference room, small dining room. AE, DC, MC, V. $$$*

Navarredonda de Gredos
Lodging

Parador Nacional de Gredos. Built in 1926 on a site chosen by Alfonso XIII, this was the first of the parador chain; it was enlarged in 1941 and again in 1975. Though modern, the stone architecture has a sturdy, traditional look and blends well with the magnificent surroundings. The rooms are standard parador, with heavy dark furniture and light walls. It has excellent views of the Gredos range and is the ideal base for a hiking or climbing holiday. *Carretera Barraco–Béjar, 05001, tel. 918/34–80–48, fax 918/34–82–05. 77 rooms with bath. Facilities: restaurant, parking, garden, conference room, tennis courts, bookshop. AE, DC, MC, V. $$$*

Pedraza
Dining

El Yantar de Pedraza. This traditional establishment, with wooden tables and beamed ceilings on the village's enchanting main square, is famous for its roast meats. It is certainly the place to come to for that most celebrated of Pedraza's specialties—*corderito lechal en horno de leña* (baby lamb roasted in a wood oven). *Plaza Mayor, tel. 911/50–98–42. Reservations advised on weekends. AE, MC, V. Closed evenings Sept. 15–July 15, and Mon. $$$*

Lodging

La Posada de Don Mariano. Opened in 1989, this hotel was originally a farmer's home. Each of the rooms in the picturesque old building has been carefully decorated in a different style with rustic furniture and antiques. The atmosphere is intimate, but the prices are grand. *Plaza Mayor 14, 40172, tel. 911/50–98–86/87. 18 rooms with bath. AE, DC, MC, V. $$$*

Salamanca
Dining

Chez Victor. If you are tired of traditional Castilian cuisine, this chic, modern restaurant is the place to come to. The owner and cook, Victoriano Salvador, learned his trade in France and now adapts

French food to Spanish taste, with numerous whimsical touches quite his own—for instance, *sesos de cordero al vinagre de frambuesa* (lamb brains in raspberry vinegar) and *raviolis rellenos de marisco* (ravioli stuffed with shellfish). The desserts are outstanding—in particular, the chocolate ones. *Espoz y Mina 26, tel. 923/21–31–23. AE, DC, MC, V. Closed Sun. evening, Mon., and Aug. $$$*

Río de la Plata. This tiny basement restaurant, dating back to 1958, has a friendly, old-fashioned character; the elegant, gilded decor is a pleasant change from the ubiquitous Castilian-style interiors typical of this region. The food is simple but carefully prepared, with good-quality fish and meat. *Plaza Peso 1, tel. 923/21–90–05. AE, MC, V. Closed Mon. and July. $$*

Lodging **Gran Hotel.** The *grande dame* of Salamanca's hotels got a facelift in 1994 and now offers stylishly baroque lounges and refurbished yet old-fashioned oversize rooms just steps from the Plaza Mayor. *Plaza Poeta Iglesias 3, 37001, tel. 923/21–35–00, fax 923/21–35–01. 109 rooms with bath. Facilities: restaurant, bar, garage. AE, DC, MC, V. $$$*

Palacio del Castellanos. Opened in 1992 in an immaculately restored 15th-century palace, this hotel offers a much needed altenative to Salamanca's national parador (probably the ugliest in the chain). This palacio has an exquisite interior patio and an equally beautiful restaurant. *San Pablo 58, tel. 923/26–18–18, fax 923/26–18–19. 69 rooms. AE, DC, MC, V. $$$*

Las Torres. Situated on the Plaza Mayor above the lively café of this name (*see* Tour 3 in Exploring Around Madrid, *above*), this slightly seedy and depressing place with pale green rooms may well be where you choose to end up in Salamanca. Its position could not be bettered, and if you are given a room overlooking the square, the view will make up for everything else. *Plaza Mayor 26, 37001, tel. 923/21–21–00 or 923/21–21–01. 26 rooms. No credit cards. $$*

Segovia **Casa Duque.** Founded by Dionisio Duque in 1895 and still in the fami-
Dining ly, this is the second most famous restaurant in town. The intimate interior, homey wood-beam decoration, and plethora of beautiful and fascinating objects hanging everywhere give it a look similar to Cándido's. It is smaller and friendlier, though, and benefits greatly from the charismatic presence of Julian Duque, the owner. Never still for a moment, Duque attends to all his clients with eccentric but not obsequious charm. Roasts are the specialty, but you should also try the *judiones de La Granja Duque*—the excellent kidney beans from nearby La Granja, served with sausages. *Cervantes 12, tel. 911/43–05–37. Reservations required weekends, advised other times. AE, DC, MC, V. $$$*

Mesón de Cándido. More than a restaurant, this is a national monument; it was declared such in 1941. Situated under the aqueduct and comprising a quaint medley of small, irregular dining rooms covered with memorabilia, it has served as an inn since at least the 18th century. Cándido took over the running in 1931 and, with his energy and flair for publicity, managed to make it the Spanish restaurant best known abroad: Hung everywhere are photographs of the countless celebrities who have been here, ranging from Salvador Dalí to Princess Grace of Monaco. The place is now run by Cándido's son, but Cándido regularly pokes in his famous bald head to see how things are going. All first-time visitors are virtually obliged to eat the *cochinillo* (suckling pig), the delicacy of which used to be attested by Cándido's slicing it with the edge of a plate; the trout here is also renowned. *Plaza de Azoguejo 5, tel. 911/42–59–11. Reservations required weekends, advised other times. AE, DC, MC, V. $$$*

★ **Mesón de José María.** The exceptionally lively bar through which you must pass to reach the restaurant augurs well for the rest of the establishment. Though of relatively recent date in Segovian terms, this place has already surpassed its formidable rivals and deserves to be considered one of Spain's finest restaurants. The hospitable and passionately dedicated owner is devoted to maintaining the traditional specialties of his region while making innovations of his own. The emphasis is on freshness and quality of produce, and the menu changes constantly. The large old-style dining room is always packed, and the waiters are uncommonly friendly. *Cronista Lecea 11, tel. 911/43–44–84. AE, DC, MC, V. $$$*

Dining and **Parador Nacional de Segovia.** Architecturally one of the most inter-
Lodging esting and beautiful of the modern paradors, this low building, which was recently expanded substantially, is spaciously arranged amid greenery on a hillside. The rooms are light, with generous amounts of glass. The panorama of Segovia and its aqueduct is unbeatable, but there are disadvantages in staying so far from the town center. The restaurant serves traditional Segovian and international dishes—for instance, *lomo de merluza al aroma de estragón* (hake fillet with tarragon and shrimp). *Carretera de Valladolid s/n, 40003, tel. 911/44–37–37, fax 911/43–73–62. 103 rooms with bath. Facilities: restaurant, garage, garden, indoor and outdoor pools, conference hall with simultaneous translation facilities. AE, DC, MC, V. $$$$*

Lodging **Los Linajes.** The only luxury hotel within the old walls of Segovia,
★ this is also by far the best hotel in town. Part of the well-modernized building belongs to a medieval palace; there are wonderful views over the town's northern ramparts and out into the countryside. *Doctor Velasco 9, 40003, tel. 911/43–12–01, fax 911/43–15–01. 53 rooms. Facilities: restaurant, bar, conference room, parking. AE, MC, V. $$$*

Infanta Isabel. A recently restored building with a Victorian feel houses this small and central hotel. It's just two steps off the Plaza Mayor and offers great views of Segovia's cathedral. The rooms are feminine and light with painted white furnishings. *Plaza Mayor s/n, 40001, tel. 911/44–31–05, fax 911/43–32–40. 29 rooms. Facilities: coffee shop, garage. AE, MC, V. $$*

Sigüenza **Parador Nacional Castillo de Sigüenza.** Of the many castles belong-
Lodging ing to the parador chain, this is one of the most impressive and his-
★ torically important. At the very top of the beautiful town of Sigüenza, this mighty, crenellated structure has hosted royalty over the centuries, from Ferdinand and Isabella right up to the present king, Juan Carlos. Some of the rooms have four-poster beds and balconies perched over the wild landscape. *Subida al Castillo s/n, 19250, tel. 911/39–01–00, fax 911/39–13–64. 77 rooms with bath. Facilities: restaurant, parking, garden, conference room. AE, DC, MC, V. $$$*

Soria **Mesón Castellano.** The most traditional restaurant in town, this cozy
Dining establishment has a large open fire over which succulent *chuletón de ternera* (veal chops) are cooked. Another specialty is its *migas pastoriles* (soaked bread crumbs fried with peppers and bacon), a local dish. *Plaza Mayor 2, tel. 911/21–30–45. AE, MC, V. $$*

Lodging **Parador Nacional Antonio Machado.** This modern building has a superb hilltop setting, surrounded by trees and parkland, and excellent views of the hilly Duero Valley. It is named after the poet who came often to this site for inspiration. *Parque del Castillo, 42005,*

tel. 911/21–34–45, fax 911/21–28–49. 34 rooms with bath. Facilities:
restaurant, parking, garden. AE, MC, V. $$$

Toledo **Asador Adolfo.** Only a few steps from the cathedral, but discreetly
Dining hidden away and making no attempt to attract the passing tourist
★ trade, this is unquestionably the best and most dignified restaurant
in town. The modern main entrance shields an old and intimate inte-
rior featuring in its principal dining room a wood-beam ceiling with
extensive painted decoration from the 14th century. The emphasis is
on freshness of produce and traditional Toledan dishes, but there is
also much innovation. Especially good starters are the *pimientos
rellenos* (stuffed peppers). For a main course, try the *merluza al
azafrán* (hake subtly flavored with saffron from the area). You
should finish with another Toledan specialty, *delicias de mazapan*
(marzipan), which is cooked here in a wooden oven and is the finest
and lightest to be found in the whole town. *Granada 6 and Hombre
de Palo 7, tel. 925/22–73–21. Reservations required on weekends.
AE, DC, MC, V. Closed Sun. evening. $$$

Hierbabuena. Dine on an enclosed Moorish patio with plenty of natural light, at tables covered with crocheted cloths. The food here is
just as inviting as the setting, and it is surprisingly reasonably
priced; try artichokes stuffed with seafood or steak with blue-
cheese sauce. *Cristo de la Luz 9, tel. 925/22–34–63. Reservations
advised. MC, V. $$

Hostal del Cardenal. The restaurant of this famous hotel adjoining
the northern walls of the town has a long-standing reputation and is
very popular with tourists. The setting is beautiful (*see* Lodging, *be-
low*), but the food is not quite what it used to be. The dishes are
mainly local, and in season you will find delicious asparagus and
strawberries from Aranjuez. *Paseo Recaredo 24, tel. 925/22–08–62.
AE, DC, MC, V. $$

Lodging **Parador Nacional Conde de Orgaz.** This modern building on the outskirts of Toledo blends well with its rural surroundings and has an
unbeatable panorama of the town. The architecture and furnishings,
emphasizing brick and wood, make concessions to the traditional
Toledan style. *Paseo Emperador s/n, 45001, tel. 925/22–18–50, fax
925/22–51–66. 77 rooms with bath. Facilities: garden, pool. AE,
DC, MC, V. $$$$

Hostal del Cardenal. Built in the 18th century as a summer palace for
Cardinal Lorenzana, this is a quiet and beautiful hotel with light-
colored rooms decorated with old furniture; some rooms overlook
the hotel's enchanting wooded garden, which lies at the foot of the
town's walls. It is difficult to believe that the main Madrid road is
only a short distance away. *Paseo de Recaredo 24, 45004, tel. 925/
22–49–00, fax 925/22–29–91. 27 rooms. Facilities: restaurant, gar-
den. AE. $$$

Pintor El Greco. Next door to the famous painter's house-museum
(closed for restoration until 1996), this friendly hotel is in what was
once a 17th-century bakery. Extensive renovation has resulted in a
light and modern interior, with some antique touches such as ex-
posed brick vaulting. *Alamillos del Transito 13, 45002, tel. 925/21–
42–50, fax 925/21–58–19. 35 rooms. AE, DC, MC, V. $$

Valladolid **La Fragua.** In a modern building with a traditional Castilian interior
Dining of white walls and wood-beam ceilings, Valladolid's most famous and
stylish restaurant counts members of the Spanish royal family
among its patrons. Specialties include meat roasted in a wood oven
and dishes more imaginative than those of the standard Castilian table, such as *rape Castellano Gran Mesón* (breaded skate served
with clams and peppers) and *lengua empiñonada* (tongue coated in

pine nuts). *Paseo Zorrilla 10, tel. 983/33–71–02. AE, DC, MC, V. Closed Sun. evening in winter, all Sun. in summer. $$$*

Lodging **Olid Melia.** A characterless modern block, the Hotel Olid Melia is situated in the middle of one of Valladolid's most attractive old districts. The building was erected in the early 1970s, and its pale green curtains and dark, heavy furniture have a somewhat dated look. The ground and first floors, however, have recently been dramatically remodeled and given a marbled, pristine elegance. *Plaza de San Miguel 10, 47003, tel. 983/35–72–00, fax 983/33–68–28. 226 rooms with bath. Facilities: garage, conference hall, hairdresser. AE, DC, MC, V. $$$*

Zamora **Parador Nacional Condes de Alba y Aliste.** This pleasing establish-
Lodging ment offers a central but quiet location, a historic building with a distinctive Renaissance patio, good landscape views, and a friendly and intelligent staff. *Plaza Viriato 5, 49014, tel. 988/51–44–97, fax 988/53–00–63. 27 rooms with bath. Facilities: garage, garden, pool. AE, DC, MC, V. Expensive.*

The Arts and Nightlife

The Arts

Outside Madrid, the arts do not flourish in Castile. A renowned **annual theater festival** does take place in the La Mancha town of **Almagro.** Information on performances is available from the tourist office at Almagro (Carnicería 11, tel. 926/86–07–17).

Nightlife

Nightlife, though provincial in comparison to Madrid, flourishes in a number of Castilian towns. The liveliest places are the university towns of Salamanca and Valladolid.

Ávila For a fashionable bar in Ávila—almost a contradiction in terms— you should try the unappealingly named **El Rincón del Jamón** (Ham Corner) at Calle Vicente Manzaredo 11.

Salamanca The main area in Salamanca (*see* Tour 3 in Exploring Around Madrid, *above*) is around the Calle Bermejeros, but for a stylish and fashionable bar/discothèque, try **Camelot,** on the Calle Bordadores.

Segovia Segovia's main nocturnal district is around the Plaza San Martín, where the activity is concentrated in three loud and exceptionally lively bars: **El Gimnasio, El Ojo,** and **El Narziotas.**

Toledo Toledo's nightlife is concentrated around the Plaza Zocodover. Some of the best night bars are to the west of this square, lining the Calle Sillería and its continuation, Alfileritos. Just to the south of the square is the recently reopened **Amsterdam,** a lively and friendly bar filled mainly with young people. For discothèques you should go to the underground complex known as the Miradero, to the north of the plaza; try the newly revamped **La Máscara.**

Valladolid Valladolid has a wide choice of places to go to at night. The Zona Francisco Suarez and the Zona Iglesia La Antigua are the two districts that are popular with students. Livelier and more fashionable still are the Zona Cantarranas (in particular, the **Inoxidable**) and around the Plaza Mayor.

5 Barcelona

By Philip Eade

Updated by George Semler

Capital of Catalunya (Catalonia) and Spain's second-largest city, Barcelona has long rivaled, even surpassed, Madrid in industrial muscle and business acumen. Though Madrid has now finally well and truly taken up the mantle of capital city, Barcelona has relinquished none of its former prowess. The city witnessed a massive building program in anticipation of the big event of 1992, the long-cherished goal of hosting the Olympics, during which world attention focused on Barcelona. It ranks as one of Europe's most beautiful cities: Few places can rival the narrow alleys of the Gothic Quarter for medieval atmosphere or the elegance and distinction of the boulevards in its Moderniste Eixample.

Barcelona enjoys an active cultural life and heritage. It was the home of the architect Antoni Gaudí i Cornet (1852–1926), whose buildings form the most startling statements of Modernisme, a Spanish and mainly Catalan offshoot of Art Nouveau, whose other leading exponents were the architects Lluís Domènech i Montaner and Josep Puig i Cadafalch. The painters Joan Miró (1893–1983) and Antoni Tàpies (born 1923) also began their careers here. It is the place where Pablo Picasso spent his formative years, and it has a museum devoted to his works. It can claim Spain's oldest and best opera house, the Liceu, and acknowledges with pride contributions to the arts of such native Catalans as cellist Pablo (Pau, in Catalán) Casals (1876–1973), surrealist Salvador Dalí (1904–1989), and opera singers Montserrat Caballé and Josep (José) Carreras. It flaunts a fashion industry hard on the heels of those of Paris and Milan, as well as one of the world's most glamorous soccer clubs.

In 133 BC the Romans conquered the city built by the Iberian tribe known as the Laietans and founded a colony they called Colonia Favencia Julia Augusta Paterna Barcino. In the 5th century, Barcelona was established as the Visigothic capital, the Moors invaded during the 8th century, and in 801 the Franks under Charlemagne captured Barcelona and made it their frontier with the Moorish empire on the Iberian Peninsula. By 988, the autonomous Catalonian counties had gained independence from the Franks, and in 1137 they were united through marriage with the House of Aragón. In 1474 the marriage of Ferdinand of Aragón and Isabella of Castile brought Aragón and Catalonia into a united Spain. As the capital of Aragón's Mediterranean empire, Barcelona had grown in importance between the 12th and the 14th centuries, and began to falter only when maritime emphasis shifted to the Atlantic after 1492. Despite Madrid's becoming the permanent seat of government in 1562, Catalonia continued to enjoy autonomous rights and privileges until 1714 when, in reprisal for having backed the pretender to the Spanish throne, all institutions and expressions of Catalonian nationalism were suppressed by the triumphant Felip V. Not until the 19th century would Barcelona's industrial growth bring about a *Renaixença* (renaissance) of nationalism and a cultural flowering redolent of the city's former opulence.

The tradition of independence nevertheless survived intact, and on numerous occasions Catalonia has revolted against the central authority of Madrid. During the civil war, Barcelona was a Republican stronghold and base for many anarchists and Communists. As a result, during the Franco dictatorship, Catalan identity and language were both suppressed, through such devices as book burning, the renaming of streets and towns, and the banning of the use of Catalan in schools and the media. But this repression had little lasting effect, for the Catalans have jealously guarded their language and culture and still only reluctantly think of themselves as Spaniards.

Catalonian home rule was granted after Franco's death in 1975, and in 1980 the ancient Generalitat, Catalunya's autonomous parliament, was reinstated. Catalan is now heard on every street, eagerly promoted through free classes funded by the Generalitat. Street names are now in Catalan, and newspapers, radio stations, and a TV channel publish and broadcast in Catalan. The circular Catalan *sardana* is danced regularly all over town. The triumphant culmination of this rebirth has, of course, been the staging of the Olympics in 1992. Stadia and pools were renovated, new harborside promenades created, and an entire set of railway tracks moved to make way for the Olympic Village. Not content to limit themselves to Olympics building projects, Barcelona's last two mayors have presided over the creation of an architecture student's paradise.

It's best not to visit in summer, when Barcelona swelters. Winters are characterized by clear blue skies and relatively mild temperatures. Rains tend to come only during the change of seasons in early November and late February.

Essential Information

Arriving and Departing by Plane

All international and domestic flights arrive at the stunning glass, steel, and marble **El Prat de Llobregat Airport,** 14 km (8½ mi) south of Barcelona, just off the main highway to Castelldefels and Sitges. For information on arrival and departure times, call Iberia at the airport (tel. 93/401–3131, 401–3535 at night; for general information, tel. 93/301–3993 for InforIberia, or 93/302–7656 for Iberia international reservations and reconfirmations). The only airlines with direct flights from the United States to Barcelona are TWA and Delta.

Between the Airport and Downtown Check first to see if your hotel provides a free shuttle service. Otherwise, you have the option of train, bus, taxi, or renting a car to drive yourself in.

By Train The train from the airport to Sants Station in the city leaves every 30 minutes between 6:12 AM and 10:42 PM (Sants–airport 5:40 AM–10:12 PM) and takes 20 minutes. There are also trains every 30 minutes to and from Plaça de Catalunya Station: airport–Plaça de Catalunya 6:12 AM–10:12 PM and Plaça de Catalunya–airport 6:05 AM–10:05 PM. The fare is 400 pesetas.

By Bus The Aerobus leaves the airport for Plaça de Catalunya every 15 minutes (6:25 AM–11 PM) on weekdays and every 30 minutes (6:45 AM–10:45 PM) on weekends. From Plaça de Catalunya to the airport, it leaves every 15 minutes (5:30 AM–10 PM) on weekdays and every 30 minutes (6:00 AM–10 PM) on weekends. The fare is 450 pesetas.

By Taxi A cab from the airport to downtown costs from 2,500 to 3,000 pesetas.

By Car By following signs to the Centre Ciutat, you will enter the city along Gran Via. The journey to the center of town can take anywhere from 15 to 45 minutes depending on traffic conditions.

Arriving and Departing by Car, Train, and Bus

By Car Barcelona is notorious for its parking difficulties, so there is a lot to be said for not coming by car. However, if you are prepared to pay 3,000 pesetas per day for a parking lot, of which there are plenty, and brave the hectic driving conditions, a car can be a convenient and independent way of seeing the city.

By Train Almost all long-distance and international trains arrive and depart from **Estació de Sants** (Sants Station; Plaça Països Catalans, tel. 93/490–0202). There is another station on Passeig de Gràcia (corner of Aragó, tel. 93/490–0202), where some trains stop before going on to, or after leaving, Sants. The **Estació de França,** near the port, handles long-distance trains to and from France.

By Bus Barcelona has no central bus station, but most buses to Spanish destinations operate from the **Estació Norte–Vilanova** (at the end of Av. Vilanova, a couple of blocks east of the Arc de Triomf, tel. 93/245–2528). Most international buses arrive at and depart from **Estació Autobuses de Sants** (Carrer Viriato, next to Sants train station, tel. 93/490–4000). Scores of independent companies operate from depots dispersed about town (*see* Barcelona Excursions, *below*).

Getting Around

Modern Barcelona, above the Plaça de Catalunya, is built on a grid system, though there's no helpful coordinated numbering system. The old town, from the Plaça de Catalunya to the port, is a labyrinth of narrow streets, and you'll need a good street map to get around. Most sightseeing can be done on foot—you won't have any choice in the Gothic Quarter—but you'll need to use the metro or buses to link sightseeing areas. If you're using an old map, you'll find that all the street names are now written in Catalan. For general information on the city's public transport, call 93/412–0000. Public-transport maps showing bus and metro routes are available free from booths in Plaça de Catalunya.

By Metro The subway is the fastest and cheapest way of getting around, as well as the easiest to use. You pay a flat fare of 125 pesetas, no matter how far you travel, but it is more economical to buy a Targeta T-2 (valid for metro and FF. CC. Generalitat trains, Tramvía Blau [blue tram], and Montjuïc Funicular; *see below*) costing 650 pesetas for 10 rides. It runs 5 AM–11 PM (until 1 AM on weekends and holidays).

By Bus City buses run daily from 5:30 AM to 11:30 PM. Fares are 125 pesetas (140 pesetas Sundays and holidays); for multiple journeys purchase a Targeta T-1, costing 700 pesetas and good for 10 rides (valid for the same as T-2 plus buses). Route maps are displayed at bus stops. Note that those with a red band always have a stop at a central square— Catalunya, Universitat, or Urquinaona—and blue indicates a night bus. From June 23 to September 17, 10 AM–7 PM, bus No. 100 operates on a circuit that takes in all the important sights. A day's ticket, which you can buy on the bus, costs 1,000 pesetas (750 pesetas half-day) and also covers the fare for the Tramvía Blau, funicular, and Montjuïc cable car across the port.

By Taxi Taxis are black and yellow and, when available for hire, show a green light. The meter starts at 350 pesetas (lasts for 6 minutes), and there are supplements for luggage, night travel, Sundays and fiestas, rides from a station or to the airport, and for going to or from the bullring or a soccer match. There are cab stands all over town; cabs may also be flagged down on the street. Make sure the driver puts on his meter. To phone a cab, try 93/387–1000, 93/490–2222, or 93/357–7755.

By Cable Car and Funicular Montjuïc Funicular is a cog railroad that runs from the junction of Avinguda Paral.lel and Nou de la Rambla to the Miramar Amusement Park on Montjuïc (Paral.lel metro). It operates weekends and

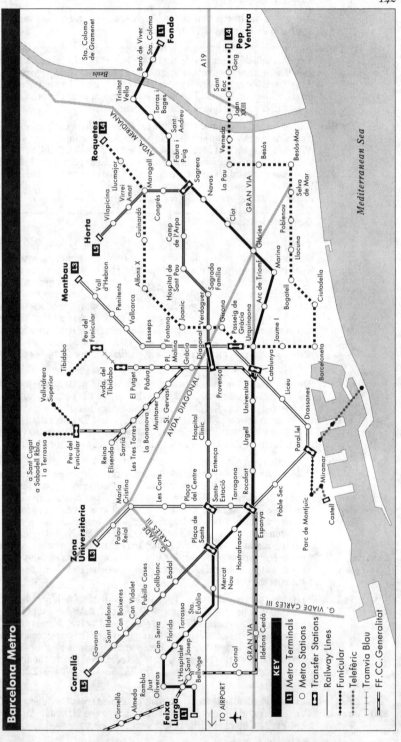

Barcelona Metro

fiestas 11 AM–8 PM in winter, and daily 11 AM–9:30 PM in summer; the fare is 125 pesetas. A cable car (*teleféric*) then takes you from the amusement park up to Montjuïc Castle (in winter, operates weekends and fiestas 11–2:45 and 4–7:30; in summer, daily 11:30 AM–9 PM; fare: 350 pesetas).

A Transbordador Aeri Harbor Cable Car runs between Miramar and Montjuïc across the harbor to Torre de Jaume I on Barcelona *moll* (jetty), and on to Torre de Sant Sebastià at the end of Passeig Nacional in Barceloneta. You can board at either stage. Fare: 700 pesetas (850 pesetas round-trip). Operates Oct.–June, weekdays noon–5:45, weekends noon–6:15; June–Oct., daily 11–9.

To reach Tibidabo summit, take the metro to Avinguda de Tibidabo, then the Tramvía Blau (single fare: 150 pesetas) to Peu del Funicular, and the Tibidabo Funicular (single fare: 300 pesetas) from there to the Tibidabo fairground. It runs every 30 minutes, 7:05 AM–9:35 PM ascending, 7:25 AM–9:55 PM descending.

By Boat Golondrinas harbor boats operate short harbor trips from the Portal de la Pau, near the Columbus Monument. Fare: 350 pesetas for a half-hour trip. Depart fall and winter, daily 11–5 (6 on weekends); spring, daily 11–6 (7 on weekends); summer, daily 11–9.

Important Addresses and Numbers

Tourist Information Tourist offices dealing with Barcelona itself are at **Sants Estació** (open daily 8–8), **Estació França** (open daily 8–8), **Palau de Congressos** (Av. María Cristina s/n, open 10–8 during trade fares and congresses only), **Ajuntament** (Plaça Sant Jaume, open June 24–Sept., Mon.–Fri. 9–8; Sat. 8:30–2:30), and **Palau de la Virreina** (La Rambla 99, open June 24–Sept., Mon.–Sat. 9–9; Sun. 10–2). Those with information about Catalunya and Spain are at **El Prat Airport** (tel. 93/478–4704, open Mon.–Sat. 9:30–8; Sun. 9:30–3) and **Gran Via de les Corts Catalanes 658,** near the Ritz Hotel (tel. 93/301–7443, open weekdays and Sun. 9–7; Sat. 9–2).

In summer (July 24–September 15), **tourist information aides** patrol the Gothic Quarter and Ramblas area 9 AM–9 PM; they travel in pairs (one of each sex), and you can recognize them by their uniforms of red shirts, white trousers or skirts, and *i* badges.

American Visitors' Bureau: Gran Via 591, between Rambla de Catalunya and Balmes, 3rd floor (tel. 93/301–0150/0032).

Consulates **U.S.:** Pg. Reina Elisenda 23, tel. 93/280–2227; **Canadian:** Via Augusta 125, tel. 93/209–0634; **U.K.:** Diagonal 477, tel. 93/419–9044.

Emergencies **Tourist Attention,** a service provided by the local police department (Guardia Urbana; Ramblas 43, tel. 93/317–7016; open 24 hours), will provide assistance if you've been the victim of a crime, need medical or psychological help, or need temporary documents in the event of loss of the originals. It has English interpreters.

Other emergency services are as follows. **Police:** National Police, tel. 091; Municipal Police, tel. 092; main police station, Via Laietana 43, tel. 93/301–6666. **Ambulance:** Creu Roja, tel. 93/300–2020. **Hospital:** Hospital Clinic (metro: Hospital Clinic, blue line), Villarroel 170, tel. 93/454–6000/7000. **Emergency Doctors:** tel. 061.

English-language Bookstores **El Corte Inglés** in Plaça Catalunya sells a few English guidebooks and novels, but the selection is very limited. For more variety, try **English Bookshop** (Calaf 52, tel. 93/239–9908), **Jaimes Bookshop** (Passeig de Gràcia 64, tel. 93/215–3626), **Laie** (Pau Claris 85, tel. 93/

318–1357), **Llibreria Francesa** (Passeig de Gràcia 91, tel. 93/215–1417), **Come In** (Provença 203, tel. 93/253–1204), or **Llibreria Bosch** (Ronda Universitat 11, tel. 93/317–5308, and Roselló 24, tel. 93/321–3341). The bookstore at the **Palau de la Virreina** at La Rambla 99 also offers a selection of some of the better books on Barcelona in English.

Late-night Pharmacies Look in any of the local newspapers under "Farmacias de Guardia" for addresses of those whose turn it is to be open late night and 24 hours.

Travel Agencies **American Express** (Roselló 257, on the corner of Passeig de Gràcia, tel. 93/217–0070), **Iberia**'s central office (Passeig de Gràcia 30, Diputació 258, tel. 93/410–3382), **Wagons-Lits Cook** (Passeig de Gràcia 8, tel. 93/317–5500), and **Bestours** (Diputación 241, tel. 93/487–8580).

Car and Motorcycle Rental **Atesa** (Balmes 141, tel. 93/237–8140), **Avis** (Casanova 209, tel. 93/209–9533), **Hertz** (Tuset 10, tel. 93/217–3248), and **Vanguard** (cars and motorcycles, Londres 31, tel. 93/439–3880).

Bicycle Rental **Bicitram** (Marquès de l'Argentera 15, tel. 93/792–2841) and **Los Filicletos** (Passeig de Picasso 38, tel. 93/319–7811).

Guided Tours

Orientation Tours City sightseeing tours are run by **Julià Tours** (Ronda Universitat 5, tel. 93/317–6454) and **Pullmantur** (Gran Via 635, tel. 93/318–5195). Tours leave from these terminals, though it may be possible to be picked up from your hotel. Prices are 3,300 pesetas (a half day) and 8,000 pesetas (a full day).

Special-Interest and Walking Tours The main organization for walking tours is **Terra Endins** (Ausias Marc 49, tel. 93/232–2413). Every month this excellent group produces a new agenda of cultural visits. There's usually one visit per day (but not every day), and the cost for nonmembers is 350 pesetas. If you are a serious Gaudí enthusiast, contact **Amics de Gaudí** (Friends of Gaudí; Av. Pedralbes 7, tel. 93/204–5250) well ahead of your visit. The Tourist Information office in the Palau de la Virreina at La Rambla 99 also rents cassettes with walking tours that follow footprints painted—different colors for different tours—on sidewalks through Barcelona's most interesting spots. The do-it-yourself method is to pick up the guides produced by the Tourist Office, *Discovering Romanesque Art* and *Discovering Modernist Art*, which outline itineraries for all of Catalunya.

Personal Guides Contact the **Barcelona Tourist Guide Association** (tel. 93/345–4221) or the **Barcelona Guide Bureau** (tel. 93/268–2422) for a list of English-speaking guides.

Excursions These are run by **Julià Tours** and **Pullmantur** and are booked as above. The principal trips are either full- or half-day tours to Montserrat to visit the monastery and shrine of the famous Moreneta, Catalonia's beloved Black Virgin; or a full-day trip to the Costa Brava resorts, including a boat cruise to Lloret de Mar.

Exploring Barcelona

Orientation

Barcelona is made up of two distinct and contrasting parts. The old city lies between Plaça de Catalunya and the port. Above it is the grid-patterned extension built after the city's third set of walls were torn down in 1860, known as Eixample, where most of the Moderniste architecture is to be found.

Tour 1 explores the Gothic Quarter, with its wealth of medieval buildings, among them the cathedral and the Picasso Museum. Tour 2 leads you along the Ramblas, Barcelona's most famous street, taking in such highlights as the Columbus Monument and Gaudí's Palau Güell. Tour 3 works its way up Passeig de Gràcia, past numerous Moderniste buildings, and ends with a visit to Gaudí's famous cathedral of the Sagrada Família. Tour 4 starts with Gaudí's Parc Güell and continues to Tibidabo and then Pedralbes. Our final two circuits take you to the city's two downtown parks, Ciutadella and Montjuïc, flanking the old city and linked by a cable-car ride high across the port. Montjuïc was the hub of Olympic activity in 1992.

Highlights for First-time Visitors

Casa Milà (*see* Tour 3)
Cathedral (*see* Tour 1)
Miró Foundation (*see* Tour 6)
National Museum of Catalan Art (*see* Tour 6)
Olympic Stadium (*see* Tour 6)
Palau Güell (*see* Tour 2)
Palau de la Música (*see* Tour 5)
Parc Güell (*see* Tour 4)
Picasso Museum (*see* Tour 1)
The Ramblas (*see* Tour 2)
Sagrada Família (*see* Tour 3)
Santa Maria del Mar (*see* Tour 1)
Tibidabo, on a clear day (*see* Tour 4)

Tour 1: The Barri Gòtic (Gothic Quarter)

Numbers in the margin correspond to points of interest on the Tour 1: The Barri Gòtic map.

Parts of the Barri Gòtic and the Barri Xines (*see* Tour 2) received a spectacular sprucing up as part of the Olympic preparations. Wandering off into the heart of the quarter, you will come across squares freshly begot by the demolition of whole blocks and the planting of fully grown palms. Bag-snatching, alas, is common in these parts, so exercise caution at all times.

We begin on **Plaça de la Seu,** where on Saturday afternoon and Sunday morning the citizens of Barcelona gather to dance the *sardana,* a somewhat demure circular dance, though a great symbol of Catalan pride. Climb the steps to the magnificent Gothic **catedral** (cathedral), built from 1298 to 1450 (the spire and neo-Gothic facade were added in 1892). Architects of Catalan Gothic churches strove to make the high altar visible to the entire congregation—hence, the unusually wide central nave and slender side columns. Highlights are the beautifully carved choir stalls, Santa Eulàlia's tomb in the crypt, the battle-scarred crucifix in the Lepanto Chapel, and the tall cloisters surrounding a tropical garden. *Open daily 7:45–1:30 and 4–7:45.*

❷ Around the corner is the **Museu Frederic Marès** (Frederic Marès Museum), where you can browse for hours among the miscellany assembled by sculptor-collector Frederic Marés. Displayed here are everything from paintings and polychrome crucifixes to pipes and

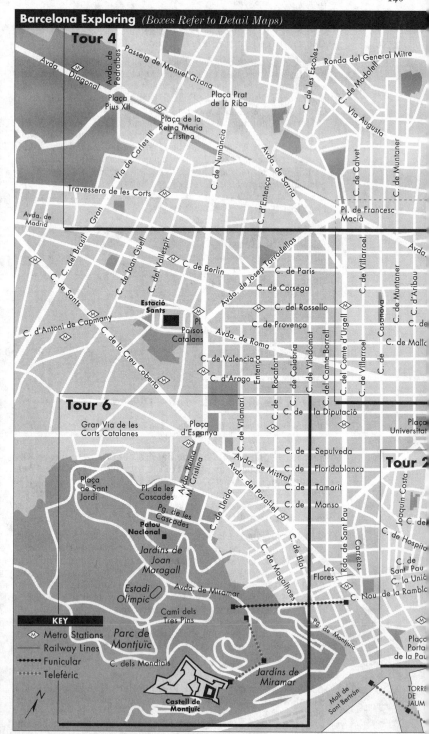

Barcelona Exploring *(Boxes Refer to Detail Maps)*

Tour 4

Avda. Diagonal

Avda. de Pedralbes

Passeig de Manuel Girona

Ronda del General Mitre

C. de les Escoles

C. de Modolell

Via Augusta

Plaça Pius XII

Plaça Prat de la Riba

Plaça de la Reina Maria Cristina

Via de Carles III

C. de Numància

Avda. de Sarrià

C. de Calvet

C. de Muntaner

Travessera de les Corts

Gran

Pl. de Francesc Macià

Avda. de Madrid

C. del Brasil

C. de Sants

C. de Joan Güell

C. del Vallespir

C. de Berlín

Avda. de Josep Tarradellas

C. de París

C. de Villarroel

Avda.

C. de Muntaner

C. d'Aribau

C. de Corsega

Estació Sants

Pl. Països Catalans

C. del Rossello

C. de Provença

Casanova

C. de

C. d'Antoni de Capmany

C. de la Creu Coberta

Avda. de Roma

C. del Comte d'Urgell

C. de Villarroel

C. de Mallo

C. de Valencia

Entença

Rocafort

de Calabria

C. de Viladomat

C. del Comte Borrell

C. de

C. d'Arago

C. de

C. de

la Diputació

Plaça Universitat

Tour 6

Gran Vía de les Corts Catalanes

Plaça d'Espanya

C. de Vilamari

C. de Sepulveda

Avda. de Mistral

C. de Floridablanca

Tour 2

Plaça de Sant Jordi

Pl. de les Cascades

Avda. Reina M. Cristina

Avda. del Paral·lel

C. de Tamarit

C. de Manso

Joaquin Costa

C. del

C. de Hospita

Pg. de les Cascades

Palau Nacional

C. de Lleida

Rda. de Sant Pau

C. de Sant Pau

C. la Unió

de la Rambla

Jardins de Joan Maragall

Estadi Olímpic

Avda. de Miramar

C. de Magalhaes

Carretes

Les Flores

C. Nou

Camí dels Tres Pins

C. de Blai

Plaça Porta de la Pau

Parc de Montjuïc

C. dels Mondials

Pg. de Montjuïc

Jardins de Miramar

Moll de Sant Bertrán

TORRE DE JAUM

Castell de Montjuïc

KEY

- ⓜ Metro Stations
- —— Railway Lines
- ●●● Funicular
- ····· Telefèric

N

TO TIBIDABO

Parc Güell

Parc del Guinardó

Plaça de Lesseps

Trav. de Dalt

C. Gran de Gràcia

Menéndez Pelayo

Verdi

C. de Sant Salvador

C. de la Providència

C. de les Camèlies

Plaça Alfons el Savi

C. de L'Escorial

C. de Pl. I Margall

Ronda del Guinardó

Travessera de Gràcia

Trav. de Gràcia

Tour 3

Diagonal

Plaça de Joan Carles I

C. de Còrsega

C. del Rosselló

C. de Indústria

C. de Bailén

Passeig de S. Joan

C. de Nápoles

C. de Sicília

C. de Sardenya

C. de Marina

Avda. de Gaudí

C. de Indústria

C. del Rosselló

C. de Provença

C. de Cartagena

venca

C. de Balmes

Rambla de Catalunya

Passeig de Gràcia

C. de Pau Claris

C. de Roger Llúria

C. de València

C. d'Aragó

Consell de Cent

C. de Roger de Flor

Avda. Diagonal

Temple Expiatori de la Sagrada Família

C. de València

C. d'Aragó

C. de Consell de Cent

C. de la Diputació

Plaça Tetuán

C. del Bruc

C. de Girona

C. de Bailén

P. de Carles I

Gran Vía de les Corts Catalanes

C. de Ribes

i

Pelai

Plaça de Catalunya

C. Sta. Anna

Pl. Urquinaona

Ronda S. Pere

Jonqueres

S. Pere Més Alt

S. Pere Més Baix

C. de Casp

Arc del Triomf

C. d'Ausias Marc

Estació Norte Vilanova (Bus Station)

C. Dels

Avda. de la Meridiana

C. de Tànger

C. de Sancho de Avila

C. dels Almogàvers

La Rambla

arme

Avda. Catedral

Tour 1

Pl. St. Jaume

C. Ferran

Via Laietana

C. Princesa

C. del Comerç

Passeig de Lluís Companys

Passeig Pujadas

Pg. Picasso

Passeig de Carles I

C. de Pamplona

C. d'Alaba

C. de Pere IV

C. de Pujades

C. de Lutxana

C. Ciutat

Passeig del Born

Plaça Reial

C. Ample

Pl. d'Antoni López

Pg. de Colom

i **Estació França**

Parc de la Ciutadella

C. de Wellington

Avda. del Bogatell

C. de Llull

Avda. d'Icària

Vila Olímpica

Avda. Litoral Costat Muntanya

Moll d'Espanya

Moll de Barceloneta

BARCELONETA

Passeig Marítim

Avda. d'Icària

Parc de Mar

Tour 5

0   450 yards

0   450 meters

Mediterranean Sea

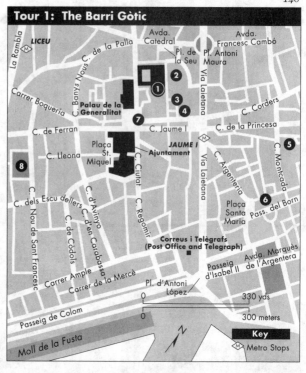

Tour 1: The Barri Gòtic

walking sticks. *Plaça Sant Iu 5. Admission: 350 pesetas, children under 18 and students free. Open Tues.–Sun. 10–7:30; closed Mon.*

❸ The neighboring **Plaça del Rei** embodies the very essence of the Gothic Quarter. After Columbus's first voyage to America, the Catholic Monarchs received him in the Saló del Tinell, a magnificent banquet hall built in 1362. Other ancient buildings around the square are the Palau Lloctinent (Lieutenant's Palace), the 14th-century chapel of Santa Àgata, and the Palau Padellàs.

❹ The latter houses the **Museu d'Història de la Ciutat** (City History Museum), which allows you to trace the evolution of the city. Founded by a Carthaginian, Hamilcar Barca, in about 230 BC, Barcelona shortly passed into the hands of the Romans during the Punic Wars. It didn't expand much until the Middle Ages, when trading links with Genoa and Venice began its long and illustrious mercantile tradition. Look for the plans submitted for the 19th-century extension, Eixample, to see how different the city would have looked had the radial plan of Antoni Rovira Trias not been blocked by cost-conscious bureaucrats in Madrid. Downstairs are some well-lighted Roman excavations. *Palau Padellàs, Carrer del Veguer 2. Admission: 350 pesetas. Open Tues.–Sat. 9–8, Sun. 9–1:30, Mon. 3:30–8.*

Cross Via Laietana, walk down Carrer de la Princesa, and turn right into Carrer Montcada. This narrow street contains one of
❺ Barcelona's most popular attractions, the **Museu Picasso** (Picasso Museum). Two 15th-century palaces provide a handsome, if somewhat inappropriate, setting for collections donated in 1963 and 1970, first by Picasso's secretary, and then by the artist himself. Although it contains very few of his major works, there is plenty here

to warrant a visit, including childhood sketches, pictures from his Blue Period, and his famous 1950s Cubist variations on Velázquez's *Las Meninas. Carrer Montcada 15–19. Admission: 650 pesetas, children under 18 and students free. Open Tues.–Sat. 10–8, Sun. 10–3; closed Mon.*

Time Out At the bottom of Carrer Montcada, a cluster of leather wineskins announces **Xampanyet,** a traditional tiled bar, popular for its house *cava* (sparkling white wine) and delicious Catalan *tapas* (savory tidbits). Opposite is **La Pizza Nostra,** a good place for a cup of coffee or a pizza and a glass of wine.

Carrer Montcada leads to Passeig del Born, an avenue lined with
❻ late-night cocktail bars. Adjoining the near end is the apse of **Santa Maria del Mar,** the most perfect of all Barcelona's Gothic churches. It was built from 1329 to 1383 in fulfillment of a vow made a century earlier by Jaume I to build a church for the Virgin of the Sailors. Its stark beauty is enhanced by a lovely rose window, soaring columns, and unusually wide vaulting. It is a fashionable place for weddings, and if you pass by on a Saturday afternoon, you are very likely to discover how Catalans perform this ceremony. *Open Mon.–Fri. 9–12:30 and 5–8; closed weekends.*

Walk up Carrer Argenteria to Via Laietana, recross it, and walk up
❼ Carrer de Ferran to **Plaça Sant Jaume,** a cobbled square in the heart of the Gothic Quarter, built in the 1840s. The two imposing buildings facing each other across the square are much older. The 15th-century **Ajuntament** (City Hall) to the left has an impressive black and burnished gold mural (1928) by Josep Maria Sert and the famous Saló de Cent, from which the Council of One Hundred ruled the city between 1372 and 1714. You can wander into the courtyard, but to visit the interior, you will need to ask permission in the office beforehand. The **Palau de la Generalitat,** opposite, seat of the autonomous Catalan government, is an elegant 15th-century palace with a lovely courtyard and first-floor patio with orange trees. The room whose windows you can see at the front is the Saló de Sant Jordi (St. George), dragon-slaying patron saint of Catalunya, as well as of England. For security reasons, you can visit the Generalitat only on the day of Sant Jordi, April 23.

Continue along Carrer de Ferran, with its attractive 19th-century shops and numerous Moderniste touches, and turn left at the end,
❽ through arches to the **Plaça Reial.** In this beautiful 19th-century arcaded square, newly repainted yellow houses overlook the wrought-iron Fountain of the Three Graces and lamp posts designed by a young Gaudí in 1879. Sidewalk cafés line the whole square. It has acquired quite a reputation for drug pushers, who form a lethargic barrier at the entrances to the square. They're easily avoided, and a heavy police presence discourages all but the most determined, so don't be put off. The most colorful time to come is on Sunday morning, when crowds gather at the stamp and coin stalls and listen to soapbox orators. At night it is the center for downtown nightlife. From here, you can saunter through to the Rambla.

Tour 2: La Rambla (Les Rambles)

Numbers in the margin correspond to points of interest on the Tour 2: La Rambla map.

Barcelona's most famous street is a snaking avenue of 24-hour newspaper kiosks, flower stalls, and bird sellers, along which traffic plays second fiddle to the endless *paseo* (stroll) of locals and visitors alike; it is the street that Federico García Lorca called the only one in the world he wished would never end. The whole avenue is referred to as Les Rambles (in Catalan) or **La Rambla** but each section has its own name: Rambla Santa Monica is at the southern end.

As you walk south from Plaça Reial toward the sea, Barri Xines (Chinatown), the notorious red-light district, is on your right. The Chinese never had much of a presence there, and the area is ill-famed for prostitutes, drug pushers, and street thieves.

❾ At the foot of the Rambla, take an elevator to the top of the **Monument a Colom** (Columbus Monument) for a breathtaking view over the city. The entrance is on the harbor side of the monument. *Admission: 350 pesetas adults, 150 pesetas children. Open June 24–Sept. 24, daily 9–9; Sept. 25–June 23, Tues.–Sat. 10–2 and 4–8, Sun. 10–7; closed Mon.*

Ahead on Moll de Barcelona you can see part of the redeveloped port area, comprising offices, fountains, shopping arcades, and new ferry terminals. You can also board the cable car that crosses the harbor to Montjuïc or board a Golondrina boat for a trip around the port (*see* Getting Around, *above*).

❿ Heading by land toward Montjuïc brings you to the **Museu Marítim** (Maritime Museum), housed in the 13th-century Drassanes Reials (Royal Dockyards). This superb museum is full of ships, including a spectacular life-size reconstructed galley, figureheads, nautical gear, and several early navigational charts. *Plaça Portal de la Pau 1. Admission: 350 pesetas. Open Tues.–Sat. 10–2 and 4–7, Sun. 10–2; closed Mon.*

⓫ Turn back up the Rambla, and a little way up turn left into Carrer Nou de la Rambla. At No. 3 is **Palau Güell.** Antoni Gaudí built this mansion in 1886–89 for his patron, a textile baron named Count Eusebi de Güell, and it projected the architect into the international limelight. The prominent Catalan emblem between the parabolic entrance gates attests to the nationalist leanings that Gaudí shared with Güell. The facade is a dramatic foil for the treasure house inside, where spear-shaped Art Nouveau columns frame the windows and prop up a series of minutely detailed wood ceilings. On the roof you can see good examples of Gaudí's decorative chimneys. *Admission: 350 pesetas. Temporarily open only at special hours due to renovations; afternoons 4–8 are a good time to try.*

⓬ Return to the Rambla and continue to the corner of Carrer de Sant Pau to view what remains of the **Gran Teatre del Liceu** (Opera House). Long considered one of Barcelona's most cherished jewels, the Liceu was gutted by fire in early 1994. Diva Montserrat Caballé stood on the Rambla in tears as this beloved venue was consumed by a mid-morning fire, the origins of which have been the subject of much speculation. The restoration of this landmark, one of world's oldest and most beautiful opera houses, will continue into 1996.

⓭ The next stretch of the Rambla is the most fascinating. The colorful paving stones on the Pla de la Boqueria were designed by Joan Miró. Turn right here to the adjoining squares, **Plaça del Pi** and **Plaça de Sant Josep Oriol,** among the Gothic Quarter's most tranquil. The church of **Santa Maria del Pi** is another good example of Catalan Gothic.

Time Out The **Bar del Pi** is a stylish and popular venue for better-heeled bohemians from the world over. The chairs outside move from one square

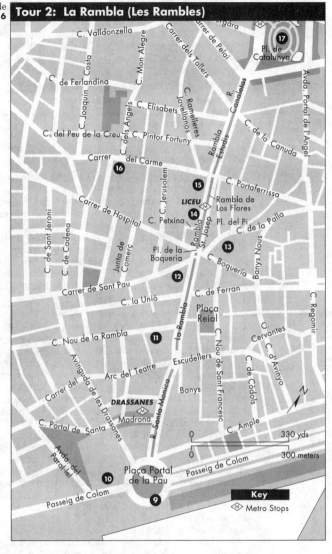

Tour 2: La Rambla (Les Rambles)

to another, following the sun, and are particularly popular on a Sunday morning.

⑭ Back on the Rambla, take a look inside the food market, **Mercat de Sant Josep o de la Boqueria** and at the **Antigua Casa Figueres,** a fine grocery and pastry store on the corner of Petxina, with a splendid mosaic facade and exquisite old fittings.

⑮ Farther on is the neoclassical **Palau de la Virreina,** built by a viceroy to Peru in 1778. It has recently been converted into a major exhibition center, and you should check out what's showing while you're here. *Rambla de les Flores 99, tel. 93/301–7775. Open Tues.–Sat. 10–2 and 4:30–9, Sun. 10–2, Mon. 4:30–9.*

⑯ Turn left down Carrer del Carme to the **Antic Hospital de la Santa Creu** (old hospital), surrounded by a cluster of other 15th-century buildings, today home to cultural and educational institutions. Particularly impressive and lovely is the courtyard of the Casa de Convalescència, with its Renaissance columns and scenes portrayed in *azulejos* (ceramic tiles).

⑰ The final stretch of the Rambla brings you to the **Plaça de Catalunya**, the banking and transport center of the city.

Tour 3: Eixample

Numbers in the margin correspond to points of interest on the Tour 3: Eixample map.

Above the Plaça de Catalunya, you come to an elegant area known as the Eixample. With the dismantling of the city walls in 1860, Barcelona embarked upon a vast expansion scheme, fueled by the return of rich colonials from America and an influx of provincial aristocrats who had sold their estates after the debilitating second Carlist War (1847–49). The grid street plan was the work of Ildefons Cerdà. Much of the building here was done at the height of the Modernisme movement. The principal thoroughfares of the Eixample are the Rambla de Catalunya and the Passeig de Gràcia, where some of the city's most elegant shops and cafés are to be found.

Moderniste houses are among Barcelona's special drawing cards, so
⑱ walk up Passeig de Gràcia until you come to the **Manzana de la Discòrdia** (Block of Discord), between Consell de Cent and Aragó. Its name is a pun on the word *manzana*, which means both "block" and "apple," alluding to the discordant architectural styles on the block and to the classical myth of the Apple of Discord. The houses here are quite fantastic: The floral Casa Lleó Morera (No. 35) was extensively rebuilt (1902–6) by Domènech i Montaner, and with permission you can visit the ornate interior, which now houses the Patronat de Turisme (tel. 93/302–0608). The pseudo-Gothic, pseudo-Flemish Casa Amatller (No. 41) is by Puig i Cadafalch and features a terraced gable. Next door is Gaudí's Casa Batlló, with a mottled facade that resembles a breaking wave. Nationalist symbolism is at work here: The scaly roof line represents St. George's dragon with his cross stuck into its tail. Walking left 1½ blocks down
⑲ Carrer d' Aragó, you come to Domènech's **Casa Montaner i Simó**, a former publishing house that has been beautifully converted to hold the work of the preeminent postwar Catalan painter Antoni Tàpies. Atop the building, Tàpies has added a tangled metal hairdo, entitled *Núvol i cadira (Cloud and Chair)*. The airy split-level Fundació Tàpies has temporary exhibitions and a library strong on Tàpies and Oriental art. *Admission: 450 pesetas. Open Tues.–Sun. 11–8; closed Mon.*

Back to Passeig de Gràcia, and our next stop—this time, on the
⑳ right—is Gaudí's **Casa Milà**, nicknamed La Pedrera (The Quarry), whose remarkable curving stone facade with ornamental balconies actually ripples its way around the corner of the block. In 1910 Barcelona's bourgeoisie were quite taken aback by the appearance of these cavelike apartments on their most fashionable street. From the roof, you have as good an opportunity as any of peering into the courtyards of Eixample blocks. *Passeig de Gràcia 92. Admission free. Open for guided visits Tues.–Sat. at 10, 11, noon, 1, and 4; closed Sun. and Mon.*

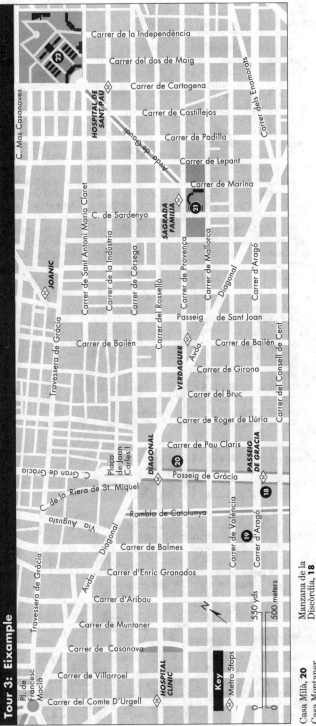

Tour 3: Eixample

Carrer de la Independència

Carrer del dos de Maig

Carrer de Cartagena

Carrer de Castillejos

Carrer de Padilla

Carrer de Lepant

Carrer de Marina

HOSPITAL DE SANT PAU

Carrer dels Enamorats

C. Mas Casanoves

Avda. de Gaudí

SAGRADA FAMILIA

C. de Sardenya

C. de Sant Antoni Maria Claret

JOANIC

Carrer de Sant Antoni Maria Claret

Carrer de la Indústria

Carrer de Còrsega

Carrer del Rosselló

Carrer de Provença

Carrer de Mallorca

Diagonal

Carrer d'Aragó

Passeig de Sant Joan

Travessera de Gràcia

Carrer de Bailèn

VERDAGUER

Avda.

Carrer de Bailèn

Carrer del Consell de Cent

Carrer de Girona

Carrer del Bruc

Carrer de Roger de Llúria

Carrer de Pau Claris

DIAGONAL

Plaça de Joan Carles I

C. Gran de Gràcia

PASSEIG DE GRACIA

Passeig de Gràcia

C. de la Riera de St. Miquel

Rambla de Catalunya

Carrer de València

Carrer d'Aragó

Via Augusta

Diagonal

Avda.

Carrer de Balmes

Carrer d'Enric Granados

Carrer d'Aribau

N

Carrer de Muntaner

Carrer de Casanova

Carrer de Villarroel

HOSPITAL CLINIC

Carrer del Comte D'Urgell

Travessera de Gràcia

Pl. de Francesc Macià

Key

◈ Metro Stops

0 ——— 550 yds

0 ——— 500 meters

Casa Milà, **20**
Casa Montaner
i Simó, **19**
Hospital de Sant
Pau, **22**

Manzana de la
Discòrdia, **18**
Temple Expiatori de la
Sagrada Família, **21**

Time Out You can ponder the vagaries of Gaudí's work over a drink in **Amarcord,** a terrace café in La Pedrera.

㉑ Now, take the metro from Diagonal (blue line) to Barcelona's most eccentric landmark, Antoni Gaudí's **Temple Expiatori de la Sagrada Família** (Expiatory Church of the Holy Family). Unfinished at his untimely death—Gaudí was run over by a tram and, unrecognized for several days, died in a pauper's ward in 1926—this striking and surreal creation will cause consternation or wonder, shrieks of protest or cries of rapture. During the civil war, in 1936, the citizens of Barcelona loved their crazy temple enough to spare it from the flames that engulfed all the other churches (except the cathedral). Gaudí envisaged three facades: Faith, Hope, and Charity, each with four towers collectively representing the 12 apostles. These, in turn, would be dwarfed by a giant central tower some 155 meters (500 ft) high, which is not yet in existence. An elevator (100 pesetas) takes visitors to the top of the east towers (or there are steps) for a spectacular bird's-eye view. Construction began again in 1940 but faltered due to confusion over Gaudí's plans. Current controversy centers on the sculptor Subirach's angular figures on the western facade, condemned by the city's intellectual elite as kitsch and the antithesis of Gaudí's lyrical style, and by religious leaders for depicting Christ in the nude.

Also visit the crypt, with a museum of Gaudí's scale models, photographs showing the progress of construction, and photographs of Gaudí's funeral, which, in terms of crowds lining the streets, would have satisfied a senior statesman. Gaudí, 74 when he died, is buried here. *Admission: 500 pesetas, children under 10 free. Open Nov.– Mar., daily 9–6; Apr.–June and Sept.–Oct., daily 9–7; July–Aug., daily 8–9.*

㉒ From here, stroll down Avinguda de Gaudí to Domènech's **Hospital de Sant Pau,** which demonstrates his preference for bricks over stone and is notable for its Mudéjar motifs and wards set individually among the gardens. You can board the metro here back to Diagonal.

Tour 4: Parc Güell, Tibidabo, and Pedralbes

Numbers in the margin correspond to points of interest on the Tour 4: Parc Güell, Tibidabo, and Pedralbes map.

㉓ Take the metro to Lesseps, where you can catch bus No. 24 to Gaudí's **Parc Güell.** Named after his main patron, it was originally intended as a hillside garden suburb on the English model, but only two of the houses were ever built. It is an Art Nouveau extravaganza, with a mosaic pagoda, undulating benches, and large multicolored lizards guarding a Moderniste grotto. *Open Oct.–Mar., daily 10–6, Apr.–June, daily 10–7, and July–Sept., daily 10–9.*

There's a small museum in an Alice in Wonderland house where Gaudí lived from 1906 to 1926, containing some of his eccentric furniture, decoration, and drawings. *Admission: 300 pesetas. Open Apr.–Oct., daily 10–2 and 4–7, Nov.–Mar., daily 10–2 and 4–6:30.*

㉔ Next, make for **Tibidabo** by a combination of bus Nos. 24 and 22, changing at the Plaça de Lesseps, or by taxi, which is a lot easier. At Avinguda Tibidabo, catch the Tramvia Blau, which connects with the funicular (for details, *see* Getting Around, *above*) to the summit. The views from this hill are legendary, but clear days are few and far between. The shapes that distinguish Tibidabo from below turn out

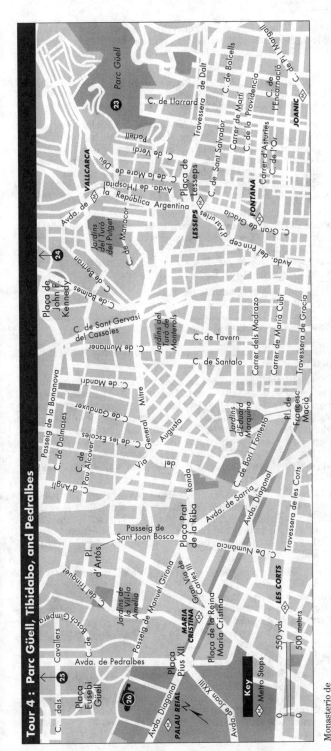

Tour 4 : Parc Güell, Tibidabo, and Pedralbes

Parc Güell

C. de Llarrard

Travessera de Dalt

C. de Balcells

Carrer de Martí

C. de la Providència

C. de l'Encarnació

JOANIC

VALLCARCA

C. de Verdi

C. del Portell

C. de la Mare de Déu

Avda. de l'Hospital

Plaça de Lesseps

C. de Sant Salvador

Carrer d'Astúries

FONTANA

C. de l'Or

Avda. de la República Argentina

LESSEPS

Gran de Gràcia

C. de Manacor

Jardins del Turó del Putget

Avda. del Príncep d'Astúries

Avda. de

Plaça de John F. Kennedy

C. de Balmes

C. de Berlvon

C. de Sant Gervasi del Cassoles

Jardins del Turó de Monterols

C. de Tavern

Carrer dels Madrazo

Carrer de Maria Cubí

Passeig de la Bonanova

C. de Muntaner

C. de Mandri

C. de Santaló

Carrer de Maria Cubí

Travessera de Gràcia

C. de Dalmases

C. de Ganduxer

Mitre

C. de les Escoles

C. de Pau Alcover

Via Augusta

General

Jardins d'Eduard Marquina

Pl. de Francesc Macià

C. d'Anglí

del

Ronda

C. de Bori i Fontestà

Passeig de Sant Joan Bosco

Plaça Prat de la Riba

Avda. de Sarrià

Avda. Diagonal

Cavallers

C. de Bosch i Gimpera

C. del Tinguet

Pl. d'Artós

Jardins de la Vil·la Amèlia

Passeig de Manuel Girona

Gran Via de Carles III

Travessera de les Corts

C. De Numància

LES CORTS

C. dels

Plaça Eusebi Güell

Avda. de Pedralbes

Plaça Pius XII

MARIA CRISTINA

Plaça de la Reina Maria Cristina

Avda. de Joan XXIII

PALAU REIAL

Avda. Diagonal

Key
Ⓜ Metro Stops

550 yds
500 meters

to be an ugly commercialized church, a vast radio mast, and the new 260-m (850-ft) communications tower. The misguided exploitation of this natural beauty spot is completed by a rather brash amusement park.

From Avinguda de Tibidabo (Plaça John F. Kennedy), take bus No. 22 to the end of the line. You pass through the picturesque suburb of Sarrià, at its heart an old village.

㉕ The bus drops you close to the **Monasterio de Pedralbes.** Founded by Reina (Queen) Elisenda for Clarist nuns in 1326, the convent has a triple-story Gothic cloister that is the finest in Barcelona. In the chapel are a beautiful stained-glass rose window and famous murals painted in 1346 by Ferrer Bassa, a Catalan much influenced by the Italian Renaissance. You can also visit the old living quarters. *Admission: 300 pesetas. Open Tues.–Sun. 9:30–2; closed Mon.*

Saunter down Avinguda de Pedralbes (or take bus No. 75) to the **㉖** **Palau Reial de Pedralbes,** built in the 1920s for King Alfonso XII and now home to the **Ceramics Museum,** a wide sweep of Spanish ceramic art from the 14th to the 18th century, with the influence of Moorish design techniques carefully documented. *Tel. 93/203–7501. Admission: 300 pesetas. Open Tues.–Sun. 9–2; closed Mon.*

From here you can board the metro (Palau Reial, green line) back to the center of town.

Tour 5: Ciutadella and Barceloneta

Numbers in the margin correspond to points of interest on the Tour 5: Ciutadella and Barceloneta map.

㉗ Start with the **Palau de la Música** on Carrer Amadeus Vives, just off the top of Via Laietana (metro: Urquinaona), a fantastic and flamboyant Moderniste building by Domènech i Montaner (1908) that rivals the best of Gaudí. The tiny ticket booths in the richly embellished columns are sadly now out of use. Try to get to a concert here, if only to see the interior, with its inverted stained-glass cupola (*see* The Arts and Nightlife, *below*). Otherwise you can make an appointment to see inside on Tuesday, Thursday, or Saturday (tel. 93/268–1000).

Continue along Carrer Sant Pere Més Alt to the Plaça Sant Pere and one of the oldest medieval churches in Barcelona, Sant Pere de les Puelles, which has beautiful stained glass and a stark interior. Make **㉘** your way out of this labyrinth to the **Arc del Triomf,** an imposing redbrick Moderniste arch built by Josep Vilaseca for the 1888 exhibition.

Stroll down the green center of Passeig Lluís Companys to the **Parc de la Ciutadella** (Citadel), Barcelona's main downtown park. The clearing dates from shortly after the War of the Spanish Succession, when Felipe V demolished some 2,000 houses to build a fortress and barracks for his soldiers, which, in turn, were pulled down in 1868 and replaced by gardens laid out by Josep Fontserè. In the park are a cluster of museums; the Catalan Parliament; and a zoo.

㉙ The arresting building as you enter the park is the **Castell dels Tres Dragons** (Castle of the Three Dragons), built by Domènech i Montaner as the café-restaurant for the 1888 exhibition. This became a workshop where Moderniste architects met to experiment with traditional crafts and exchange ideas. It is now home to the Zoological Museum. *Admission: 300 pesetas. Open Tues.–Sun. 9–2; closed Mon.*

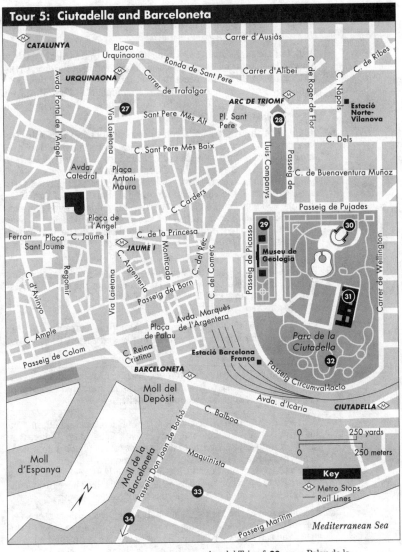

Tour 5: Ciutadella and Barceloneta

Arc del Triomf, **28**
Barceloneta, **33**
Castell dels Tres Dragons, **29**
Font de la Senyoreta del Paraïgua/Font d'Aurora, **30**

Palau de la Ciutadella, **31**
Palau de la Música, **27**
Telefèric, **34**
Zoo, **32**

Adjacent stand the Geology Museum and the beautiful Umbracle, whose black slats help create a jungle light for the valuable collection of tropical plants growing here.

Walk left through exotic trees and shrubs, not quite thickly enough planted to enable you to escape the sight and sound of the city, to the ③⓪ lake and **Font de la Senyoreta del Paraïgua** (Fountain of the Lady with the Umbrella) and behind it the monumental **Font d' Aurora** (Fountain of Aurora), Gaudí's first work while still a student, and the centerpiece of the 1888 exhibition.

③① Heading to the right brings you to the **Palau de la Ciutadella,** the only surviving remnant of Felipe's fortress, now shared by the Catalan Parliament and the Museu d'Art Modern (Museum of Modern Art). The latter is something of a misnomer because only a small handful of rooms are given over to contemporary Catalan artists. Its main strength is the collection produced in Barcelona of late-19th-century and early 20th-century works. This golden period of painting and bohemianism in Barcelona saw Picasso living here, famous artistic tertulias in Els Quatre Gats, and the rise of the Moderniste movement. *Admission: 500 pesetas. Open Mon. 3–7:30, Tues.–Sat. 9–7:30, Sun. 9–3.*

③② The excellent **zoo,** home to Snowflake, the world's only captive albino gorilla, occupies the whole bottom section of the park. *Admission: 1,000 pesetas, children under 3 free. Open Oct.–Mar., daily 10–5; Apr.–Sept., daily 9:30–7:30.*

The west gate of the park leads to Avinguda Marquès de l'Argentera, on the left of which is the lovely and recently renovated Estacío de França. Go left at Pla del Palau.

Time Out   Across the Pla del Palau, on Reina Cristina, **Can Paixano** is legendary for its inexpensive cavas, delicious tapas, and rapid turnover of customers. It doubles as an expensive delicatessen.

③③ Our next destination is the Old Quarter of **Barceloneta,** built in 1755 and traditionally the home of workers and fishermen. Today, it is rather run-down, and many of its interior streets have a deserted, somewhat threatening air. But at lunchtime its main thoroughfare, the Passeig Don Joan de Borbó, or Moll de la Barceloneta, comes strikingly to life when the citizens of Barcelona flock here to feast on the delicious seafood of its numerous no-frills restaurants.

③④ From the end of the Passeig Nacional, a **telefèric** (cable car) crosses the port to Montjuïc, offering a spectacular bird's-eye view of the city. (You can also board the cable car at the Torre de Jaume I near the Columbus Monument; *see* Tour 2: La Rambla, *above*.)

Tour 6: Montjuïc

Numbers in the margin correspond to points of interest on the Tour 6: Montjuïc map.

Montjuïc, the hill to the south of town, was named for the Jewish cemetery once located on its slopes, although an alternate explanation has it being named for the Roman deity Jove or Jupiter. The most dramatic approach is by way of the cross-harbor telefèric, but you can reach it from the Paral.lel or Espanya metro stop.

The telefèric drops you at the Jardins de Miramar, a 10-minute walk, straight ahead, to the Plaça de Dante and the entrance to the amusement park. If you are nostalgic for the days of rock and roll, you may want to look up Chus Martínez, onetime colleague of Bill Haley ánd Eddie Cochrane, who runs the Bali restaurant here. It's not unheard of for him to give an impromptu concert for his guests, so check this out when you get here.

From here, another small cable car (fare: 300 pesetas; Oct.–June 21, weekends 11–2:45 and 4–7:30; June 22–Sept., daily 11:30–9) takes 🟢**35** you up to the **Castell de Montjuïc.** Built in 1640 by rebels against Felipe IV, the castle has been stormed several times, most famously in 1705 by Lord Peterborough for Archduke Carlos of Austria. In 1808, during the Peninsular War, the castle was seized by the French under General Dufresne. Later, during an 1842 civil disturbance, Barcelona was bombed by a Spanish artillery battery from its heights. Today, it functions as a military museum housing the weapon collection of Frederic Marés. *Admission: 100 pesetas. Open Oct.–Mar., Tues.–Sat. 10–2 and 4–7, Sun. 10–2; Apr.–Sept., Tues.–Sat. 10–2 and 4–7, Sun. 10–8.*

The moat has been made into attractive gardens, with one side given over to an archery range. From the various terraces, there are panoramic views over the city and out to sea.

Descend by the same cable car or walk and continue along the 🟢**36** Avinguda de Miramar to the **Fundació Miró** (Miró Foundation), a gift from the artist Joan Miró to his native city and one of Barcelona's most exciting contemporary art galleries. The white, airy building was designed by Josep Lluís Sert and opened in 1975; an extension was added by Sert's pupil, Jaume Freixa, in 1988. Miró himself now rests in the cemetery on the southern slopes of Montjuïc. During the Franco regime, which he strongly opposed, Miró lived in self-imposed exile in Paris and in 1956 moved to Mallorca. When he died in 1983, the Catalans gave him a send-off amounting to a state funeral. *Admission: 600 pesetas. Open Tues.–Sat. 11–7 (Thurs. 11–9:30), Sun. 10:30–2:30; closed Mon.*

🟢**37** Farther along this avenue you arrive at the **Estadi Olímpic** (Olympic Stadium; tel. 93/424–0508: open weekdays 10–2 and 4–7, weekends 10–6). It was originally built for the Great Exhibition of 1929, with the idea that Barcelona would then host the 1936 Olympics (ultimately staged in Hitler's Berlin). After twice failing to gain the nomination, Barcelona celebrated the capture of its long-cherished goal by renovating the semiderelict stadium in time for 1992 and giving it a seating capacity of 70,000 people. Next door stands the futuristic Palau Sant Jordi Sports Palace, designed by the Japanese architect Arata Isozaki and built from the roof downward.

🟢**38** Descend now to the **Museu Nacional d'Art de Catalunya** (National Museum of Catalan Art), in the imposing **Palau Nacional,** also built in 1929 and recently renovated by Gae Aulenti, architect of the Musée d'Orsay in Paris. The Romanesque and Gothic art treasures, medieval frescoes, and altarpieces here are simply staggering. Many were removed from small churches and chapels in the Pyrenees during the 1920s to ward off the threat of exportation by art dealers. When possible, the works are being returned to their original homes or are being replicated, as with the famous *Pantocrator* fresco, a copy of which is now back in the Church of Sant Climent de Taüll. The museum also contains works by El Greco, Velázquez, and Zurbarán. *Admission: 600 pesetas. Open Tues.–Sun. 9–2; closed Mon.*

Downhill, to the right of the Palau Nacional as you leave it, is the 🟢**39** **Museu Arqueològic** (Archaeological Museum), which contains many important finds from the Greek ruins at Empúries, on the Costa

Tour 6: Montjuïc

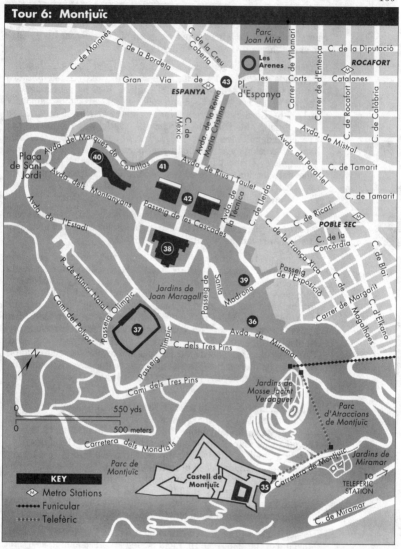

Brava. These are exhibited, along with fascinating objects from, and explanations of, Megalithic Spain. *Admission: 300 pesetas. Open Tues.–Sat. 9:30–1 and 4–7; Sun. 9:30–1; closed Mon.*

40 To the other side of the Palau Nacional is the **Poble Espanyol** (Spanish Village), created again for the 1929 Exhibition. It is a kind of Spain-in-a-bottle, with the local architectural styles of each province faithfully reproduced, enabling you to wander from the walls of Ávila to the wine cellars of Jerez. The most lively time to come is at night, for a concert or flamenco show. *Admission: 500 pesetas adults, 250 pesetas children under 14. Open daily 9 AM–3:30 AM.*

On the way down to Plaça d'Espanya, you pass the reconstructed
41 **Mies van der Rohe pavilion** (open daily 10–6), the German contribution to the 1929 Exhibition: interlocking planes of white marble, green onyx, and glass. Next comes the multicolored fountain in the
42 **Plaça de les Cascades.** Stroll down the wide esplanade past more exhibition halls to the large and somber **Plaça d'Espanya.** Across the
43 square is Les Arenes bullring, now the venue for theater performances and political rallies rather than bullfights. From here, you can take the metro or bus No. 38 back to Plaça de Catalunya.

What to See and Do with Children

Take the children to the **zoo** in Ciutadella to visit the world's only captive albino gorilla (*see* Tour 5: Ciutadella and Barceloneta, *above*). They'll also enjoy taking a trip across the harbor in one of the **Golondrinas boats.** Ride the **cable car** across the harbor to the **Amusement Park** on Montjuïc (*see* Tour 6: Montjuïc, *above*) or the Tramvia Blau (tram) and **funicular** up to the **fun fair** on Tibidabo (*see* Tour 4: Parc Güell, Tibidabo, and Pedralbes, *above*).

Young scientific minds work overtime in the **Museu de la Ciència** (Science Museum), just below Tibidabo, many of whose displays and activities are designed for children (over age 7). *Teodor Roviralta 55 (metro: Avinguda de Tibidabo and Tramvia Blau halfway), tel. 93/ 212–6050. Admission: 400 pesetas. Open Tues.–Sun. 10–8; closed Mon.*

Children also appreciate the sightseeing time saved by a visit to **Catalunya en Miniature** (Catalunya in Miniature), which comprises 60,000 square meters of the province's most famous buildings, including the complete works of Gaudí, scaled down. *Torrelles de Llobregat (17 km/10½ mi west of Barcelona), tel. 93/689–0960. Admission: weekdays, 750 pesetas adults, 300 pesetas children; weekends, 1,000 pesetas adults, 500 pesetas children.*

Above all, don't miss the fairy-tale extravaganza of the **Parc Güell** (*see* Tour 4: Parc Güell, Tibidabo, and Pedralbes, *above*); it's a popular playground for Barcelona's children.

Off the Beaten Track

Go to see the soccer club **F.C. Barcelona** play, preferably against Real Madrid. The massive Camp Nou stadium seats 130,000 spectators, and crowds frequently number over 100,000. Look in the museum, with its impressive array of trophies and five-screen video showing memorable goals in the history of one of Europe's most glamorous soccer clubs. *Arístides Maillol, tel. 93/330–9411. Museum admission: 350 pesetas, 100 pesetas students. Open Oct.–Mar., Tues.–Fri. 10–1 and 4–6, weekends 10–1 and 3–6, closed Mon.; Apr.–Sept., Mon.–Sat. 10–1 and 3–6; closed Sun.*

The **Collserola Tower** that now dwarfs Tibidabo is an architectural triumph erected during the 1992 Olympics amid a certain amount of controversy. What is incontrovertible is the splendid panorama over the city that this lookout point provides. To reach the tower, take the funicular up to Tibidabo; there is free transport to the tower from Plaza Tibidabo. *Tel. 93/211–7942. Admission: 600 pesetas. Open weekdays 11–9; Sat., Sun., and holidays 11–7.*

Explore the **Gràcia** area, above Diagonal. This used to be a separate village, and it retains a distinctive air of independence.

Hunt out the tiny **Shoe Museum** (Museu del Calçat) in a hidden corner of the Gothic Quarter, between the cathedral and the Bishop's Palace. The collection includes a pair of clown's shoes and a pair worn by Pablo Casals. *Plaça de Sant Felip Neri. Admission: 250 pesetas. Open Tues.–Sun. 11–2; closed Mon.*

Shopping

Shopping Districts Elegant shopping districts are the Passeig de Gràcia, Rambla de Catalunya, and Avinguda Diagonal up as far as Carrer Ganduxer. Try Carrer Tuset, above Diagonal, for small boutiques. For more affordable, more old-fashioned, and typically Spanish-style shops, explore the area between the Ramblas and Via Laietana, especially around Carrer de Ferran. The area around Plaça del Pi, from the Boqueria to Carrer Portaferrissa and Carrer de la Canuda, has fashionable stores, jewelry, and gift shops. Most shops are open weekdays 9–1:30 and 5–8; Saturday hours are generally the same, but some don't open in the afternoon; on Sundays virtually all are closed.

Specialty Stores
Antiques Carrer de la Palla and Carrer Banys Nous in the Gothic Quarter are lined with antiques shops full of old maps, books, paintings, and furniture. An antiques market is held every Thursday, 10–8, in Plaça del Pi. The **Centre d'Antiquaris** (Passeig de Gràcia 57) contains 75 antiques stores. Try **Gothsland** (Consell de Cent 331) for Moderniste design.

Art The greatest concentration of prestigious galleries is along Carrer Consell de Cent, between Passeig de Gràcia and Carrer Balmes. The best known are **Sala Gaspar** at 323, and **Galeria Ciento** at 347. Carrer Petritxol, which leads down into Plaça del Pi (*see* Tour 2, La Rambla) is also lined with art galleries, as are the Carrer Montcada (*see* Tour 1, Barri Gòtic) and around the Passeig del Born (also *see* Tour 1).

Boutiques/Fashion If you are after fashion and jewelry, you've come to the right place, because Barcelona makes all the headlines on Spain's booming fashion front. Check out **El Bulevard Rosa** (Passeig de Gràcia 53–55), a collection of boutiques that stock the very latest outfits. Others are on Avinguda Diagonal between Passeig de Gràcia and Carrer Ganduxer. **Adolfo Domínguez,** Spain's top designer, is at Passeig de Gràcia 35 and Diagonal 570; **Joaquim Berao,** a top jewelry designer, is at Roselló 277.

Design/Interiors At Passeig de Gràcia 102 is **Gimeno,** whose elegant displays range from unusual suitcases to the latest in furniture design. A couple of doors down, at 96, **Vinçon** is equally chic. Some 50 years old, it has steadily expanded through a rambling Moderniste house that was once the home of Moderniste poet/artist Santiago Rusiñol as well as the site of the studio of his colleague the painter Ramón Casas. It stocks everything from Filofaxes to handsome kitchenware. **Bd** (*Barcelona design*), at 291–293 Carrer Mallorca, located in another

Moderniste gem, Domènechi Muntaner's Casa Thomas, is another spectacular design store.

Department Stores The ubiquitous **El Corte Inglés** is at Plaça de Catalunya 14 and Diagonal 617 (metro: Maria Cristina). **Galerías Preciados,** now colonized by a host of English stores, from Dorothy Perkins to Marks and Spencer, is on Portal de L'Àngel and Plaça de Francesc Macià.

Food and Flea Markets The **Boqueria,** or Sant Josep Market, on the Rambla between Carrer del Carme and Carrer de Hospital, is a colorful and bustling food market, open Monday–Saturday. **Els Encants,** Barcelona's biggest flea market, is held Monday, Wednesday, Friday, and Saturday 8–7, at the end of Dos de Maig, on Plaça de les Glòries (metro: Glòries, red line). **Sant Antoni** market, at the end of Ronda Sant Antoni, is an old-fashioned food and clothes market, best on Sunday.

Sports

Participant Sports

Golf Barcelona is fortunate enough to be ringed by some excellent golf courses; be sure to call ahead to reserve tee times.

Around Barcelona **Reial Club de Golf El Prat** (08820 El Prat de Llobregat, tel. 93/379–0278), greens fees 6,000 pesetas and up. **Club de Golf de Sant Cugat** (08190 Sant Cugat del Vallès, tel. 93/674–3958), greens fees 5,000 pesetas. **Club de Golf Vallromanes** (08188 Vallromanes, tel. 93/568–0362), greens fees 3,500 pesetas weekdays, 6,000 pesetas weekends. **Club de Golf Terramar** (08870 Sitges, tel. 93/894–0580), greens fees 3,500–5,000 pesetas.

Farther Afield **Club de Golf Costa Brava.** La Masía, 17246 Santa Cristina d'Aro, tel. 972/83–71–50. Greens fees: 4,000–6,000 pesetas. **Club de Golf Pals.** Platja de Pals, 17256 Pals, tel. 972/63–70–09. Greens fees: 7,000 pesetas.

Gymnasiums Catalans are keen on fitness: You will see gymnasiums everywhere and in the Páginas Amarillas/Pàgines Grogues (Yellow Pages) under "Gimnasios/Gimnasis." Recommended is the new and exciting **Crack,** which has gym, sauna, pool, six squash courts, and paddle tennis. *Pasaje Domingo 7, tel. 93/215–2755. Admission: 2,000 pesetas for a day's membership plus small supplements for the courts.*

Swimming **Indoor** Try the **Club Natació Barceloneta** (Passeig Marítim, tel. 93/309–3412; admission: 500 pesetas) or the **Piscines Pau Negre-Can Toda** (Ramiro de Maetzu, tel. 93/213–4344; admission: 500 pesetas).

Outdoor Uphill from Parc Güell is the **Parc de la Creueta del Coll** (Castellterçol, tel. 93/416–2625; admission: 300 pesetas), which has a huge outdoor swimming pool (*see also* Tennis, *below*).

Tennis The cheapest place to play tennis is the **Complejo Deportivo Can Caralleu** (Can Caralleu Sports Complex), above Pedralbes. The complex includes two pools, indoor and out (cost: 500 pesetas). *Tel. 93/203-7874. Admission: 700 pesetas per hour daytime, 1,000 pesetas per hour at night. Open daily 8 AM–11 PM.*

There is also the upscale **Club Vall Parc.** *Carretera de la Rabassada 79, tel. 93/212-6789. Admission: 2,750 pesetas per hour daytime, 3,250 pesetas per hour at night. Open daily 8 AM–midnight.*

Beaches

Barceloneta This is the city's main beach and has become quite popular since being cleaned up for the Barcelona Olympics of 1992. There is now clean sand, surf, and perfectly decent swimming to be found just a 20-minute walk from the Rambla.

Others As you go north, the first fine beaches you come to are Arenys, Sant Pol, and Calella, reached by train from Passeig de Gràcia. **Sant Pol** is the pick, with a sandy bathing beach and a lovely old town. Generally, the farther north you go toward the Costa Brava, the better the beaches become.

Ten km (6 mi) south is the popular day resort of **Castelldefels**, with a series of good beachside restaurants and bars and a long, sandy beach for sunning and bathing, though it's windy.

Topless bathing is fine on all these beaches, but nudists should head up the Costa Brava or down the Costa Dorada.

Dining

Combining many of the best elements of France and Spain, Catalan cuisine is wholesome and served in hearty portions. Spicy sauces are more prevalent here than elsewhere in Spain—for instance, you will come across garlicky *all i oli*, used to dress a wide variety of dishes. Typical entrées include *habas á la catalana* (a spicy broad-bean stew) and *bullabesa* (fish soup-stew similar to the French *bouillabaisse)*, as well as macaroni: Pasta dishes are more popular here than in the rest of Spain. Bread is doused with olive oil and spread with tomato to make *pa amb tomaquet*, delicious on its own or as an accompaniment. Above all, *zarzuela de mariscos* (literally "operetta" of seafood) tastes better in Catalunya than anywhere else. You can accompany it with excellent wine from the Penedès region just to the south or the famous Catalan *cava* (champagne).

Menús del día offer good value, though they vary in quality and are generally served only at lunchtime. Restaurants usually serve lunch 1–4 and dinner 9–1. It is normal but by no means a requirement to tip; 10% is generous.

Highly recommended restaurants are indicated by a star ★.

Category	Cost*
$$$$	over 7,000 ptas
$$$	5,000–7,000 ptas
$$	2,400–5,000 ptas
$	under 2,400 ptas

**per person, excluding drinks, service, and tax*

$$$$ **Beltxenea.** Previously a smart Eixample apartment, Beltxenea, es-
★ tablished in 1987, retains an atmosphere of privacy in its elegant dining rooms. In summer you can dine outside in the formal garden. Chef Miguel Ezcurra's outstanding cooking hails from the Basque country. His specialty is *merluza con kokotxas y almejas* (hake fried in garlic, simmered in stock, added to clams, and garnished with parsley). If the wine list defeats you, narrow it down to the Riojas. *Mallorca 275, tel. 93/215-3024. Reservations required.*

Dress: neat but casual. AE, DC, MC, V. Closed Sat. lunch, Sun., and July–Aug.

Botafumeiro. Up on Gràcia's main thoroughfare is Barcelona's finest shellfish restaurant, with dishes prepared according to traditional recipes. The waiters will impress you with their soldierly white outfits and superquick service. The tone set is maritime, with white tablecloths and pale varnished wood paneling. The obvious highlights are the *mariscos Botafumeiro* (myriad plates of shellfish that arrive one after the other). *Gran de Gràcia 81, tel. 93/218–42–30. Reservations advised. Dress: neat but casual. AE, DC, MC, V. Closed Sun. evening and Mon.*

★ **La Dama.** Manager-chef Josep Bullich, previously at Vía Veneto and Agut d'Avignon, has converted a Moderniste house into the chicest restaurant in town, with green walls, orange tablecloths, and a polished wood floor. The building was designed by the "amateur," Manuel Sayrach, who built only three buildings during his life. His Art Nouveau interior is perfect for Bullich, who likens his cooking to a movement in modern art. Try the *ensalada tibia de cigalas al vinagre de naranja* (langoustine salad with orange vinegar). *Diagonal 423/425, tel. 93/202–0686. Reservations required. Jacket advised. AE, DC, MC, V.*

★ **Eldorado Petit.** In 1984 Luis Cruañas moved to Barcelona from the Costa Brava and opened this restaurant, which rapidly became known as the best in Barcelona and one of the top restaurants in Spain. The setting—a private villa in Sarrià, with an exotic garden for summer dining up in the hills—is simply beautiful, as is the diverse international cuisine. Try the *pichón relleno* (roast pigeon with truffles and foie gras). *Dolors Monserdà 51, tel. 93/204–5153. Reservations required. Dress: neat but casual. AE, MC, V. Closed Sun. and 2 weeks in Aug.*

Orotava. A 50th-anniversary painting by Miró and an acclaimed copy of Velázquez's *Los Borrachos (The Drunkards)* adorn this intimate baroque-style dining room. Game is the chef's special drawing card, and he is well supplied by clients who bring back the results of their sport from as far afield as Albacete. In season try the *faisán royal* (roast pheasant in a cream and truffle sauce). *Consell de Cent 335, tel. 93/302–3128. Reservations required. Jacket advised. AE, DC, MC, V. Closed Sun. year-round and Sat. June–Sept.*

Reno. Fish is smoked on the premises and meat is cooked on charcoal in this respected haute cuisine restaurant, just north of Diagonal. Game specialties are recommended in season; try the *perdiz a la moda Alcantara* (partridge in wine or port). The tasting (*de gustació*)menu allows you to sample several of the best dishes. Semicircular black sofas surround white-clothed tables, and dark paneling, interspersed with mirrors, extends to the ceiling. *Tuset 27, tel. 93/200–1390. Reservations strongly advised. Jacket and tie required. AE, DC, MC, V.*

Vía Veneto. A Baroque dining room with pink tablecloths, located just above Plaça de Francesc Macià, provides the setting for one of the city's more traditional restaurants. New and exciting Catalan recipes are forever forthcoming; try the *salmón marinado al vinagre de frambuesa* (salmon marinated in raspberry vinegar and aromatic herbs). *Ganduxer 10–12, tel. 93/200–7024. Reservations required. Jacket and tie required. AE, DC, MC, V. Closed Sat. lunch, Sun., and Aug. 1–20.*

$$$ **Agut d'Avignon.** This venerable Barcelona institution (since 1962) takes a bit of finding; head down Carrer Ferran from the Plaça de Sant Jaume, turn left down Carrer Avinyó, and Carrer Trinitat is the first alley off to the right. White walls, heavy wood tables, and

Dining

Agut, **51**
Agut d' Avignon, **44**
Arcs de Sant
Gervasi, **7**
Beltxenea, **20**
Bilbao, **16**
Botafumeiro, **13**
Brasserie Flo, **37**
Can Isidre, **53**
Egipte, **31**
El Asador de
Aranda, **14**
El Glop, **15**
Eldorado Petit, **5**
Jaume de
Provença, **11**
La Cuineta, **46**
La Dama, **12**
La Odisea, **39**
La Tomaquera, **54**
La Vaqueria, **8**
Los Caracoles, **49**
Neichel, **3**
Orotava, **23**
Quo Vadis, **32**
Reno, **10**
Set Portes, **52**
Sopeta Una, **38**
Tram-Tram, **4**
Vía Veneto, **6**

Lodging

Alexandra, **18**
Avenida Palace, **25**
Calderón, **24**
Colón, **40**
Condes de
Barcelona, **19**
Continental, **29**
Duques de
Bergara, **28**
España, **42**
Gótico, **47**
Gran Derby, **9**
Gran Vía, **27**
Hotel Rey Juan
Carlos I, **2**
Jardí, **34**
Le Meridien, **33**
Majestic, **22**
Metropol, **50**
Montecarlo, **35**
Nouvel, **36**

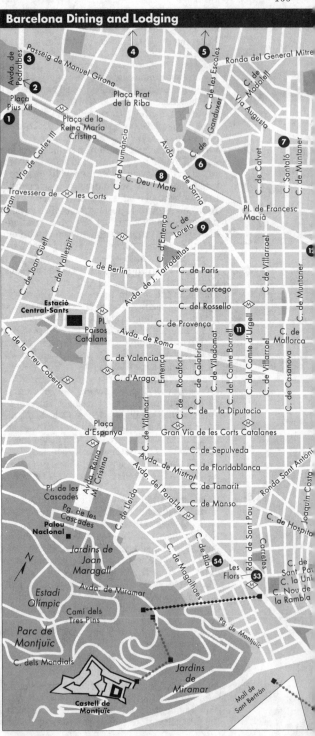

Barcelona Dining and Lodging

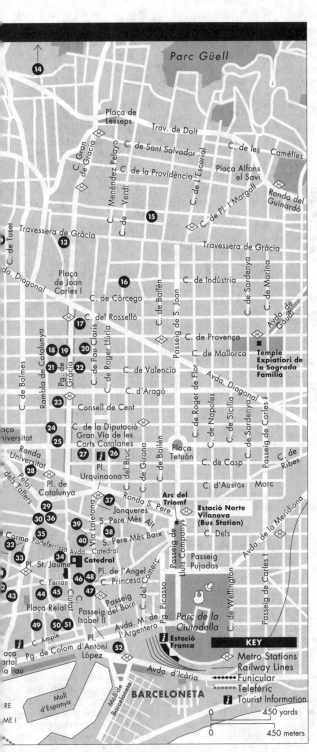

KEY

◇ Metro Stations
— Railway Lines
••••• Funicular
········ Teleféric
ℹ Tourist Information

0 ——————— 450 yards

0 ——————— 450 meters

terra-cotta urns give the place a rustic air, and it's a favorite with businesspeople and politicians from across the road in the Generalitat. The cooking is traditional Catalan and specialties change with the season; from September to May, try the *pato con higos* (roast wild duck in a fig sauce). *Trinitat 3, tel. 93/317–3693. Reservations advised. Jacket advised. AE, DC, MC, V. Closed Holy Week and Christmas.*

Can Isidre. This small restaurant located just inside the Raval from Avinguda del Paral.lel has a long-standing tradition with Barcelona's artistic elite. Pictures and engravings by Dalí and other prominent artists line the walls. The traditional Catalan cooking with a slight French accent draws on the nearby Boqueria's fresh produce. The homemade foie gras is superb. Come and go by cab at night; the area's not the best. *Les Flors 12, tel. 93/441–1139. Reservations required. Dress: casual but stylish. AE, MC, V. Closed Sun., Holy Week, and mid-July–mid-Aug.*

La Cuineta. When the Madolell family converted their antiques business into a restaurant in the late 1960s, it soon gained respect for its neobaroque elegance, intimacy, and Catalan nouvelle cuisine. The clientele encompasses a wide range of foreigners and locals alike. Fish is the house specialty; try the *bacalao La Cuineta* (cod with spinach, raisins, pine nuts, and white sauce). The restaurant is located in two neighboring premises behind the cathedral's apse. *Paradís 4, tel. 93/315–0111 (closed Mon.), and Pietat 12, tel. 93/315–4156 (closed Tues.). No reservations. Dress: casual. AE, DC, MC, V.*

Jaume de Provença. People come here because of the very high reputation of the chef, Jaume Bargués. From his haute cuisine repertoire, try the *lenguado relleno de setas* (sole stuffed with mushrooms) or *lubina* (sea bass) soufflé. The restaurant, situated in the Hospital Clinic area of Eixample, has been recently redecorated in modern black and bottle green. *Provença 88, tel. 93/430–0029. Reservations required. Jacket advised. AE, DC, MC. Closed Sun. evening, Mon., and Aug.*

★ **Neichel.** Hailing from Alsace-Lorraine, chef Jean-Louis Neichel is not bashful about his reputation as he explains such French delicacies as the *ensalada de gambas al sésamo con puernas fritas* (shrimp in sesame-seed sauce with fried leeks). The prices fluctuate widely, depending on your choice. The setting is the ground floor of a Pedralbes apartment block, mundane modernity compared with the cooking. *Calle Bertran i Rozpide 16 bis (just off Av. Pedralbes), tel. 93/203–8408. Reservations required. Jacket advised. AE, DC, MC, V. Closed Sun., Christmas week, Holy Week, and Aug.*

★ **La Odisea.** The dark red walls of this small restaurant, near the cathedral front, are crowded with contemporary Catalan paintings, and a colorful portrait of the chef as you enter. The artistic sense translates to the cooking, adventurously concocted from myriad Mediterranean ingredients and brought to your table by friendly waiters. Try the *merluza al vapor con salsa de tomate fresco* (steamed sea bass with fresh tomato sauce) or *ensaladilla de higado* (liver salad served with mushrooms and Modena vinegar). *Copons 7, tel. 93/302–3692. Reservations required. Dress: neat but casual. AE, DC, MC, V. Closed Sat. lunch, Sun., Holy Week, and Aug.*

Quo Vadis. Just off the Ramblas, near the Boqueria market and Betlem Church, a shiny gray facade camouflages one of Barcelona's most respected restaurants. A succession of small dining rooms decorated in grays and greens provides an atmosphere of sleek intimacy. Its much-praised cuisine includes *pot pourri de setas* (mushrooms) and *higado de ganso con ciruelas* (fried goose liver with prunes). *Carme 7, tel. 93/317-7447. Reservations advised. Dress: neat but casual. AE, DC, MC, V. Closed Sun.*

★ **Tram-Tram.** At the end of the old tram line just uphill from the village of Sarrià, Isidre Soler and his stunning wife Reyes have put together one of the finest and most original of Barcelona's new culinary opportunities. Try the *menu de desgustació* and you might be lucky enough to get the marinated tuna salad, the cod medallions, and the venison filet mignons, among other tasty creations. Perfect-size portions, and the graceful setting—especially in or near the garden out back—make this a popular spot, and although having reservations is a good idea, Reyes can always invent a table on the spur of the moment, so don't pass up the chance to eat here because of lack of planning. *Major de Sarrià 121, tel. 93/204-8518. Reservations advised. Dress: as you wish. AE, MC, V. Closed Sun. and Dec. 24-Jan. 6.*

$$ **Arcs de Sant Gervasi.** Situated up the hill toward Muntaner, Arcs is a modern restaurant that has beige walls with frequently changed artwork, salmon pink tablecloths, and plentiful mirrors. The cooking is *cucina de mercat* (based upon what fresh produce is available in the market) and includes very good fish. Try the *lenguado a las almendras* (sole with almonds). *Santaló 103, tel. 93/201-9277. Reservations advised. Dress: neat but casual. AE, DC, MC, V.*

★ **El Asador de Aranda.** Few restaurants can compete with the setting here—a large, detached, redbrick castle above the Avenida Tibidabo metro. The dining room is large and airy, with a terracotta floor and traditional Castellano furnishings. The traditional Castilian cooking here has won high praise since the restaurant opened in 1988. Try *pimientos de piquillo* (hot spicy peppers) and then *chorizo de la olla* (chorizo sausage stew). *Av. Tibidabo 31, tel. 93/417-0115. Dinner reservations advised. Dress: casual. AE, DC, MC, V. Closed Sun. evening.*

Bilbao. Located at the corner of Venus and Perill (danger) this cozy bistro is indeed perilous to abstinence of all kinds. The overhanging balcony seems to place all diners on stage and it gets fun and foolish quickly. The Catalan cuisine is excellent and the value is among the best in Barcelona. A good place for earlyish dining at lunch or dinner. *Carrer de Perill 33, tel. 93/458-9624. Reservations held until nine o'clock only, after which it's first come, first served. Dress: casual. MC, V. Closed Sun. and holidays.*

Brasserie Flo. A block above the Palau de la Música, this used to be a textiles factory; you dine in a large, elegantly restored warehouse with arched vaulting, steel columns, and wood paneling. Opened in 1982 by a group of Frenchmen, the Brasserie serves an exciting combination of French and Catalan dishes. Try the freshly made foie gras and *choucroûte. Jonqueres 10, tel. 93/317-8037. Reservations advised. Dress: neat but casual. AE, DC, MC, V.*

Los Caracoles. Just below Plaça Reial, a wall of roasting chickens announces one of Barcelona's most famous tourist haunts, which, despite catering primarily to visitors, has great food and real atmosphere. At night you are likely to be serenaded at your table. The walls are hung thickly with azulejos and photos of bullfighters and visiting celebrities. House specialties are *suquillo de pescadores* (an assortment of fish fried in oil and butter and added to a sauce); paella; *mejillones* (mussels); and, of course, *caracoles* (snails). *Escudellers 14, tel. 93/302-3185. No reservations. Dress: casual. AE, DC, MC, V.*

Set Portes. A high-ceilinged dining room, black-and-white marble floor, and numerous mirrors hide behind these seven doors near the waterfront. Going strong since 1836, this restaurant fills up during the week with people from the Bolsa (Stock Exchange) across the way, but at night and on weekends it draws all sorts. The cooking is Catalan, the portions are enormous, and specialties are *paella de peix* (fish) and *sarsuela Set Portes* (seafood casserole). *Passeig Isabel II 14, tel. 93/319-3033. Reservations advised. Jacket advised. AE, DC, MC, V.*

La Vaqueria. This onetime cow shed has been wonderfully converted into an unusual eating place where tables for romantic couples and boisterous groups seem to coexist in perfect harmony. The feed bins and watering troughs have been left in place, and the country design has a certain urban elegance, along with a veneer of humor. The food is delicious and, for the most part, uncomplicated. The *solomillo de buey* (filet mignon) can be prepared with wild mushrooms, green peppers, or blue cheese and is always superb. *Deu i Mata 141, tel. 93/419-0346. Closed for lunch on Sat. and Sun. AE, DC, MC, V.*

$ ★ **Agut.** Wood paneling surmounted by white walls on which hang 1950s canvases forms the setting for the mostly Catalan diners in this homey restaurant in the lower reaches of the Gothic Quarter. It was founded in 1924, and its popularity has never waned, not least because the hearty Catalan fare offers fantastic value. In season (September–May), try the *pato silvestre agridulce* (sweet-and-sour wild duck). There's a good selection of wine but no frills such as coffee or liqueurs. *Gignas 16, tel. 93/315-1709. No reservations. Dress: casual. AE, MC, V. Closed Sun. evening, Mon., and July.*

Egipte. The Egipte, hidden away behind the Boqueria market, has become more and more popular over the last few years, especially with the young. The traditional Catalan home cooking (featuring such favorites as *habas a la catalana*—spicy broad-bean stew) emanates from an overstretched but resourceful kitchen, and the results can be uneven. Nevertheless, the many-tiered dining rooms with marble-top tables and Egyptian motifs continue to entice a lively and sophisticated crowd. The best time to come is lunchtime, when there is a good-value menú del día. There are sister branches at Jerusalem 3 and Rambla 79. *Jerusalem 12, tel. 93/317-7480. No reservations. Dress: casual. AE, DC, MC, V. Closed Sun.*

El Glop. Noisy, hectic, and full of jolly diners from all over Barcelona, El Glop's specialties are *calçotades* (giant spring onions baked in a clay oven) and *asados* (barbecued meats). House wine arrives in a porró (porrón in Spanish)—unless you're a practiced at pouring wine into your mouth from some distance, save your blushes by using the wider opening and a glass. Bright and simply furnished, this restaurant is located a few blocks north of Plaça del Sol in Gràcia. *Sant Lluís 24, tel. 93/213-7058. Reservations required. Dress: casual. MC, V. Closed Mon.*

★ **Sopeta Una.** Dining in this delightful, minuscule restaurant, with old-fashioned earthy decor and cozy ambience, is more like eating in a private house. The menu is in Catalan, all the dishes are Catalan, and everything is very genteel. Try the *cors de carxofes* (artichoke hearts with prawns and tomato and mayonnaise sauce) and for dessert, the traditional Catalan *música*—a plate of raisins, almonds, and dried fruit, served with a glass of Muscatel. *Verdaguer i Callis 6, tel. 93/319-6131. No reservations. Dress: neat but casual. AE, V. Closed Sun., Mon. AM, and Aug.*

La Tomaquera. Situated amid the fading glory of the Paral.lel theater district, this small and unpretentious restaurant is renowned across the city for its superb caracoles and *carns a la brasa* (charcoal-grilled meats), which arrive in giant portions and are accompanied by *all i oli* sauce. *Margarit 58, no tel. No reservations. Dress: casual. No credit cards. Closed Mon. and Aug.*

Bars and Cafés

Barcelona abounds in colorful old tapas bars; smart, trendy cafés; and a whole range of stylish in-vogue bars glorifying in the titles of *coctelerias* (cocktail bars), *whiskerias*, or *xampanyerias* (champagne bars). Below, we list just a few, but on the whole it is best to wander at will and try out any that take your fancy. Most stay open till 2:30 AM (*see* The Arts and Nightlife, *below*, for later spots).

Xampanyerias **La Cava del Palau.** Very handy for the Palau de la Música, this champagne bar serves a wide selection of cavas, wines, and cocktails, with cheeses, pâtés, smoked fish, or caviar on a series of stepped balconies adorned with shiny azulejos. *Verdaguer i Callis 10. Open Mon.–Sat. 7 PM–2:30 AM; closed Sun.*

El Xampanyet. Just down the street from the Picasso Museum, hanging *botas* (leather wineskins), but no sign, announce one of Barcelona's liveliest xampanyerias, packed full most of the time. The house cava, cider, and pan con tomate are served on marble-top tables surrounded by barrels and walls decorated with colored tiles (azulejos) and fading yellow paint. *Montcada 22. Open Tues.–Sun. 8:30 AM–4 PM and 6:30–midnight; closed Mon.*

Tapas Bars **Bar Rodrigo.** Next to the church of Santa Maria del Mar is this popular tapas bar of mirrors, marble-top tables, and steel columns. The specialty is the *vermut* (vermouth) cocktail. There is also a good-value menu for lunch. *L'Argenteria 67. Open 8 AM–1 AM; closed Wed. evening and Thurs.*

Cap Pep. This lively spot has an excellent selection of tapas served fresh and piping hot. *Plaça de les Olles 8. Closed Sun. and Mon. lunch.*

La Palma. Between the Ajuntament and Via Laietana, this has marble tables reminiscent of a Paris bistro, tapas to nibble, and newspapers to read. *Palma Sant Just 7. Open daily 7 AM–10 PM.*

Pla de la Garsa. Serving cheeses, pâtés, wines, and cava, this is a typically Catalan locale. If you just want a drink, come after midnight. *Assonadors 13 (off Montcada). Open daily 7 PM–1 AM.*

Cafés **Café de l'Acadèmia.** Said to serve the best *bocadillos* (French bread sandwiches) in town, this is a sophisto-rustic spot with wicker chairs and stone walls, frequented by politicians from the nearby Generalitat who come here to listen to classical music. *Lledó 1. Open daily 9 AM–4 PM and 9–11:30 PM.*

Café de l'Opera. Right opposite the Liceu, the high-ceilinged Art Nouveau interior plays host to opera goers and performers, but it's also right on the tourist trail, and you won't be the only visitor here. *Ramblas 74. Open Apr.–Sept., daily 24 hrs; Oct.–Mar., daily 10 AM–2 AM.*

Café Zurich. Few avoid a drink in Barcelona's best-known meeting place, a sea of alfresco tables perfectly placed to watch the world emerge from the top end of the Ramblas. *Corner of Pelai and Plaça Catalunya. Open daily 10 AM–midnight.*

Els Quatre Gats. This is the café where Picasso staged his first exhibition and met fellow Modernistes. Don't confuse it with the modern one next door. *Montsió 3. Open daily 8 PM–3 AM.*

Coctelerias **El Copetín.** On Barcelona's best-known cocktail avenue, this bar has exciting decor and good cocktails. *Passeig del Born 19. Open daily 7 PM–3 AM.*

Miramelindo. This bar offers a large selection of herbal liquors, fruit cocktails, pâtés, cheeses, and music, usually jazz. *Passeig del Born 15. Open daily 8 PM–3 AM.*

El Paraigua. Behind the Ajuntament, this rather pricey bar serves cocktails in a stylish setting with classical music. *Plaça Sant Miquel. Open daily 7 PM–1 AM.*

Lodging

The staging of the 1992 Olympic Games here caused a massive boom in hotel construction. New hotels shot up in the ferment, and existing ones underwent extensive renovations. The most spectacular new lodging place in Barcelona is the Hotel Rey Juan Carlos I, which now accompanies—and to some degree has replaced—the Princesa Sofía as the Barcelona luxury hotel closest to the airport. Room rates across the board have increased well above the rate of inflation in recent years, meaning that there are very few real bargains left. Don't give up too easily, however, as most receptionists will become flexible about rates if they suspect you might leave in search of cheaper accommodations. Write or fax ahead asking for a discount; you may be pleasantly surprised.

Generally speaking, hotels in the Gothic Quarter and Ramblas are convenient for sightseeing, have plenty of Old World charm, but, with some notable exceptions, are not as strong on creature comforts. Those in the Eixample are generally set in late-19th-century to 1950s town houses, often Moderniste in design; they all offer a choice between street and inner courtyard rooms, so be sure to specify when you book. The newest hotels, with the widest range of facilities, are out to the west along the Diagonal.

Reservations are a good idea, if only to make your bid for a good rate, but the pre-Olympics hotel-shortage days are over, and in the forseeable future there will be few times when lodging cannot be found with relative ease. Ask for weekend rates, which are often half-price.

Highly recommended hotels are indicated by a star ★.

Category	Cost*
$$$$	over 25,000 ptas
$$$	17,000–25,000 ptas
$$	9,000–17,000 ptas
$	under 9,000 ptas

All prices are for a standard double room, excluding tax.

$$$$ **Avenida Palace.** At the bottom of the Eixample, between the Rambla de Catalunya and Passeig de Gràcia, this hotel manages to convey a feeling of elegance and antiquated style despite dating only from 1952. The lobby is wonderfully ornate, with curving staircases leading off in many directions. Everything is patterned, from the carpets to the plasterwork, a style largely echoed in the bedrooms, although some have been modernized and the wallpaper subdued. Nevertheless, if you prefer contemporary simplicity, go elsewhere. *Gran Via 605–607, 08007, tel. 93/301–9600, fax 93/318–1234. 160 rooms with bath. Facilities: restaurant, bar, gym, health club, sauna. AE, DC, MC, V.*

★ **Condes de Barcelona.** Installed in the old Batlló house (the annex across the street is in the old Duarella house), this hotel is one of the city's most popular hotels—rooms need to be booked well in advance. The stunning pentagonal lobby features a marble floor and the columns and courtyard of the original 1891 building. The modern rooms have Jacuzzis and terraces over interior gardens. An affiliated fitness club around the corner offers facilities including squash courts and a pool. *Passeig de Gràcia 75, 08008, tel. 93/484–8600, fax 93/488–0614. 110 rooms with bath in the Batlló house and 73 in the newly opened Daurella house. Facilities: restaurant, bar, parking. AE, DC, MC, V.*

Le Meridien. Formerly the Manila and then Ramada Renaissance, the French-owned Le Meridien vies with the Colón and Rivoli Ramblas as the premier hotel in the Barri Gòtic. Bedrooms are light, spacious, and decorated in pastel shades. As well as hosting visiting rock stars such as Michael Jackson, the hotel is very popular with business people; facsimiles and computers in your room are available on request. A room overlooking the Ramblas is probably worth the extra noise. *Rambla 111, 08002, tel. 93/318–6200, fax 93/301–7776. 209 rooms with bath. Facilities: bar, restaurant, parking. AE, DC, MC, V.*

Princesa Sofía. Long regarded as the city's foremost modern hotel despite its slightly out-of-the-way location on Avda. Diagonal, this towering high rise offers a wide range of facilities and everything from shops to three different restaurants, including one of the city's finest, Le Gourmet, and the 19th-floor Top City, with breathtaking views. Modern bedrooms are ultracomfortable and decorated in soft colors. *Plaça Pius XII 4, 08028, tel. 93/330–7111, fax 93/411–2106. 505 rooms with bath. Facilities: 3 restaurants, bars, shops, hairdresser, gym, health club, sauna, 2 pools (indoor and outdoor), gardens, parking. AE, DC, MC, V.*

★ **Ritz.** Founded in 1919 by Caesar Ritz, this is the *grande dame* of Barcelona hotels. Extensive refurbishment has restored it to its former splendor. The imperial entrance lobby is awe-inspiring, the rooms contain Regency furniture, some have Roman baths and mosaics, and the service is impeccable. As for the price, you can almost double that of its nearest competitor. *Gran Via 668, 08010, tel. 93/318–5200, fax 93/318–0148. 158 rooms with bath. Facilities: restaurant, bar. AE, DC, MC, V.*

$$$ **Alexandra.** Behind a reconstructed Eixample facade, everything here is slick and contemporary. The rooms are spacious, attractively furnished with dark wood chairs and thatch screens on the balconies to give privacy to the inward-facing rooms. From the airy white marble hall up, the Alexandra is perfectly suited to modern Martini-sipping folk. *Mallorca 251, 08008, tel. 93/487–0505, fax 93/488–0258. 81 rooms with bath. Facilities: restaurant-grill and bar, parking. AE, DC, MC, V.*

Calderón. Ideally placed on the chic uptown extension of the Ramblas, this modern high rise possesses the range of facilities normally expected only of those farther out of town. Public rooms are huge, with cool white marble floors, a style continued in the bedrooms. Don't forgo one of the higher rooms, from which the views from sea to mountains and over the city are breathtaking. *Rambla de Catalunya 26, 08007, tel. 93/301–0000. 264 rooms with bath. Facilities: restaurant, piano bar, 2 pools (1 indoor, 1 outdoor on roof), 2 squash courts, gym, sauna, parking. AE, DC, MC, V.*

★ **Colón.** This cozy, older town-house hotel has a unique charm and intimacy reminiscent of an English country inn. It lays claim to the sightseer's ideal location, with many of the rooms overlooking the floodlit main facade of the cathedral. The rooms are comfortable and tastefully furnished; those to the back are quiet. The Colón was a great favorite of Joan Miró, and if you're not going to be disturbed by the cathedral bells, it's an excellent choice. *Av. Catedral 7,*

08002, tel. 93/301–1404, fax 93/317–2915. 147 rooms with bath. Facilities: restaurant, bar. AE, DC, MC, V.

Duques de Bergara. This hotel is set in a stately Moderniste mansion with high ceilings and the full range of art nouveau trappings. The public rooms successfully combine old and new, Persian rugs and glass tables. The bedrooms display restraint and elegance in their mingling of functional contemporary with antiques, though some are smaller and have thinner walls than one would wish. *Bergara 11, 08002, tel. 93/301–5151, fax 93/317–3442. 54 rooms with bath. Facilities: restaurant, bar. AE, DC, MC, V.*

Gran Derby. Every bedroom in this modern Eixample hotel has its own sitting room, and each is decorated with modern black-and-white tile floors, plain light walls, and coral bedspreads. Some have an extra bedroom, making this an ideal choice for a family. If it weren't for the location, some way out (for sightseeing purposes), just below Plaça Francesc Macià, it would be unreservedly recommended. *Loreto 28, 08029, tel. 93/322–3215, fax 93/419–6820. 44 rooms with sitting room and bath. Facilities: café, bar, parking. AE, DC, MC, V.*

Hotel Rey Juan Carlos I. This modern complex towering over the western end of Barcelona's Avinguda Diagonal is as much shopping mall as luxury hotel. Jewelry, furs, caviar, art, flowers and fashions, even limousines are for sale or hire at this giant concentration of hospitality and design. The lush garden, including a pond complete with swans, is the setting of an Olympic-sized swimming pool, and the green expanses of Barcelona's finest in-town country club, El Polo, spread luxuriantly out beyond. Hotel dining facilities include three restaurants, the luxurious French "Chez Vous," the Japanese Kokoro, and a buffet, as well as an American bar. Lecture halls and seminar rooms are abundant. *Avinguda Diagonal 661–671, 08028, tel. 93/448–0808, fax 93/448–0607. 375 rooms with bath, 37 suites, 2 presidential suites, 1 royal suite. Facilities: 3 restaurants, bar, parking, garden, swimming pool, hairdressers, boutiques. AE, DC, MC, V.*

★ **Majestic.** With an unbeatable location on the city's most stylish boulevard and a great rooftop pool, this is a near-perfect place to stay. The different combinations of wallpaper, pastels, and vintage furniture in the rooms and the leather sofas, marble, and mirrors in the reception area all suit the place rather well—and the jet set still comes here. The building is part Eixample town house and part modern extension, so bear this in mind when booking your room. *Passeig de Gràcia 70, 08008, tel. 93/488–1717, fax 93/488–1880. 335 rooms with bath. Facilities: restaurant, bar, health club, pool, parking. AE, DC, MC, V.*

Rivoli Ramblas. Behind the upper-Rambla facade lies imaginative slick, modern decor, marble floors, elegant pastel bedrooms, and a roof-terrace bar with panoramic views. *Ramblas 128, 08002, tel. 93/302–6643, fax 93/317–5053. 87 rooms with bath. Facilities: restaurant, cocktail bar, fitness center, spa, sauna, solarium. AE, DC, MC, V.*

$$ **España.** They've completely modernized the large bedrooms here—
★ the best and quietest overlook the bright interior patio—and now this erstwhile budget hotel, with already stunning public rooms, is a real winner. Its main attraction remains the Moderniste ground-floor decor, designed by Domènech i Montaner, and featuring a superbly sculpted hearth by Eusebi Arnau, elaborate woodwork, and a mermaid-populated Ramón Casas mural in the breakfast room. The restaurant is likewise beautiful. Don't miss this lovely concentration of Art Nouveau, even if you only stop in for lunch or dinner.

Sant Pau 9–11, 08001, tel. 93/318–1758, fax 93/317–1134. 76 rooms with bath. Facilities: restaurant, breakfast room, cafeteria. AE, DC, MC, V.

Gótico. Along with the neighboring Rialto and Suizo hotels, this now belongs to the Gargallo group, which has done a good job of renovating these three old favorites, popular with tour groups. Just off Plaça Sant Jaume, the Gótico is central for exploring the Gothic Quarter. The rooms have wood beams, white walls, heavy wood furniture, white tile floors, and walnut doors; ask for an exterior one. *Jaume I 14, 08002, tel. 93/315–2211, fax 93/315–3819. 80 rooms with bath. Facilities: cafeteria, bar. AE, DC, MC, V.*

★ **Gran Via.** Architectural features are the attraction of this grand 19th-century town house, close to the main tourist office. The original chapel has been preserved; also, you can have breakfast in a hall of mirrors, climb its elaborate Moderniste staircase, and call from the Belle Epoque phone booths. The rooms have plain alcoved walls, bottle green carpets, and Regency-style furniture; those overlooking Gran Via itself have better views but are quite noisy. *Gran Via 642, 08007, tel. 93/318–1900, fax 93/318–9997. 53 rooms with bath. Facilities: breakfast room, parking. AE, DC, MC, V.*

★ **Metropol.** Located between the lower reaches of the Rambla and Via Laietana, this town house offers easy access to the marina while being pleasantly off the tourist trail. Bedrooms are cozily decorated with plain orange carpets, green bedspreads, and modern prints. *Ample 31, 08002, tel. 93/315–4011, fax 93/319–1276. 68 rooms with bath. Facilities: cafeteria, bar. AE, DC, MC, V.*

Montecarlo. Entrance from the Rambla is through an enticing marble hall, and upstairs is a sumptuous large reception room with a dark wood Moderniste ceiling. The rooms are modern, bright, and functional; ask for a view of the Rambla if you don't mind the higher noise level. *Rambla 124, 08002, tel. 93/412–0404, fax 93/318–7323. 76 rooms with bath. Facilities: bar, cafeteria, buffet, parking. AE, DC, MC, V.*

Nouvel. Centrally located just below Plaça de Catalunya, this hotel blends white marble, etched glass, elaborate plasterwork, and carved dark woodwork in its handsome Art Nouveau interior. Renovated and upgraded to cash in on the recent Olympics, the bedrooms now have pristine marble floors, firm beds, and smart bathrooms. The narrow street is pedestrian-only and therefore quiet, but views are non-existent. *Santa Anna 18–20, 08002, tel. 93/301–8274, fax 93/301–8370. 74 rooms with bath. Facilities: breakfast room. AE, DC, MC, V.*

Oriente. Down toward the seamier side of the city's action, Barcelona's oldest hotel has nevertheless retained all its style and charm. Its ornate public rooms and glowing chandeliers recall a bygone era. The only drawback is the somewhat functional decor of the rooms, some of which have an extra bed for families. It is popular with businesspeople, though, and located just below the Liceu Opera House. *Rambla 45–47, 08002, tel. 93/302–2558, fax 93/412–3819. 142 rooms with bath. Facilities: restaurant, bar. AE, DC, MC, V.*

Regente. The Moderniste decor and plentiful stained glass lend style and charm to this smallish hotel. The public rooms have been renovated over the last two years and are carpeted with many different patterns. The bedrooms, fortunately, are elegantly restrained; the verdant roof-terrace with a pool and the prime position on the Rambla de Catalunya complete the positive verdict. *Rambla de Catalunya 76, 08008, tel. 93/487–5989, fax 93/487–3227. 78 rooms with bath. Facilities: 2 restaurants, bar, pool. AE, DC, MC, V.*

Rialto. This hotel seems to have taken a leaf from the paradors' book with its subdued and classy decor of pine floors, white walls, and walnut doors. The rooms (ask for an exterior one) echo this look, with heavy furniture set against light walls, and they have all the same fittings as the Gótico. There is a vaulted bar in the basement and a modern mirrored *salón* by the lobby. *Ferran 42, 08002, tel. 93/318–5212, fax 93/315–3819. 132 rooms with bath. Facilities: cafeteria, bar. AE, DC, MC, V.*

Suizo. The last of the Gargallo hotels lacks the spacious corridors of the Rialto, but its public rooms are preferable, with elegant modern seating at the front of the hotel, either near the reception area or one floor up, with good views over the noisy square. The bedrooms have bright walls and either wood or tile floors. *Plaça del Àngel 12, 08002, tel. 93/315–4111, fax 93/315–3819. 48 rooms with bath. Facilities: restaurant, bar, cafeteria. AE, DC, MC, V.*

$ Continental. Something of a legend among cost-conscious travelers, this comfortable hotel with canopied balconies stands at the top of the Rambla, just below Plaça de Catalunya. Everything is cramped, but the bedrooms manage to accommodate large, firm beds. The green swirly patterns on the walls match those on the fast-fading carpets. Ask for a room on the Rambla side. A good breakfast is served overlooking the famous street. *Rambla 138, 08002, tel. 93/301–2508, fax 93/302–7360. 35 rooms with bath. Facilities: breakfast room. AE, DC, MC, V.*

★ Jardí. With views over the adjoining traffic-free and charming squares, Plaça del Pi and Plaça Sant Josep Oriol, this hotel's newly renovated bedrooms have immaculate white-tile floors, modern pine furniture, white walls, and powerful, hot showers. Be sure to get an exterior room—they're quiet and represent excellent value. The alfresco tables of the Bar del Pi downstairs are ideal for breakfasting. *Plaça Sant Josep Oriol 1, 08002, tel. 93/301–5900, fax 93/318–3664. 40 rooms with bath. Facilities: breakfast room. AE, DC, MC, V.*

Paseo de Gràcia. Formerly a hostel, this hotel has good-quality plain carpets and sturdy wooden furniture adorning the soft-color bedrooms. Add to this the location on the handsomest of Eixample's boulevards and this is an excellent budget option if you want to stay uptown. Half the rooms have superb rooftop terraces, with great views up to Tibidabo. *Passeig de Gràcia 102, 08008, tel. 93/215–5828, fax 93/215–3724. 33 rooms with bath. Facilities: breakfast room, bar. AE, DC, MC, V.*

★ Peninsular. Built for the 1890 Exposition, this hotel in the Barri Xines features an impressive coral marble lobby and an appealing interior courtyard, painted white and pale green and adorned with numerous hanging plants. The bedrooms have tile floors, good showers, and firm beds. Look at a few before choosing because all are different; some have views, others give onto the courtyard. *Sant Pau 34, 08001, tel. 93/302–3138, fax 93/302–3138. 80 rooms with bath, 20 rooms without bath. Facilities: breakfast room. MC, V.*

The Arts and Nightlife

With music halls, theaters, and some of Europe's trendiest nightclubs, Barcelona has a wide-ranging arts and nightlife scene. To find out what's on, look in newspapers or the weekly *Guía Del Ocio*, available from newsstands all over town. *Activitats* is a monthly list of cultural events, published by the Ajuntament and available from its information office in Palau de la Virreina (Rambla 99).

The Arts

Concerts Catalans are great music lovers, and their main concert hall is the **Palau de la Música** (Sant Francesc de Paula 2, tel. 93/268–1000). The ticket office is open weekdays 11–1 and 5–8, Saturday 5–8 only. Sunday morning concerts (11 AM) are a popular tradition. Tickets range from 450 to 9,000 pesetas and are best purchased in advance. Concerts are held September–June. In September the city hosts an **International Music Festival** as part of its celebrations for the festival of the Mercè.

Dance **L'Espai de Dansa i Música de la Generalitat de Catalunya,** generally listed as **L'Espai** (The Space; Travessera de Gràcia 63, tel. 93/414–3133), was opened by the Catalonian government in February 1992 and is now Barcelona's prime venue for ballet, contemporary dance, and musical performances of varying kinds. **El Mercat de les Flors** (Lleida 59, tel. 93/426–1875) near Plaça de Espanya, is the more traditional setting for modern dance and theater.

Film Though some foreign films will be dubbed, there is always a good selection of films showing in their original language. Look in listing magazines for movies marked *v.o. subtitulada* (subtitled). The **Filmoteca** (Av. Sarrià 33, tel. 93/430–5007) shows three films daily in their original language, often English.

Flamenco Barcelona is not richly endowed with flamenco spots, as Catalans are only moderately fond of this very Andalucían spectacle. The best place is **El Patio Andaluz** (Aribau 242, tel. 93/209–3378), with *sevillanas* rather than flamenco and some audience participation, but it is quite expensive. **El Cordobés** (Rambla 35, tel. 93/317–6653) is the place most visited by tour groups, but it can be colorful and fun. Others are **El Tablao de Carmen** (Poble Espanyol, tel. 93/325–6895) and **Los Tarantos** (Plaça Reial 17, tel. 93/318–3067).

Opera Barcelona's opulent and beloved **Gran Teatre del Liceu** was gutted by flames in early 1994 and will in all probability not be restored until 1996. Originally constructed in 1848, the Liceu was destroyed by fire once before, in 1861. Considered one of Europe's finest opera houses, the Liceu was a Barcelona landmark. The box office, according to present plans, will remain open at San Pau 1 (tel. 93/318–9277); operas and musical events will be staged at the **Palau Sant Jordi** sports hall on Montjuïc, at the **Palacio Nacional** above Plaza España, or at the **Palau de la Música.** Some of the most spectacular halls and rooms of the Liceu were unharmed by the fire, and there may be some tours of these areas during the restoration.

Rock and Roll Keep an eye out for posters; in addition to some good Spanish bands (Radio Futura, El Ultimo de la Fila), many international bands pass through Barcelona. Major concerts are held in sports stadia or nightclubs such as Zeleste and K.G.B. For tickets, try any record shop; **Discos Castelló** (Tallers 79), just off Plaça Universitat, sells most concert tickets.

Theater Most theater performances are in Catalan, but Barcelona is also well known for its mime troupes (**Els Joglars** and **La Claca**). An international mime festival is held most years, as is the **Festival de Títeres** (Puppet Festival).

The best-known modern theaters are the **Teatre Lliure** (Montseny 47, in Gràcia, tel. 93/218–9251), **Mercat de les Flors** (Lleida 59, tel. 93/318–8599), **Teatre Romea** (Hospital 51, tel. 93/317–7189), **Teatre Tívoli** (Casp 10, tel. 93/412–2063), and **Teatre Poliorama** (Rambla

Estudios 115, tel. 93/317–7599) all of which offer a dynamic variety of classical, contemporary, and experimental theater.

Many of the older theaters specializing in big musicals are along the Paral.lel. They include **Apolo** (Paral.lel 56, tel. 93/241–9007) and **Victòria** (Paral.lel 67–69, tel. 93/441–3979). There is an open-air summer theater festival in July and August, when plays, music, song, and dance performances are held in the **Teatre Grec** (Greek Theater) on Montjuïc, as well as in other venues.

Nightlife

Cabaret Take in the venerable **Bodega Bohemia** (Lancaster 2, tel. 93/302–5061), where a variety of singers perform to an upright piano, or the minuscule **Bar Pastis** (Santa Mònica 4, tel. 93/318–7980), where the habitués form the cabaret and a phonograph plays the music of Edith Piaf.

Arnau (Paral.lel 60, tel. 93/242–2804) and **El Molino** (Vila i Vila 99, tel. 93/329–8854) are both traditional old-time music halls that have retained their popularity. **Belle Epoque** (Muntaner 246, tel. 93/209–7711), a richly decorated music hall, stages the most sophisticated shows.

Casinos The **Gran Casino de Barcelona** (tel. 93/893–3666), 42 km (26 mi) south in Sant Pere de Ribes, near Sitges, also has a dance hall and some excellent international shows in a 19th-century setting. The only others in Catalunya are in Lloret del Mar (tel. 972/36–65–12) and Perelada (tel. 972/53–81–25), both in Girona province up the coast north of Barcelona.

Jazz Clubs Try **La Cova del Drac** (Vallmajor 33, tel. 93/200–7032); **L'Auditori** (Balmes 245); or the Gothic Quarter's **Harlem Jazz Club** (Comtessa Sobradiel 8, tel. 93/310–0755), which is small but puts on atmospheric bands. The Palau de la Música stages an important **international jazz festival** in November, and the nearby city of Terrassa has its own jazz festival in March.

Nightclubs/ Barcelona is currently so hip that it is difficult to keep track of the
Discotheques trendiest places to go at night. Most clubs have a discretionary entrance charge that they like to inflict on foreigners, so dress up and be prepared to talk your way past the doorman.

Top ranked recently has been the prison decor–mimicking **Otto Zutz** (Lincoln 15, tel. 93/238–0722), just off Via Augusta. **K.G.B.** (Alegre de Dalt 55, tel. 93/210–5906) is another hot spot, while **Fibra Optica** (Beethoven 9, tel. 93/202–0069) and the city's nearly classic **Up and Down** (pronounced "Pendow") (Numancia 179, tel. 93/280–2922) are both anything but calm. **Oliver y Hardy** (Diagonal 593, tel. 93/419–3181) next to the Barcelona Hilton is a recent invention more popular with the older set (you won't stand out if you're over 35) while **La Tierra** (Aribau 230, tel. 93/200–7346) and **El Otro** (Valencia 166, tel. 93/323–6759) also accept post-graduates with open arms. **Zeleste** (Almogavers 122, tel. 93/309–1204) is one more standard hangout, especially popular with jazz and rock buffs.

For an old-fashioned *sala de baile* (dance hall) with a big band playing tangos, head to **La Paloma** (Tigre 27, tel. 93/301–6897); the kitsch 1950s decor creates a peculiar atmosphere that's great fun.

Late-night *Bar musical* is Spanish for any bar that plays modern music loud
Bars enough to drown out conversation. The pick of these are **Universal** (Marià Cubí 182–184, tel. 93/200–7470), **Mas i Mas** (Marià Cubí 199,

tel. 93/209–4502), and **Nick Havanna** (Rosselló 208, tel. 93/215–6591).

For a more laid-back locale, tall ceilings, billiards, tapas, and hundreds of students, visit the popular **Velodrom** (Muntaner 211–213, tel. 93/230–6022), just below Diagonal. Two blocks away is the intriguing *bar-museo* (bar-cum-museum) **La Fira** (Provença 171, tel. 93/323–7271). Downtown, deep in the Barrio Chino, try the **London Bar** (Nou de la Rambla 34, tel. 93/302–3102), an Art Nouveau old circus haunt with a trapeze suspended above the bar.

Barcelona Excursions

Numbers in the margin correspond to points of interest on the Barcelona Excursions map.

Montserrat

An almost obligatory side trip while you are in Barcelona is to the shrine of La Moreneta, the Black Virgin of **Montserrat,** 50 km (30 mi) west, high in the peaks of the Serra de Montserrat. These weird sawtoothed peaks have given rise to countless legends: Here, Parsifal found the Holy Grail, St. Peter left a statue of the Virgin Mary carved by St. Luke, and Wagner sought inspiration for his opera. A monastery has stood on the site since the early Middle Ages, though the present 19th-century building replaced the rubble left by Napoleon's troops in 1812. Montserrat is a world-famous shrine and one of Catalunya's spiritual sanctuaries. Honeymooning couples flock here by the thousands, seeking La Moreneta's blessing upon their marriage, and twice a year, on April 27 and September 8, the diminutive statue of Montserrat's Black Virgin becomes the object of one of Spain's greatest pilgrimages.

Follow the A2/A7 autopista on the new upper ring road (Ronda de Dalt) or from the western end of Diagonal as far as salida 25 to Martorell. Bypass this industrial center and follow signs to Montserrat. There is also train and bus service from Sants station to Montserrat, as well as guided tours (Pullmantur and Julià).

Only the Basilica and museum are readily open to the public. The **Basilica** (open daily 6–10:30 and noon–6:30) is dark and ornate, its blackness pierced by the glow of hundreds of votive lamps. Above the high altar stands the famous polychrome statue of the Virgin and Child to which the faithful can pay their respects by way of a separate door.

The monastery's **museum** has two sections: The Secció Antiga (open Tues.–Sat. 10:30–2) contains old masters, among them paintings by El Greco, Correggio, and Caravaggio, and the amassed gifts to the Virgin; the Secció Moderna (open Tues.–Sat. 3–6) concentrates on recent Catalan painters.

Time Out   Amid a string of overpriced buffet establishments, the pick of lunching spots is the unremarkably named **Montserrat** (Plaça Apòstols, lunch only).

Montserrat is as memorable for its setting as for its religious treasures, so be sure to explore these strange pink hills. The vast monastic complex is dwarfed by the grandeur of the jagged peaks, and the crests are dotted with hermitages: Sant Joan hermitage can be reached by funicular. The views over the mountains away to the

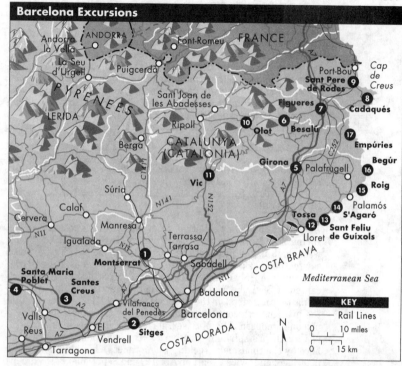

Barcelona Excursions

Mediterranean and, on a clear day, to the Pyrenees are breathtaking, and the rugged boulder-strewn setting makes for dramatic walking and hiking country.

Sitges, Santes Creus, and Poblet

These three attractions to the south and west of Barcelona can be seen comfortably in a day. Sitges is the prettiest and most popular resort in Barcelona's immediate environs and flaunts, apart from an excellent beach, a picturesque Old Quarter and some interesting Moderniste touches. The Cistercian monasteries west of here are characterized by restrained Romanesque architecture and beautiful cloisters.

Head southwest along Gran Via or Passeig de Colón to the freeway that passes the airport on its way to Castelldefels. From here, the new freeway and tunnels will get you to Sitges in 20 minutes. From Sitges, drive inland toward Vilafranca del Penedès and the A7 freeway. The A2 (Lleida) is the road for the monasteries.

Regular trains leave Sants and Passeig de Gràcia for Sitges; the ride takes a half hour. From Sitges, trains go to L'Espluga de Francolí, 4 km (2½ mi) from Poblet (Lleida line). For Poblet, stay with the train to Tarragona and catch a bus to the monastery (Autotransports Perelada, tel. 973/20–20–58).

② In **Sitges**, head for the museums. Most interesting is the **Cau-Ferrat**, founded by the artist Russinyol, which contains some of his own paintings, together with two works by El Greco. Connoisseurs of wrought iron will be delighted to find here a beautiful collection of *cruces terminales,* crosses once erected to mark town boundaries. *Fonollar s/n, tel. 93/894-0364. Admission: 250 pesetas (free Sundays and holidays). Open Tues.-Sun. 9:30-2.*

Time Out You will find fine moderately priced seafood at **Vivero** (Passeig Balmins s/n, tel. 93/894-2149; closed Tues. from Dec. to May).

On leaving Sitges, make straight for the A2 autopista by way of Vilafranca del Penedès. If you are a wine buff, you may want to stop here to taste the excellent Penedès wine. You can visit and taste at the **Bodega Miguel Torres** (Comercio 22, tel. 93/890-0100), and there's an interesting **Museu del Vi** (Wine Museum; admission: 250 pesetas; open Tues.-Sun. 10-2 and 4-7; closed Mon.) in the Royal Palace, with descriptions of wine-making history.

❸ As it branches west to the province of Lleida, A2 passes two monasteries. The first you come to (salida 11) is **Santes Creus,** founded in 1157. Three austere aisles and an unusual 14th-century apse combine with the newly restored cloisters and the courtyard of the royal palace. *Admission: 350 pesetas. Open Oct.-Mar., daily 10-1 and 3-6; Apr.-Sept., daily 10-1 and 3-7.*

Another turning off the highway (salida 9) leads to the town of **Montblanc,** whose ancient gates are too narrow for cars. A walk through its tiny streets reveals Gothic churches with intricate stained-glass windows, a 16th-century hospital, and fine medieval mansions.

❹ Eight km (5 mi) farther on is the second and older monastery, **Santa Maria Poblet.** This splendid Cistercian foundation at the foot of the Prades Mountains is the most complete and representative masterpiece of Spanish monastic architecture. Founded in 1150 by Ramón Berenguer IV in gratitude for the Reconquest, it was initially inhabited by 12 Cistercians from Narbonne in France. The kings of Aragón used it for religious retreat and burial. It suffered extensive damage in the 1836 revolution, but since 1940 the monks of the reformed Cistercian order have successfully managed the difficult task of restoration. Today, monks and novices again pray before the splendid retable over the tombs of Aragonese rulers, restored to their former glory by sculptor Frederic Marés; sleep in the cold, barren dormitory; and eat their frugal meals in the stark refectory. The cloister is outstanding for its lightness and severity, two elements you rarely find blended so deftly as at Poblet. *Admission: 600 pesetas. Open for guided tours 10-12:30 and 3-6 (5:30 Oct.-Mar.).*

Girona and Northern Catalunya

The ancient city of Girona, often ignored by visitors who use its airport for the resorts of the Costa Brava, is full of interest and within easy day-tripping distance of Barcelona. The narrow medieval streets, with frequent stairways as required by the steep terrain, are what give Girona much of its charm. The historic buildings here include the cathedral, dominating the city from atop 90 steps; Arab baths; and an antique and charming Jewish Quarter.

Northern Catalunya boasts green rolling hills, the Aberes mountain range at the eastern tip of the Pyrenees, and the rugged Costa Brava. Meandering off into the countryside you see charming *masias* (farmhouses), whose austere grayish or pinkish stone, staggered rooftops, and ubiquitous square towers give them a look of fortresses. Churches confer dignity on the villages, and the tiniest of these contains its main arcaded square and *rambla* (promenade), where villagers stroll during the sacred evening paseo.

Arriving and Departing

By Car Barcelona is now completely surrounded by a new network of *rondas*, or ring roads, with quick access from every corner of the city. Look for signs for these *rondas*, then follow signs to France (Francia); Girona; and the A7 autopista, which goes all the way. Leave the autopista at salida 7 for Girona. The 100 km (62 mi) to Girona takes 1½ hours.

By Train Trains leave **Sants** and **Passeig de Gràcia** every 1½ hours for Girona, Figueres, and Port Bou. Some trains for northern Catalunya and France also leave from the França Station. Always double-check which station your train is leaving from. For Vic and Ripoll, catch a Puigcerdà train (every hour or two) from Sants or Plaça de Catalunya.

By Bus **Sarfa** (Plaça Medinaceli 4, tel. 93/318–9434) has buses every 1½ hours to Girona, Figueres, and Cadaqués. For Vic try **Segalés** (at Fabra i Puig subway stop, tel. 93/231–2756) and for Ripoll call **Teisa** (Pau Claris 118, tel. 93/488–2837).

Guided Tours **Trenes Turísticos de RENFE** (tel. 93/490–0202) operates guided tours to Girona by train May through September, leaving Sants at 10 AM and returning at 7:30 PM. It also has train tours to Vic and Ripoll, leaving Sants at 9 AM and returning at 8:40 PM. The cost for each is 1,500 pesetas for adults, 1,000 pesetas for children. Call RENFE to confirm these tours.

Exploring 5 In **Girona** you can park in the Plaça Independencia and find your way to the Tourist Information Office at Rambla Llibertad 1. Ask for their *oferta*, a card that will get you discount prices all over town. Then head to the Old Quarter across the River Onyar, past Girona's best-known view: the orange waterfront houses and their windows, draped with a colorful array of drying laundry, reflected in the waters of the Onyar. Use the cathedral's huge Baroque facade to guide you up through the labyrinth of streets.

At the base of 90 steps go left through the Sobreportes gate to the **Banys Arabs** (Arab Baths). Built by Morisco craftsmen in the late 12th century, long after Girona's Islamic occupation (795–1015) had ended, the baths are both Romanesque and Moorish in design. *Admission: 300 pesetas. Open May–Sept., Tues.–Sat., 10–2 and 4–7, Sun. 10–2; Oct.–Apr., Tues.–Sun. 10–1; closed Mon.*

Cross the River Galligants to visit the church of **Sant Pere** (Holy Father; finished 1131), notable for its octagonal Romanesque belfry and the finely detailed capitals atop the columns of the cloister. Next door is the **Museu Arqueològic**, which documents the region's history since Paleolithic times. *Admission free. Church and museum open daily 10–1 and 4:30–7.*

Stroll back to and up the stepped Passeig Arqueològic, which runs below the Old City walls. Climb to the highest **ramparts** through the Jardins de la Francesa. You get a good view from here of the 11th-century Romanesque Tower of Charlemagne, the oldest part of the cathedral.

Complete the loop around the **cathedral** to visit the interior. Designed by Guillem Bofill in 1416, it is famous for its immense, uncluttered Gothic nave—at 23 m (75½ ft), the widest in the world and the epitome of the goal of Catalan Gothic architects. The cathedral's museum contains the famous *Tapis de la Creació* (Tapestry of Creation) and a 10th-century copy of Beatus's manuscript *Commentary on the*

Apocalypse. Admission: 300 pesetas. Open Oct.–June, daily 9:30–1:15 and 3:30–7; July–Sept., daily 9:30–8.

The adjacent **Palau Episcopal** (Bishop's Palace) houses the **Museu d'Art,** a good mix of Romanesque, Catalan Gothic, and modern art. *Open Tues.–Sat. 10–1 and 4:30–7, Sun. 10–1; closed Mon. Same ticket as for Arab baths.*

Leave Plaça dels Apòstols along Carrer Claveria and turn right down Carrer Lluis Batlle i Prats. Plunge right down the tiny Carrer Sant Llorenç, formerly the cramped and squalid center of the 13th-century *Call,* or Jewish Quarter. Halfway down on the left is the small **Monastruc Çaporta,** a museum of Jewish history (open Tues.–Sat. 10–2 and 4–7, Sun. 10–2; closed Mon.), and the **Pati dels Rabís** (Rabbis' Courtyard).

Three km (2 mi) north of Girona, turn left along C150. You pass through Banyoles by a large lake and countryside that grows steadily greener as you rise. The Pyrenees come into view on clear days, providing a spectacular backdrop to the ancient town of **Besalú,** capital of a feudal county from the 9th until the 12th century. Look for the carved, fortified bridge as you drive in, the porticoed **Plaça Llibertat,** the ruined **convent of Santa Maria** up on the hill, and the **church of Sant Pere,** whose window above the main portal is guarded by beautifully carved lions. The convent and churches can be visited by arrangement with the tourist office on Plaça Llibertat, with tours starting on the hour.

Now follow C260, which runs through woods before descending to the ugly built-up plain and **Figueres.** Even if you aren't a great fan of Salvador Dalí's work, Figueres's **Museu Dalí** commands a halt. It's installed in a former theater, adjacent to the bizarre red Islamic-looking fortress where Dalí lived until his death in 1989. The remarkable collection includes a vintage Cadillac whose ivy-cloaked passengers you can water by putting 25 pesetas in a box at the side. Dalí is buried in a self-designed tomb beneath the museum. *Admission: 600 pesetas. Open Oct.–Mar., Tues.–Sun. 11:30–5:30; Apr.–Sept., Tues.–Sun. 9–8:30.*

Our next destination is **Cadaqués,** 34 km (21 mi) away. Head past Roses and over the bleak heathland of the Sierra Alseda. Cadaqués's clustered, whitewashed houses set around a bay make it the most attractive of all Costa Brava resorts. The tiny beach is of a special kind of reddish-blue slate, used most decoratively in houses, walls, and streets, but uncomfortable to sit on and agony to walk over. The town has a strikingly situated 16th-century parish church and many steep, picturesque streets. It became an artists' haunt in the 1950s.

In summer, visit the **Museu Perrot-Moore** in the old town, which has an important collection of graphic arts dating from the 15th to the 20th century, including works by Dalí. *Admission: 400 pesetas. Open June 15–Oct. 15, daily 5–9.*

A few small, sandy beaches hug the side of the legendary **Cap** (Cape) **de Creus.** There remain only **Port de la Selva, Port de Llança,** and the frontier village of **Port-Bou** before you reach France. This road is unforgettably lovely as it winds its way around numerous bends, high above the turquoise sea, but the towns themselves are unremarkable.

From Port de la Selva a rough track leads to a parking lot from which you can walk to the 10th-century monastery of **Sant Pere de Rodes,** a 610-m (2,000-ft) hilltop site with a perfect view of the coast. Built by Benedictine monks between 972 and 1022, the monastery was abandoned in 1789 and looted by the French. The bulk of the buildings have survived and are undergoing restoration. A paved road leads from the parking area onto C252. *Admission: 400 pesetas. Open daily 10–2 and 4–dusk.*

❿ From Besalú, you can also go west to **Olot,** surrounded by basalt piles and largely destroyed by earthquakes in the 15th century. There is an interesting modern church here that flaunts a springboard-shape steeple and a gigantic monk's head sculptured by Iloret on its facade. This is the **Church of Sant Pere the Martyr.** The **Museu Comarcal de la Garrotxa** contains an important assemblage of Moderniste art and design. *Carrer Hospici 8. Admission: 300 pesetas. Open Mon. and Wed.–Sat. 11–2 and 4–7, Sun. 11–2; closed Tues.*

⓫ From Olot follow C153 over a twisting, scenic road to **Vic.** The town rests on a 488-m (1,600-ft) plateau at the confluence of the Guri and Heder rivers, the business and industrial center of the region. It boasts a mostly neoclassical **cathedral** (open summer, Mon.–Sat. 10–1 and 4–7, Sun. 10–1 and 4–5; winter, Mon.–Sat. 10–1 and 4–6, Sun. 10–1 and 4–5), whose tremendous 11th-century Romanesque tower, El Cloquer, was built by Abbot Oliva. The cathedral is decorated with powerful modern murals by Josep Maria Sert. There is a good **museum** just opposite, containing very fine Romanesque and Gothic altarfronts, collected from local churches, as well as Gothic paintings. *Admission: 300 pesetas. Open Mon.–Sat. 10–1 and 4–7, Sun. 10–1:30.*

Before you go, be sure to see the vast **Plaça Mayor,** surrounded on all sides by Gothic arcades and well served by bars. A busy market takes place here on Tuesdays and Saturdays.

Dining **Galiota** is the trendiest spot in town. Well-heeled arty types come
Cadaqués here to eat fish and study the Dalí paintings on the walls. *Narcís Monturiol 9, tel. 972/25–81–87. Reservations required. Open only Sat., Sun., and holidays Oct.–May. $$*

Figueres **Ampurdán,** 1.5 km (1 mi) north on the NII, serves huge helpings of superb French/Catalan cooking; try one of the fish mousses. *Carretera NII, tel. 972/50–05–62. AE, DC, MC, V. $$$*
Mas Pau, 1.5 km (1 mi) west on the Olot road, is set in an old *masia* with a pretty garden; try one of the game specialties in season. *Carretera de Olot, tel. 972/54–61–54. DC, MC, V. $$$*

Girona **Alvereda** has excellent Ampurdan cuisine served in a bright and pleasant setting. Try the *galleta de calabacin con langostinos glaceada* (zucchini bisque with prawns). *Alvereda 7, tel. 972/22–60–02. Closed Sun. and many holidays. AE, DC, MC. $$*
El Po del Call is well situated near the center of Girona. The cuisine ranges from original creations like *bacalao a la miel* (cod in honey) to classical dishes. *La Força 14, tel. 972/22–37–74. Closed Sun. DC, MC, V. $$*

Lodging **Hotel Playa Sol** has a pretty location—over a tiny beach, looking
Cadaqués back at the town. *Platja Pianch 5, 17488, tel. 972/25–81–00, fax 927/ 25–80–54. 49 rooms. Facilities: coffee shop, garden, swimming pool, tennis. Closed Jan. 10–Feb. 15. MC, V. $$*

Girona **Ultònia**'s attractive setting makes it Girona's best hotel. *Gran Via Jaume I 22, 08002, tel. 972/20–38–50, fax 972/20–33–34. 45 rooms. Facilities: coffee shop. AE, DC, MC, V. $$*

Vic **Parador de Vic** is 14 km (8½ mi) northeast of town on the road to Roda de Ter, with a stunning mountain setting and all the restrained good taste of the national chain. *Carretera Roda de Ter, 08500, tel. 93/888-3229 or 93/888-7211, fax 93/888-7311. 36 rooms. Facilities: coffee shop, garden, swimming pool, tennis. $$$*

The Costa Brava

The Costa Brava (rugged coast) is a jagged stretch of shoreline that begins at Lloret, northeast of Barcelona, and runs past 135 km (84 mi) of coves and beaches to the Franco-Spanish frontier town of Port-Bou. It is best to concentrate on selected pockets, just north of Tossa, around Cap de Begúr and around Cadaqués (*see above*), where the terrain is rocky and steep enough to have staved off the worst excesses of real-estate speculation. Here, on a good day, the luminous blue of the sea still contrasts with the red-brown headlands and cliffs; the distant lights of sardine boats reflect across wine-colored waters at dusk; and neat umbrella pines accompany you to the fringes of white, sandy beaches.

Arriving and Departing
By Car From Barcelona, go as if to Girona, leaving the autopista only when you are parallel with the bit you want to tackle, or you are in for a frustrating time competing with the coastal traffic.

By Train A slow train runs along the coast to Blanes, just south of Lloret, from Sants and Passeig de Gràcia.

By Bus Buses to Lloret, Tossa, Sant Feliu de Guíxols, Platja d'Aro, Palamós, Begúr, Roses, and Cadaqués are operated by **Sarfa** (Plaça Duc de Medinaceli 4, tel. 93/318-9434; metro: Drassanes).

Guided Tours Between May 1 and October 15, **Julià** and **Pullmantur** run coach and cruise tours, visiting the ports of Tossa, Lloret del Mar, and Fanals. A bus takes you from their Barcelona terminals (*see* Guided Tours, in Essential Information, above) up the coast to Tossa. From here, weather permitting, a boat will take you to the beach at Fanals, where you'll have time for swimming and lunch. Buses leave Barcelona at 9 AM, returning at 6 PM. The price per person is 9,000 pesetas, or 10,500 pesetas with lunch included.

Exploring
⑫ **Tossa** was the first place on the Costa Brava to attract foreigners, and one of the worst sufferers. It is only 23 km (15 mi) from here to Sant Feliu de Guíxols, but if you go by the beautiful coastal road, prepare for one sharp curve after another, as the road winds round innumerable deep-cut inlets. Parked cars indicate accessible coves, always involving a long walk down.

⑬ **Sant Feliu de Guíxols,** with its numerous *simpático* bars and restaurants, is much more agreeable than Tossa. Owing to the advent of plastics, the town has lost its cork industry and now lives from its port, fishing, and tourist trade. There is no beach, but a bus service runs to and from S'Agaró, 3 km (2 mi).

⑭ **S'Agaró,** one of the showpieces of the Costa Brava, is the creation of one man, José Ensesa, who bought the land to build his idea of a perfect seaside resort. Walk along the kilometer of hidden sea wall, beginning below the Hostal de la Gavina and ending at the magnificent Concha Beach.

Beyond S'Agaró, head for the rocky stretch opposite Palafrugell. Of the towns between the Cap de Sant Sebastià and Cap de Begúr, **Tamariu,** where umbrella pines fringe the silver-white strand, is the most beautiful.

⑮ Before stretching out on one of these idyllic beaches, visit **Roig,** reached by track from Calella, home to one of Spain's finest botanical gardens. *Admission: 350 pesetas. Open for guided visits, Mar.–Dec., daily 9–9; closed Jan. and Feb.*

Llafranc was an Iberian settlement in pre-Greek and pre-Roman times. From the 18th-century hermitage, with its Baroque sanctuary, set near the lighthouse that crowns the cape, you can see far along the loveliest stretch of the entire coast. From here to Aiguablava, the coast is precipitous and magnificent, but can be properly appreciated only from the sea. **Aiguablava** (Catalan for blue water) is a secluded little resort with a parador. Its beach at Fornells epitomizes what Mediterranean bathing should be—deep, clear blue water, sheltered by two headlands to form a natural yacht basin.

⑯ The neighboring town of **Begúr**, with a ruined medieval castle, contains a number of fine houses built during the last century by adventurers who went to Cuba to make their fortunes and returned to Spain rich enough to end their days in idle splendor.

⑰ If you are a devotee of the classics, don't miss visiting the Greek and Roman settlements at **Empúries**, 41 km (25 mi) north via Torroella. Emporion was founded by Greeks in 550 BC and used as an important trading station for three centuries until it was taken by the Romans, who built a larger city above the old Greek colony. *Admission: 350 pesetas. Open Apr.–Sept., Tues.–Sun. 9–7; Oct.–Mar., Tues.– Sun. 10–1 and 3–5; closed Mon.*

Dining
S'Agaró

La Gavina is a classy and elegant Relais and Chateaux hotel/restaurant. *Plaça de la Rosaleda, 08033, tel. 972/32–11–00. AE, MC, V. $$$$*

Sant Feliú

Eldorado Petit is the excellent (older) sister of its namesake in Barcelona. It serves diverse Catalan and international dishes. *Rambla Vidal 23, tel. 972/32–18–18. AE, MC, V. $$$*

Lodging
Aiguablava

Parador de la Costa Brava, stylish and modern, overlooks the bay. *Aiguablava, 08033, tel. 972/62–21–62, fax 972/62–21–66. AE, MC, V. Closed Nov. $$$*

Aiguablava has superb management and a delightful location above the beach. *Playa de Fornells, 08033, tel. 972/62–20–58, fax 972/62–21–12. AE, MC, V. $$*

Index

Personal Itinerary

Departure *Date*

Time

Transportation

Arrival *Date*   *Time*

Departure *Date*   *Time*

Transportation

Accommodations

Arrival *Date*   *Time*

Departure *Date*   *Time*

Transportation

Accommodations

Arrival *Date*   *Time*

Departure *Date*   *Time*

Transportation

Accommodations

Personal Itinerary

Arrival *Date*   *Time*

Departure *Date*   *Time*

Transportation

Accommodations

Arrival *Date*   *Time*

Departure *Date*   *Time*

Transportation

Accommodations

Arrival *Date*   *Time*

Departure *Date*   *Time*

Transportation

Accommodations

Arrival *Date*   *Time*

Departure *Date*   *Time*

Transportation

Accommodations

Personal Itinerary

Arrival *Date* *Time*

Departure *Date* *Time*

Transportation

Accommodations

Arrival *Date* *Time*

Departure *Date* *Time*

Transportation

Accommodations

Arrival *Date* *Time*

Departure *Date* *Time*

Transportation

Accommodations

Arrival *Date* *Time*

Departure *Date* *Time*

Transportation

Accommodations

Personal Itinerary

Arrival *Date*   *Time*

Departure *Date*   *Time*

Transportation

Accommodations

Arrival *Date*   *Time*

Departure *Date*   *Time*

Transportation

Accommodations

Arrival *Date*   *Time*

Departure *Date*   *Time*

Transportation

Accommodations

Arrival *Date*   *Time*

Departure *Date*   *Time*

Transportation

Accommodations

Personal Itinerary

Arrival *Date*   *Time*

Departure *Date*   *Time*

Transportation

Accommodations

Arrival *Date*   *Time*

Departure *Date*   *Time*

Transportation

Accommodations

Arrival *Date*   *Time*

Departure *Date*   *Time*

Transportation

Accommodations

Arrival *Date*   *Time*

Departure *Date*   *Time*

Transportation

Accommodations

Addresses

Name	*Name*
Address	*Address*
Telephone	*Telephone*
Name	*Name*
Address	*Address*
Telephone	*Telephone*
Name	*Name*
Address	*Address*
Telephone	*Telephone*
Name	*Name*
Address	*Address*
Telephone	*Telephone*
Name	*Name*
Address	*Address*
Telephone	*Telephone*
Name	*Name*
Address	*Address*
Telephone	*Telephone*
Name	*Name*
Address	*Address*
Telephone	*Telephone*
Name	*Name*
Address	*Address*
Telephone	*Telephone*

Addresses

Name	*Name*
Address	*Address*
Telephone	*Telephone*
Name	*Name*
Address	*Address*
Telephone	*Telephone*
Name	*Name*
Address	*Address*
Telephone	*Telephone*
Name	*Name*
Address	*Address*
Telephone	*Telephone*
Name	*Name*
Address	*Address*
Telephone	*Telephone*
Name	*Name*
Address	*Address*
Telephone	*Telephone*
Name	*Name*
Address	*Address*
Telephone	*Telephone*
Name	*Name*
Address	*Address*
Telephone	*Telephone*

Addresses

Name	Name
Address	Address
Telephone	Telephone
Name	Name
Address	Address
Telephone	Telephone
Name	Name
Address	Address
Telephone	Telephone
Name	Name
Address	Address
Telephone	Telephone
Name	Name
Address	Address
Telephone	Telephone
Name	Name
Address	Address
Telephone	Telephone
Name	Name
Address	Address
Telephone	Telephone
Name	Name
Address	Address
Telephone	Telephone

The only guide to explore a *Disney World*® you've never seen before:

The one for grown-ups.

0-679-02490-5 $14.00 ($18.50 Can)

This is the only guide written specifically for the millions of adults who visit Walt Disney World® each year <u>without</u> kids. Upscale, sophisticated, packed full of facts and maps, *Walt Disney World® for Adults* provides up-to-date information on hotels, restaurants, sports facilities, and health clubs, as well as unique itineraries for adults. With *Walt Disney World® for Adults* in hand, you'll get the most out of one of the world's most fascinating, most complex playgrounds.

At bookstores everywhere, or call **1-800-533-6478**.

Fodor's

Fodor's Travel Guides

Available at bookstores everywhere, or call 1–800–533–6478, 24 hours a day.

U.S. Guides

Alaska

Arizona

Boston

California

Cape Cod, Martha's Vineyard, Nantucket

The Carolinas & the Georgia Coast

Chicago

Colorado

Florida

Hawaii

Las Vegas, Reno, Tahoe

Los Angeles

Maine, Vermont, New Hampshire

Maui

Miami & the Keys

New England

New Orleans

New York City

Pacific North Coast

Philadelphia & the Pennsylvania Dutch Country

The Rockies

San Diego

San Francisco

Santa Fe, Taos, Albuquerque

Seattle & Vancouver

The South

The U.S. & British Virgin Islands

USA

The Upper Great Lakes Region

Virginia & Maryland

Waikiki

Walt Disney World and the Orlando Area

Washington, D.C.

Foreign Guides

Acapulco, Ixtapa, Zihuatanejo

Australia & New Zealand

Austria

The Bahamas

Baja & Mexico's Pacific Coast Resorts

Barbados

Berlin

Bermuda

Brittany & Normandy

Budapest

Canada

Cancún, Cozumel, Yucatán Peninsula

Caribbean

China

Costa Rica, Belize, Guatemala

The Czech Republic & Slovakia

Eastern Europe

Egypt

Euro Disney

Europe

Florence, Tuscany & Umbria

France

Germany

Great Britain

Greece

Hong Kong

India

Ireland

Israel

Italy

Japan

Kenya & Tanzania

Korea

London

Madrid & Barcelona

Mexico

Montréal & Québec City

Morocco

Moscow & St. Petersburg

The Netherlands, Belgium & Luxembourg

New Zealand

Norway

Nova Scotia, Prince Edward Island & New Brunswick

Paris

Portugal

Provence & the Riviera

Rome

Russia & the Baltic Countries

Scandinavia

Scotland

Singapore

South America

Southeast Asia

Spain

Sweden

Switzerland

Thailand

Tokyo

Toronto

Turkey

Vienna & the Danube Valley

Special Series

Fodor's Affordables

Caribbean

Europe

Florida

France

Germany

Great Britain

Italy

London

Paris

Fodor's Bed & Breakfast and Country Inns Guides

America's Best B&Bs

California

Canada's Great Country Inns

Cottages, B&Bs and Country Inns of England and Wales

Mid-Atlantic Region

New England

The Pacific Northwest

The South

The Southwest

The Upper Great Lakes Region

The Berkeley Guides

California

Central America

Eastern Europe

Europe

France

Germany & Austria

Great Britain & Ireland

Italy

London

Mexico

Pacific Northwest & Alaska

Paris

San Francisco

Fodor's Exploring Guides

Australia

Boston & New England

Britain

California

The Caribbean

Florence & Tuscany

Florida

France

Germany

Ireland

Italy

London

Mexico

New York City

Paris

Prague

Rome

Scotland

Singapore & Malaysia

Spain

Thailand

Turkey

Fodor's Flashmaps

Boston

New York

Washington, D.C.

Fodor's Pocket Guides

Acapulco

Bahamas

Barbados

Jamaica

London

New York City

Paris

Puerto Rico

San Francisco

Washington, D.C.

Fodor's Sports

Cycling

Golf Digest's Best Places to Play

Hiking

The Insider's Guide to the Best Canadian Skiing

Running

Sailing

Skiing in the USA & Canada

USA Today's Complete Four Sports Stadium Guide

Fodor's Three-In-Ones (guidebook, language cassette, and phrase book)

France

Germany

Italy

Mexico

Spain

Fodor's Special-Interest Guides

Complete Guide to America's National Parks

Condé Nast Traveler Caribbean Resort and Cruise Ship Finder

Cruises and Ports of Call

Euro Disney

France by Train

Halliday's New England Food Explorer

Healthy Escapes

Italy by Train

London Companion

Shadow Traffic's New York Shortcuts and Traffic Tips

Sunday in New York

Sunday in San Francisco

Touring Europe

Touring USA: Eastern Edition

Walt Disney World and the Orlando Area

Walt Disney World for Adults

Fodor's Vacation Planners

Great American Learning Vacations

Great American Sports & Adventure Vacations

Great American Vacations

Great American Vacations for Travelers with Disabilities

National Parks and Seashores of the East

National Parks of the West

The Wall Street Journal Guides to Business Travel

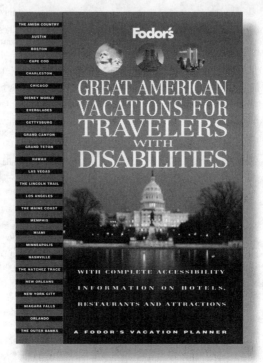